The Story of John G. Paton

Or, Thirty Years Among South Sea Cannibals

John Gibson Paton

Alpha Editions

This edition published in 2024

ISBN : 9789362921017

Design and Setting By
Alpha Editions
www.alphaedis.com
Email - info@alphaedis.com

As per information held with us this book is in Public Domain.
This book is a reproduction of an important historical work. Alpha Editions uses the best technology to reproduce historical work in the same manner it was first published to preserve its original nature. Any marks or number seen are left intentionally to preserve its true form.

Contents

PREFACE. ....- 1 -

CHAPTER I. OUR COTTAGE HOME. ....- 2 -

CHAPTER II. OUR FOREBEARS. ....- 5 -

CHAPTER III. CONSECRATED PARENTS. ....- 8 -

CHAPTER IV. SCHOOL DAYS. ....- 11 -

CHAPTER V. LEAVING THE OLD HOME. ....- 14 -

CHAPTER VI. EARLY STRUGGLES. ....- 16 -

CHAPTER VII. A CITY MISSIONARY. ....- 20 -

CHAPTER VIII. GLASGOW EXPERIENCES. ....- 24 -

CHAPTER IX. A FOREIGN MISSIONARY. ....- 28 -

CHAPTER X. TO THE NEW HEBRIDES. ....- 32 -

CHAPTER XI. FIRST IMPRESSIONS OF HEATHENDOM. ....- 35 -

CHAPTER XII. BREAKING GROUND ON TANNA. ....- 38 -

CHAPTER XIII. PIONEERS IN THE NEW HEBRIDES. - 41 -

CHAPTER XIV. THE GREAT BEREAVEMENT. - 43 -

CHAPTER XV. AT HOME WITH CANNIBALS. - 47 -

CHAPTER XVI. SUPERSTITIONS AND CRUELTIES. - 50 -

CHAPTER XVII. STREAKS OF DAWN AMIDST DEEDS OF DARKNESS. - 53 -

CHAPTER XVIII. THE VISIT OF H. M. S. "CORDELIA." - 56 -

CHAPTER XIX. "NOBLE OLD ABRAHAM." - 59 -

CHAPTER XX. A TYPICAL SOUTH SEA TRADER. - 61 -

CHAPTER XXI. UNDER AX AND MUSKET. - 63 -

CHAPTER XXII. A NATIVE SAINT AND MARTYR. - 65 -

CHAPTER XXIII. BUILDING AND PRINTING FOR GOD. - 68 -

CHAPTER XXIV. HEATHEN DANCE AND SHAM FIGHT. - 70 -

CHAPTER XXV. CANNIBALS AT WORK. - 73 -

CHAPTER XXVI. THE DEFYING OF NAHAK. ....- 75 -

CHAPTER XXVII. A PERILOUS PILGRIMAGE. ....- 78 -

CHAPTER XXVIII. THE PLAGUE OF MEASLES. ....- 82 -

CHAPTER XXIX. ATTACKED WITH CLUBS. ....- 85 -

CHAPTER XXX. KOWIA. ....- 88 -

CHAPTER XXXI. MARTYRDOM OF THE GORDONS. ....- 91 -

CHAPTER XXXII. SHADOWS DEEPENING ON TANNA. ....- 93 -

CHAPTER XXXIII. THE VISIT OF THE COMMODORE. ....- 97 -

CHAPTER XXXIV. THE WAR CHIEFS IN COUNCIL. ....- 101 -

CHAPTER XXXV. UNDER KNIFE AND TOMAHAWK. ....- 104 -

CHAPTER XXXVI. THE BEGINNING OF THE END. ....- 108 -

CHAPTER XXXVII. FIVE HOURS IN A CANOE. ....- 112 -

CHAPTER XXXVIII. A RACE FOR LIFE. ....- 115 -

CHAPTER XXXIX. FAINT YET PURSUING.................................- 117 -

CHAPTER XL. WAITING AT KWAMERA. ....- 121 -

CHAPTER XLI. THE LAST AWFUL NIGHT. ....- 124 -

CHAPTER XLII. "SAIL O! SAIL O!"..................- 126 -

CHAPTER XLIII. FAREWELL TO TANNA. ....- 129 -

CHAPTER XLIV. THE FLOATING OF THE "DAYSPRING."...........................- 132 -

CHAPTER XLV. A SHIPPING COMPANY FOR JESUS. ....- 135 -

CHAPTER XLVI. AUSTRALIAN INCIDENTS. ....- 138 -

CHAPTER XLVII. AMONGST SQUATTERS AND DIGGERS. ....- 143 -

CHAPTER XLVIII. JOHN GILPIN IN THE BUSH. ....- 147 -

CHAPTER XLIX. THE ABORIGINES OF AUSTRALIA. ....- 151 -

CHAPTER L. NORA..- 154 -

CHAPTER LI. BACK TO SCOTLAND...................- 158 -

CHAPTER LII. TOUR THROUGH THE OLD COUNTRY. ....- 160 -

CHAPTER LIII. MARRIAGE AND FAREWELL. ....- 163 -

CHAPTER LIV. FIRST PEEP AT THE "DAYSPRING." ....- 165 -

CHAPTER LV. THE FRENCH IN THE PACIFIC. ....- 169 -

CHAPTER LVI. THE GOSPEL AND GUNPOWDER. ....- 172 -

CHAPTER LVII. A PLEA FOR TANNA. ....- 176 -

CHAPTER LVIII. OUR NEW HOME ON ANIWA. ....- 179 -

CHAPTER LIX. HOUSE-BUILDING FOR GOD. ....- 181 -

CHAPTER LX. A CITY OF GOD. ....- 184 -

CHAPTER LXI. THE RELIGION OF REVENGE. ....- 187 -

CHAPTER LXII. FIRST FRUITS ON ANIWA. ....- 189 -

CHAPTER LXIII. TRADITIONS AND CUSTOMS. ....- 191 -

CHAPTER LXIV. NELWANG'S ELOPEMENT. ....- 194 -

CHAPTER LXV. THE CHRIST-SPIRIT AT WORK. ....- 198 -

CHAPTER LXVI. THE SINKING OF THE WELL. ....- 201 -

CHAPTER LXVII. RAIN FROM BELOW. ....- 204 -

CHAPTER LXVIII. THE OLD CHIEF'S SERMON. ....- 208 -

CHAPTER LXIX. THE FIRST BOOK AND THE NEW EYES. ....- 212 -

CHAPTER LXX. A ROOF-TREE FOR JESUS. ....- 215 -

CHAPTER LXXI. "KNOCK THE TEVIL OUT!" ....- 218 -

CHAPTER LXXII. THE CONVERSION OF YOUWILI. ....- 220 -

CHAPTER LXXIII. FIRST COMMUNION ON ANIWA. ....- 223 -

CHAPTER LXXIV. THE NEW SOCIAL ORDER. ....- 225 -

CHAPTER LXXV. THE ORPHANS AND THEIR BISCUITS. ....- 228 -

CHAPTER LXXVI. THE FINGER-POSTS OF GOD. ....- 231 -

CHAPTER LXXVII. THE GOSPEL IN LIVING CAPITALS. ....- 235 -

CHAPTER LXXVIII. THE DEATH OF NAMAKEI. ....- 237 -

CHAPTER LXXIX. CHRISTIANITY AND COCOANUTS. ....- 240 -

CHAPTER LXXX. NERWA'S BEAUTIFUL FAREWELL. ....- 243 -

CHAPTER LXXXI. RUWAWA. ....- 246 -

CHAPTER LXXXII. LITSI SORÉ AND MUNGAW. ....- 248 -

CHAPTER LXXXIII. THE CONVERSION OF NASI. ....- 252 -

CHAPTER LXXXIV. THE APPEAL OF LAMU. ....- 254 -

CHAPTER LXXXV. WANTED! A STEAM AUXILIARY. ....- 256 -

CHAPTER LXXXVI. MY CAMPAIGN IN IRELAND. ....- 259 -

CHAPTER LXXXVII. SCOTLAND'S FREE-WILL OFFERINGS. ....- 261 -

CHAPTER LXXXVIII. ENGLAND'S OPEN BOOK. ....- 264 -

CHAPTER LXXXIX. FAREWELL SCENES. ....- 268 -

CHAPTER XC. WELCOME TO VICTORIA AND ANIWA. ....- 271 -

CHAPTER XCI. GOOD NEWS FROM TANNA, 1891..- 273 -

PREFACE.

EVER since the story of my brother's life first appeared (January 1889) it has been constantly pressed upon me that a YOUNG FOLKS' EDITION would be highly prized. The Autobiography has therefore been re-cast and illustrated, in the hope and prayer that the Lord will use it to inspire the Boys and Girls of Christendom with a wholehearted enthusiasm for the Conversion of the Heathen World to Jesus Christ.

A few fresh incidents have been introduced; the whole contents have been rearranged to suit a new class of readers; and the service of a gifted Artist has been employed, to make the book every way attractive to the young. For *full* details as to the Missionary's work and life, the COMPLETE EDITION must still of course be referred to.

JAMES PATON.
GLASGOW, *Sept*, 1892.

CHAPTER I.
OUR COTTAGE HOME.

MY early days were all spent in the beautiful county of Dumfries, which Scotch folks call the Queen of the South. There, in a small cottage, on the farm of Braehead, in the parish of Kirkmahoe, I was born on the 24th May, 1824. My father, James Paton, was a stocking manufacturer in a small way; and he and his young wife, Janet Jardine Rogerson, lived on terms of warm personal friendship with the "gentleman farmer," so they gave me his son's name, John *Gibson*; and the curly-haired child of the cottage was soon able to toddle across to the mansion, and became a great pet of the lady there. On my visit to Scotland in 1884 I drove out to Braehead; but we found no cottage, nor trace of a cottage, and amused ourselves by supposing that we could discover by the rising of the grassy mound, the outline where the foundations once had been!

While yet a mere child, five years or so of age, my parents took me to a new home in the ancient village of Torthorwald, about four and a quarter miles from Dumfries, on the road to Lockerbie. At that time, say 1830, Torthorwald was a busy and thriving village, and comparatively populous, with its cottars and crofters, large farmers and small farmers, weavers and shoemakers, doggers and coopers, blacksmiths and tailors. Fifty-five years later, when I visited the scenes of my youth, the village proper was extinct, except for five thatched cottages where the lingering patriarchs were permitted to die slowly away,—soon they too would be swept into the large farms, and their garden plots plowed over, like sixty or seventy others that had been blotted out!

From the Bank Hill, close above our village, and accessible in a walk of fifteen minutes, a view opens to the eye which, despite several easily understood prejudices of mine that may discount any opinion that I offer, still appears to me well worth seeing amongst all the beauties of Scotland. At your feet lay a thriving village, every cottage sitting in its own plot of garden, and sending up its blue cloud of "peat reek," which never somehow seemed to pollute the blessed air; and after all has been said or sung, a beautifully situated village of healthy and happy homes for God's children is surely the finest feature in every landscape! Looking from the Bank Hill on a summer day, Dumfries with its spires shone so conspicuous that you could have believed it not more than two miles away; the splendid sweeping vale through which Nith rolls to Solway, lay all before the naked eye, beautiful with village spires, mansion houses, and white shining farms; the Galloway hills, gloomy and far-tumbling, bounded the forward view, while to the left rose Criffel, cloud-capped and majestic; then the white sands of Solway, with tides swifter than horsemen; and finally the eye rested joyfully upon the hills of Cumberland, and noticed with glee the blue curling smoke from its villages on the southern Solway shores.

There, amid this wholesome and breezy village life, our dear parents found their home for the long period of forty years. There too were born to them eight additional children, making in all a family of five sons and six daughters. Theirs was the first of the thatched cottages on the left, past the "miller's house," going up the "village gate," with a small garden in front of it, and a large garden across the road; and it is one of the few still lingering to show to a new generation what the homes of their fathers were. The architect who planned that cottage had no ideas of art, but a fine eye for durability! It consists at present of three, but originally of four, pairs of "oak couples" (Scottice *kipples*) planted like solid trees in the ground at equal intervals, and gently sloped inwards till they meet or are "coupled" at the ridge, this coupling being managed not by rusty iron, but by great solid pins of oak. A roof of oaken wattles was laid across these, till within eleven or twelve feet of the ground, and from the ground upwards a stone wall was raised, as perpendicular as was found practicable, towards these overhang-wattles, this wall being roughly "pointed" with sand and clay and lime. Now into and upon the roof was woven and intertwisted a covering of thatch, that defied all winds and weathers, and that made the cottage marvelously cozy,—being renewed year by year, and never allowed to remain in disrepair at any season. But the beauty of the construction was and is its durability, or rather the permanence of its oaken ribs! There they stand, after probably not less than four centuries, japanned with "peat reek" till they are literally shining, so hard that no ordinary nail can be driven into them, and perfectly capable of service for four centuries more on the same conditions. The walls are quite modern, having all been rebuilt in my father's time, except only the few great foundation boulders, piled around the oaken couples; and parts of the roofing also may plead guilty to having found its way thither only in recent days; but the architect's one idea survives, baffling time and change—the ribs and rafters of oak.

Our home consisted of a "but" and a "ben" and a "mid room," or chamber, called the "closet." The one end was my mother's domain, and served all the purposes of dining-room and kitchen and parlor, besides containing two large wooden erections, called by our Scotch peasantry "box beds"; not holes in the wall, as in cities, but grand, big, airy beds, adorned with many-colored counterpanes, and hung with natty curtains, showing the skill of the mistress of the house. The other end was my father's workshop, filled with five or six "stocking-frames," whirring with the constant action of five or six pairs of busy hands and feet, and producing right genuine hosiery for the merchants at Hawick and Dumfries. The "closet" was a very small apartment betwixt the other two, having room only for a bed, a little table and a chair, with a diminutive window shedding diminutive light on the scene. This was the Sanctuary of that cottage home. Thither daily, and oftentimes a day, generally after each meal, we saw our father retire, and "shut to the door"; and we children got to understand by a sort of spiritual instinct (for the thing was too sacred to be talked about) that prayers were being poured out there for us, as of old by the High Priest within the veil in the Most Holy Place. We occasionally heard the pathetic echoes of a trembling voice pleading as if for life, and we learned to slip out and in past that door on tiptoe, not to disturb the holy colloquy. The outside world might not know, but we knew, whence came that happy light as of a new-born smile that always was dawning on my father's face: it was a reflection from the Divine Presence, in the consciousness of which he lived. Never, in temple or cathedral, on mountain or in glen, can I hope to feel that the Lord God is more near, more visibly walking and talking with men, than under that humble cottage roof of thatch and oaken wattles. Though everything else in religion were by some unthinkable catastrophe to be swept out of memory, or blotted from my understanding, my soul would wander back to those early scenes, and shut itself up once again in that Sanctuary Closet, and, hearing still the echoes of those cries to God, would hurl back all doubt with the victorious appeal, "He walked with God, why may not I?"

CHAPTER II.
OUR FOREBEARS.

A FEW notes had better here be given as to our "Forebears," the kind of stock from which my father and mother sprang. My father's mother, Janet Murray, claimed to be descended from a Galloway family that fought and suffered for Christ's Crown and Covenant in Scotland's "killing time," and was herself a woman of a pronouncedly religious development. Her husband, our grandfather, William Paton, had passed through a roving and romantic career, before he settled down to be a douce deacon of the weavers of Dumfries, like his father before him.

Forced by a press-gang to serve on board a British man-of-war, he was taken prisoner by the French, and thereafter placed under Paul Jones, the pirate of the seas, and bore to his dying day the mark of a slash from the captain's sword across his shoulder for some slight disrespect or offense. Determining with two others to escape, the three were hotly pursued by Paul Jones's men. One, who could swim but little, was shot, and had to be cut adrift by the other two, who in the darkness swam into a cave and managed to evade for two nights and a day the rage of their pursuers. My grandfather, being young and gentle and yellow-haired, persuaded some kind heart to rig him out in female attire, and in this costume escaped the attentions of the press-gang more than once; till, after many hardships, he bargained with the captain of a coal sloop to stow him away amongst his black diamonds; and thus, in due time, he found his way home to Dumfries, where he tackled bravely and wisely the duties of husband, father, and citizen for the remainder of his days. The smack of the sea about the stories of his youth gave zest to the talks round their quiet fireside, and that, again, was seasoned by the warm Evangelical spirit of his Covenanting wife, her lips "dropping grace."

On the other side, my mother, Janet Rogerson, had for parents a father and mother of the Annandale stock. William Rogerson, her father, was one of many brothers, all men of uncommon strength and great force of character, quite worthy of the Border Rievers of an earlier day. Indeed, it was in some such way that he secured his wife, though the dear old lady in after days was chary about telling the story. She was a girl of good position, the ward of two unscrupulous uncles who had charge of her small estate, near Langholm; and while attending some boarding school she fell devotedly in love with the tall, fair-haired, gallant young blacksmith, William Rogerson. Her guardians, doubtless very properly, objected to the "connection"; but our young Lochinvar, with his six or seven stalwart brothers and other trusty "lads," all mounted, and with some ready tools in case of need, went boldly and claimed his bride, and she, willingly mounting at his side, was borne off in the light of open day, joyously married, and took possession of her "but and ben," as the mistress of the blacksmith's castle.

Janet Jardine bowed her neck to the self-chosen yoke, with the light of a supreme affection in her heart, and showed in her gentler ways, her love of books, her fine accomplishments with the needle, and her general air of ladyhood, that her lot had once been cast in easier, but not necessarily happier, ways. Her blacksmith lover proved not unworthy of his lady bride, and in old age found for her a quiet and modest home, the fruit of years of toil and hopeful thrift, their own little property, in which they rested and waited a happy end. Amongst those who at last wept by her grave stood, amidst many sons and daughters, her son the Rev. James J. Rogerson, clergyman of the Church of England, who, for many years thereafter, and till quite recently, was spared to occupy a distinguished position at ancient Shrewsbury and has left behind him there an honored and beloved name.

From such a home came our mother, Janet Jardine Rogerson, a bright-hearted, high-spirited, patient-toiling, and altogether heroic little woman; who, for about forty-three years, made and kept such a wholesome, independent, God-fearing, and self-reliant life for her family of five sons and six daughters, as constrains me, when I look back on it now, in the light of all I have since seen and known of others far differently situated, almost to worship her memory. She had gone with her high spirits and breezy disposition to gladden as their companion, the quiet abode of some grand or great-grand-uncle and aunt, familiarly named in all that Dalswinton neighborhood, "Old Adam and Eve." Their house was on the outskirts of the moor, and life for the young girl there had not probably too much excitement. But one thing had arrested her attention. She had noticed that a young stocking-maker from the "Brig End," James Paton, the son of William and Janet there, was in the habit of stealing alone into the quiet wood, book in hand, day after day, at certain hours, as if for private study and meditation. It was a very excusable curiosity that led the young bright heart of the girl to watch him devoutly reading and hear him reverently reciting (though she knew not then, it was Ralph Erskine's *Gospel Sonnets*, which he could say by heart sixty years afterwards, as he lay on his bed of death); and finally that curiosity awed itself into a holy respect, when she saw him lay aside his broad Scotch bonnet, kneel down under the sheltering wings of some tree, and pour out all his soul in daily prayers to God. As yet they had never spoken. What spirit moved her, let lovers tell—was it all devotion, or was it a touch of unconscious love kindling in her towards the yellow-haired and thoughtful youth? Or was there a stroke of mischief, of that teasing, which so often opens up the door to the most serious step in all our lives? Anyhow, one day she slipped in quietly, stole away his bonnet, and hung it on a branch near by, while his trance of devotion made him oblivious of all around; then, from a safe retreat, she watched and enjoyed his perplexity in seeking for and finding it! A second day this was repeated; but his manifest disturbance of mind, and his long pondering with the bonnet in hand, as if almost alarmed, seemed to touch another chord in her heart—that chord of pity which is so often the prelude of love, that finer pity that grieves to wound anything nobler or tenderer than ourselves. Next day, when he came to his accustomed place of prayer, a little card was pinned against the tree just where he knelt, and on it these words: "She who stole away your bonnet is ashamed of what she did; she has a great respect for you, and asks you to pray for her, that she may become as good a Christian as you."

Staring long at that writing, he forgot Ralph Erskine for one day! Taking down the card, and wondering who the writer could be, he was abusing himself for his stupidity in not suspecting that some one had discovered his retreat and removed his bonnet, instead of wondering whether angels had been there during his prayer,—when, suddenly raising his eyes, he saw in front of old Adam's cottage, though a lane amongst the trees, the passing of another kind of angel, swinging a milk-pail in her hand and merrily singing some snatch of old Scottish song. He knew, in that moment, by a Divine instinct, as infallible as any voice that ever came to seer of old, that she was the angel visitor that had stolen in upon his retreat—that bright-faced, clever-witted niece of old Adam and Eve, to whom he had never yet spoken, but whose praises he had often heard said and sung—"Wee Jen." I am afraid he did pray "for her," in more senses than one, that afternoon; at any rate, more than a Scotch bonnet was very effectually stolen; a good heart and true was there virtually bestowed, and the trust was never regretted on either side, and never betrayed.

Often and often, in the genial and beautiful hours of the autumntide of their long life, have I heard my dear father tease "Jen" about her maidenly intentions in the stealing of that bonnet; and often have heard her quick mother-wit in the happy retort, that had his motives for coming to that retreat been altogether and exclusively pious, he would probably have found his way to the other side of the wood, but that men who prowled about the Garden of Eden ran the risk of meeting some day with a daughter of Eve!

CHAPTER III.
CONSECRATED PARENTS.

SOMEWHERE in or about his seventeenth year, my father passed through a crisis of religious experience; and from that day he openly and very decidedly followed the Lord Jesus. His parents had belonged to one of the older branches of what is now called the United Presbyterian Church; but my father, having made an independent study of the Scotch Worthies, the Cloud of Witnesses, the Testimonies, and the Confession of Faith, resolved to cast in his lot with the oldest of all the Scotch Churches, the Reformed Presbyterian, as most nearly representing the Covenanters and the attainments of both the first and second Reformations in Scotland. This choice he deliberately made, and sincerely and intelligently adhered to; and was able at all times to give strong and clear reasons from Bible and from history for the principles he upheld.

Besides this, there was one other mark and fruit of his early religious decision, which looks even fairer through all these years. Family Worship had heretofore been held only on Sabbath Day in his father's house; but the young Christian, entering into conference with his sympathizing mother, managed to get the household persuaded that there ought to be daily morning and evening prayer and reading of the Bible and holy singing. This the more readily, as he himself agreed to take part regularly in the same, and so relieve the old warrior of what might have proved for him too arduous spiritual toils! And so began in his seventeenth year that blessed custom of Family Prayer, morning and evening, which my father practised probably without one single avoidable omission till he lay on his deathbed, seventy-seven years of age; when ever to the last day of his life, a portion of Scripture was read, and his voice was heard softly joining in the Psalm, and his lips breathed the morning and evening Prayer,—falling in sweet benediction on the heads of all his children, far away many of them over all the earth, but all meeting him there at the Throne of Grace.

Our place of worship was the Reformed Presbyterian Church at Dumfries, under the ministry, during most of these days, of Rev. John McDermid—a genuine, solemn, lovable Covenanter, who cherished towards my father a warm respect, that deepened into apostolic affection when the yellow hair turned snow-white and both of them grew patriarchal in their years. The Minister, indeed, was translated to a Glasgow charge; but that rather exalted than suspended their mutual love. Dumfries was four miles fully from our Torthorwald home; but the tradition is that during all these forty years my father was only thrice prevented from attending the worship of God—once by snow, so deep that he was baffled and had to return; once by ice on the road, so dangerous that he was forced to crawl back up the Roucan Brae on his hands and knees, after having descended it so far with many falls; and once by the terrible outbreak of cholera at Dumfries.

Each of us, from very early days, considered it no penalty, but a great joy, to go with our father to the church; the four miles were a treat to our young spirits, the company by the way was a fresh incitement, and occasionally some of the wonders of city-life rewarded our eager eyes. A few other pious men and women, of the best Evangelical type, went from the same parish to one or other favorite Minister at Dumfries; and when these God-fearing peasants "forgathered" in the way to or from the House of God, we youngsters had sometimes rare glimpses of what Christian talk may be and ought to be.

We had, too, special Bible Readings on the Lord's Day evening,—mother and children and visitors reading in turns, with fresh and interesting question, answer, and exposition, all tending to impress us with the infinite grace of a God of love and mercy in the great gift of His dear Son Jesus, our Saviour. The Shorter Catechism was gone through regularly, each answering the question asked, till the whole had been explained, and its foundation in Scripture shown by the proof-texts adduced. It has been an amazing thing to me, occasionally to meet with men who blamed this "catechizing" for giving them a distaste to religion; every one in all our circle thinks and feels exactly the opposite. It laid the solid rock-foundations of our religious life. After-years have given to these questions and their answers a deeper or a modified meaning, but none of us has ever once even dreamed of wishing that we had been otherwise trained. Of course, if the parents are not devout, sincere, and affectionate,—if the whole affair on both sides is taskwork, or worse, hypocritical and false,—results must be very different indeed!

Oh, I can remember those happy Sabbath evenings; no blinds down, and shutters up, to keep out the sun from us, as some scandalously affirm; but a holy, happy, entirely human day, for a Christian father, mother and children to spend. Others must write and say what they will, and as they feel; but so must I. There were eleven of us brought up in a home like that; and never one of the eleven, boy or girl, man or woman, has been heard, or ever will be heard, saying that Sabbath was dull and wearisome for us, or suggesting that we have heard of or seen any way more likely than that for making the Day of the Lord bright and blessed alike for parents and for children. But God help the homes where these things are done by force and not by love!

As I must, however, leave the story of my father's life—much more worthy, in many ways, of being written than my own—I may here mention that his long and upright life made him a great favorite in all religious circles far and near within the neighborhood, that at sick-beds and at funerals he was constantly sent for and much appreciated, and that this appreciation greatly increased, instead of diminishing, when years whitened his long, flowing locks, and gave him an apostolic beauty; till finally, for the last twelve years or so of his life, he became by appointment a sort of Rural Missionary for the four nearest parishes, and spent his autumn in literally sowing the good seed of the Kingdom as a Colporteur of the Tract and Book Society of Scotland. His success in this work, for a rural locality, was beyond all belief. Within a radius of five miles he was known in every home, welcomed by the children, respected by the servants, longed for eagerly by the sick and aged. He gloried in showing off the beautiful Bibles and other precious books, which he sold in amazing numbers. He sang sweet Psalms beside the sick, and prayed like the voice of God at their dying beds. He went cheerily from farm to farm, from cot to cot; and when he wearied on the moorland roads, he refreshed his soul by reciting aloud one of Ralph Erskine's "Sonnets," or crooning to the birds one of David's Psalms. His happy partner, our beloved mother, died in 1865, and he himself in 1868, having reached his seventy-seventh year, an altogether beautiful and noble episode of human existence having been enacted, amid the humblest surroundings of a Scottish peasant's home, through the influence of their united love by the grace of God; and in this world, or in any world, all their children will rise up at mention of their names and call them blessed!

CHAPTER IV.
SCHOOL DAYS.

IN my boyhood, Torthorwald had one of the grand old typical Parish Schools of Scotland; where the rich and the poor met together in perfect equality; where Bible and Catechism were taught as zealously as grammar and geography; and where capable lads from the humblest of cottages were prepared in Latin and Mathematics and Greek to go straight from their Village class to the University bench. Besides, at that time, an accomplished pedagogue of the name of Smith, a learned man of more than local fame, had added a Boarding House to the ordinary School, and had attracted some of the better class gentlemen and farmers' sons from the surrounding country; so that Torthorwald, under his *régime*, reached the zenith of its educational fame. In this School I was initiated into the mystery of letters, and all my brothers and sisters after me, though some of them under other masters than mine. My teacher punished severely—rather, I should say, savagely—especially for lessons badly prepared. Yet, that he was in some respects kindly and tender-hearted, I had the best of reasons to know.

When still under twelve years of age, I started to learn my father's trade, in which I made surprising progress. We wrought from six in the morning till ten at night, with an hour at dinner-time and half an hour at breakfast and again at supper. These spare moments every day I devoutly spent on my books, chiefly in the rudiments of Latin and Greek; for I had given my soul to God, and was resolved to aim at being a Missionary of the Cross, or a Minister of the Gospel. Yet I gladly testify that what I learned of the stocking frame was not thrown away; the facility of using tools, and of watching and keeping the machinery in order, came to be of great value to me in the Foreign Mission field.

One incident of this time I must record here, because of the lasting impression made upon my religious life. Our family, like all others of peasant rank in the land, were plunged into deep distress, and felt the pinch severely, through the failure of the potato, the badness of other crops, and the ransom-price of food. Our father had gone off with work to Hawick, and would return next evening with money and supplies; but meantime the meal barrel ran low, and our dear mother, too proud and too sensitive to let any one know, or to ask aid from any quarter, coaxed us all to rest, assuring us that she had told God everything, and that He would send us plenty in the morning. Next day, with the carrier from Lockerbie came a present from her father, who, knowing nothing of her circumstances or of this special trial, had been moved of God to send at that particular nick of time a love-offering to his daughter, such as they still send to each other in those kindly Scottish shires—a bag of new potatoes, a stone of the first ground meal or flour, or the earliest homemade cheese of the season—which largely supplied all our need. My mother, seeing our surprise at such an answer to her prayers, took us around her knees, thanked God for His goodness, and said to us:

"O my children, love your Heavenly Father, tell Him in faith and prayer all your needs, and He will supply your wants so far as it shall be for your good and His glory."

Perhaps, amidst all their struggles in rearing a family of eleven, this was the hardest time they ever had, and the only time they ever felt the actual pinch of hunger; for the little that they had was marvelously blessed of God, and was not less marvelously utilized by that noble mother of ours, whose high spirit, side by side with her humble and gracious piety, made us, under God, what we are to-day.

I saved as much at my trade as enabled me to go for six weeks to Dumfries Academy; this awoke in me again the hunger for learning, and I resolved to give up that trade and turn to something that might be made helpful to the prosecution of my education. An engagement was secured with the Sappers and Miners, who were mapping and measuring the county of Dumfries in connection with the Ordnance Survey of Scotland. The office hours were from 9 A. M. till 4 P. M.; and though my walk from home was above four miles every morning, and the same by return in the evening, I found much spare time for private study, both on the way to and from my work and also after hours. Instead of spending the mid-day hour with the rest, at football and other games, I stole away to a quiet spot on the banks of the Nith, and there pored over my book, all alone. Our lieutenant, unknown to me, had observed this from his house on the other side of the stream, and after a time called me into his office and inquired what I was studying. I told him the whole truth as to my position and my desires. After conferring with some of the other officials there, he summoned me again, and in their presence promised me promotion in the service, and special training in Woolwich at the Government's expense, on condition that I would sign an engagement for seven years. Thanking him most gratefully for his kind offer, I agreed to bind myself for three years or four, but not for seven.

Excitedly he said, "Why? Will you refuse an offer that many gentlemen's sons would be proud of?"

I said, "My life is given to another Master, so I cannot engage for seven years." He asked sharply, "To whom?" I replied, "To the Lord Jesus; and I want to prepare as soon as possible for His service in the proclaiming of the Gospel."

In great anger he sprang across the room, called the paymaster and exclaimed, "Accept my offer, or you are dismissed on the spot!"

I answered, "I am extremely sorry if you do so, but to bind myself for seven years would probably frustrate the purpose of my life; and though I am greatly obliged to you, I cannot make such an engagement."

His anger made him unwilling or unable to comprehend my difficulty; the drawing instruments were delivered up, I received my pay, and departed, without further parley. Hearing how I had been treated, and why, Mr. Maxwell, the Rector of Dumfries Academy, offered to let me attend all classes there, free of charge so long as I cared to remain; but that, in lack of means of support, was for the time impossible, as I would not and could not be a burden on my dear father, but was determined rather to help him in educating the rest. I went therefore to what was known as the Lamb Fair at Lockerbie, and for the first time in my life took a "fee" for the harvest. On arriving at the field when shearing and mowing began, the farmer asked me to bind a sheaf; when I had done so, he seized it by the band, and it fell to pieces! Instead of disheartening me, however, he gave me a careful lesson how to bind; and the second that I bound did not collapse when shaken, and the third he pitched across the field, and on finding that it still remained firm, he cried to me cheerily:

"Right now, my lad; go ahead!"

It was hard work for me at first, and my hands got very sore; but, being willing and determined, I soon got into the way of it, and kept up with the best of them. The male harvesters were told off to sleep in a large hayloft, the beds being arranged all along the side, like barracks. Many of the fellows were rough and boisterous; and I suppose my look showed that I hesitated in mingling with them, for the quick eye and kind heart of the farmer's wife prompted her to suggest that I, being so much younger than the rest, might sleep with her son George in the house—an offer, oh, how gratefully accepted! A beautiful new steading had recently been built for them; and during certain days, or portions of days, while waiting for the grain to ripen or to dry, I planned and laid out an ornamental garden in front of it, which gave great satisfaction—a taste inherited from my mother, with her joy in flowers and garden plots. They gave me, on leaving, a handsome present, as well as my fee, for I had got on very pleasantly with them all. This experience, too, came to be valuable to me, when, in long-after days, and far other lands, Mission buildings had to be erected, and garden and field cropped and cultivated without the aid of a single European hand.

CHAPTER V.
LEAVING THE OLD HOME.

BEFORE going to my first harvesting, I had applied for a situation in Glasgow, apparently exactly suited for my case; but I had little or no hope of ever hearing of it further. An offer of £50 per annum was made by the West Campbell Street Reformed Presbyterian Congregation, then under the good and noble Dr. Bates, for a young man to act as district visitor and tract distributor, especially amongst the absentees from the Sabbath School; with the privilege of receiving one year's training at the Free Church Normal Seminary, that he might qualify himself for teaching, and thereby push forward to the Holy Ministry. The candidates, along with their application and certificates, were to send an essay on some subject, of their own composition, and in their own handwriting. I sent in two long poems on the Covenanters, which must have exceedingly amused them, as I had not learned to write even decent prose. But, much to my surprise, immediately on the close of the harvesting experience, a letter arrived, intimating that I, along with another young man, had been put upon the short leet, and that both were requested to appear in Glasgow on a given day and compete for the appointment.

Two days thereafter I started out from my quiet country home on the road to Glasgow. Literally "on the road," for from Torthorwald to Kilmarnock—about forty miles—had to be done on foot, and thence to Glasgow by rail. Railways in those days were as yet few, and coach-travelling was far beyond my purse. A small bundle contained my Bible and all my personal belongings. Thus was I launched upon the ocean of life. I thought on One who says, "I know thy poverty, but thou art rich."

My dear father walked with me the first six miles of the way. His counsels and tears and heavenly conversation on that parting journey are fresh in my heart as if it had been but yesterday; and tears are on my cheeks as freely now as then, whenever memory steals me away to the scene. For the last half mile or so we walked on together in almost unbroken silence,—my father, as was often his custom, carrying hat in hand, while his long, flowing yellow hair (then yellow, but in later years white as snow) streamed like a girl's down his shoulders. His lips kept moving in silent prayers for me; and his tears fell fast when our eyes met each other in looks of which all speech was vain! We halted on reaching the appointed parting-place; he grasped my hand firmly for a minute in silence, and then solemnly and affectionately said:

"God bless you, my son! Your father's God prosper you, and keep you from all evil!"

Unable to say more, his lips kept moving in silent prayer; in tears we embraced, and parted. I ran off as fast as I could; and, when about to turn a corner in the road where he would lose sight of me, I looked back and saw him still standing with head uncovered where I had left him—gazing after me. Waving my hat in adieu, I was round the corner and out of sight in an instant. But my heart was too full and sore to carry me farther, so I darted into the side of the road and wept for a time. Then, rising up cautiously, I climbed the dyke to see if he yet stood where I had left him; and just at that moment I caught a glimpse of him climbing the dyke and looking out for me! He did not see me, and after he had gazed eagerly in my direction for a while he got down, set his face towards home, and began to return—his head still uncovered, and his heart, I felt sure, still rising in prayers for me. I watched through blinding tears, till his form faded from my gaze; and then, hastening on my way, vowed deeply and oft, by the help of God, to live and act so as never to grieve or dishonor such a father and mother as He had given me. The appearance of my father, when we parted,—his advice, prayers, and tears—the road, the dyke, the climbing up on it and then walking away, head uncovered—have often, often, all through life, risen vividly before my mind, and do so now while I am writing, as if it had been but an hour ago. In my earlier years particularly, when exposed to many temptations, his parting form rose before me as that of a guardian angel.

CHAPTER VI.
EARLY STRUGGLES.

I REACHED Glasgow on the third day, having slept one night at Thornhill, and another at New Cumnock; and having needed, owing to the kindness of acquaintances upon whom I called by the way, to spend only three halfpence of my modest funds. Safely arrived, but weary, I secured a humble room for my lodging, for which I had to pay one shilling and sixpence per week. Buoyant and full of hope and looking up to God for guidance, I appeared at the appointed hour before the examiners, as did also the other candidate; and they having carefully gone through their work, asked us to retire. When recalled, they informed us that they had great difficulty in choosing, and suggested that the one of us might withdraw in favor of the other, or that both might submit to a more testing examination. Neither seemed inclined to give it up, both were willing for a second examination; but the patrons made another suggestion. They had only £50 per annum to give; but if we would agree to divide it betwixt us, and go into one lodging, we might both be able to struggle through, they would pay our entrance fees at the Free Normal Seminary, and provide us with the books required; and perhaps they might be able to add a little to the sum promised to each of us. By dividing the mission work appointed, and each taking only the half, more time also might be secured for our studies. Though the two candidates had never seen each other before, we at once accepted this proposal, and got on famously together, never having had a dispute on anything of common interest throughout our whole career.

As our fellow-students at the Normal were all far advanced beyond us in their education, we found it killing work, and had to grind away incessantly, late and early. Both of us, before the year closed, broke down in health; partly by hard study, but principally, perhaps, for lack of nourishing diet. A severe cough seized upon me; I began spitting blood, and a doctor ordered me at once home to the country and forbade all attempts at study. My heart sank; it was a dreadful disappointment, and to me a bitter trial. Soon after, my companion, though apparently much stronger than I, was similarly seized. He, however, never entirely recovered, though for some years he taught in a humble school; and long ago he fell asleep in Jesus, a devoted and honored Christian man.

I, on the other hand, after a short rest, nourished by the hill air of Torthorwald and by the new milk of our family cow, was ere long at work again. Renting a house, I began to teach a small school at Girvan, and gradually but completely recovered my health.

Having saved £10 by my teaching, I returned to Glasgow, and was enrolled as a student at the College; but before the session was finished my money was exhausted—I had lent some to a poor student, who failed to repay me—and only nine shillings remained in my purse. There was no one from whom to borrow, had I been willing; I had been disappointed in attempting to secure private tuition; and no course seemed open for me, except to pay what little I owed, give up my College career, and seek for teaching or other work in the country. I wrote a letter to my father and mother, informing them of my circumstances; that I was leaving Glasgow in quest of work, and that they would, not hear from me again till I had found a suitable situation. I told them that if otherwise unsuccessful, I should fall back on my own trade, though I shrank from that as not tending to advance my education; but that they might rest assured I would do nothing to dishonor them or my own Christian profession. Having read that letter over again through many tears, I said,—I cannot send that, for it will grieve my darling parents; and therefore, leaving it on the table, I locked my room door and ran out to find a place where I might sell my precious books, and hold on a few weeks longer. But, as I stood on the opposite side and wondered whether these folks in a shop with the three golden balls would care to have a poor student's books, and as I hesitated, knowing how much I needed them for my studies, conscience smote me as if for doing a guilty thing; I imagined that the people were watching me like one about to commit a theft; and I made off from the scene at full speed, with a feeling of intense shame at having dreamed of such a thing! Passing through one short street into another, I marched on mechanically; but the Lord God of my father was guiding my steps, all unknown to me.

A certain notice in a window, into which I had probably never in my life looked before, here caught my eye, to this effect—"Teacher wanted, Maryhill Free Church school; apply at the Manse." A coach or bus was just passing, when I turned round; I leapt into it, saw the Minister, arranged to undertake the School, returned to Glasgow, paid my landlady's lodging score, tore up that letter to my parents and wrote another full of cheer and hope; and early next morning entered the School and began a tough and trying job. The Minister warned me that the School was a wreck, and had been broken up chiefly by coarse and bad characters from mills and coal-pits, who attended the evening classes. They had abused several masters in succession; and, laying a thick and heavy cane on the desk, he said:

"Use that freely, or you will never keep order here!"

I put it aside into the drawer of my desk, saying, "That will be my last resource."

There were very few scholars for the first week—about eighteen in the Day School and twenty in the Night School. The clerk of the mill, a good young fellow, came to the evening classes, avowedly to learn book-keeping, but privately he said he had come to save me from personal injury.

The following week, a young man and a young woman began to attend the Night School, who showed from the first moment that they were bent on mischief. On my repeated appeals for quiet and order, they became the more boisterous, and gave great merriment to a few of the scholars present. I finally urged the young man, a tall, powerful fellow, to be quiet or at once to leave, declaring that at all hazards I must and would have perfect order; but he only mocked at me, and assumed a fighting attitude. Quietly locking the door and putting the key in my pocket, I turned to my desk, armed myself with the cane, and dared any one at his peril to interfere betwixt us. It was a rough struggle—he smashing at me clumsily with his fists, I with quick movements evading and dealing him blow after blow with the heavy cane for several rounds—till at length he crouched down at his desk, exhausted and beaten, and I ordered him to turn to his book, which he did in sulky silence. Going to my desk, I addressed them and asked them to inform all who wished to come to the School,—That if they came for education, everything would be heartily done that it was in my power to do; but that any who wished for mischief had better stay away, as I was determined to conquer, not to be conquered, and to secure order and silence, whatever it might cost. Further, I assured them that that cane would not again be lifted by me, if kindness and forbearance on my part could possibly gain the day, as I wished to rule by love and not by terror. But this young man knew he was in the wrong, and it was that which had made him weak against me, though every way stronger far than I. Yet I would be his friend and helper, if he was willing to be friendly with me, the same as if this night had never been. At these words a dead silence fell on the School: every one buried face diligently in book; and the evening closed in uncommon quiet and order.

The attendance grew, till the School became crowded, both during the day and at night. During the mid-day hour even, I had a large class of young women who came to improve themselves in writing and arithmetic. By and by the cane became a forgotten implement; the sorrow and pain which I showed as to badly-done lessons, or anything blameworthy, proved the far more effectual penalty.

The School Committee had promised me at least ten shillings per week, and guaranteed to make up any deficit if the fees fell short of that sum; but if the income from fees exceeded that sum, all was to be mine. Affairs went on prosperously for a season; indeed, too much so for my selfish interest. The Committee took advantage of the large attendance and better repute of the School, to secure the services of a master of the highest grade. The parents of many of the children offered to take and seat a hall, if I would remain, but I knew too well that I had neither education nor experience to compete with an accomplished teacher. Their children, however, got up a testimonial and subscription, which was presented to me on the day before I left and this I valued chiefly because the presentation was made by the young fellows who at first behaved so badly, but were now my devoted friends.

Once more I committed my future to the Lord God of my father, assured that in my very heart I was willing and anxious to serve Him and to follow the blessed Saviour, yet feeling keenly that intense darkness had again enclosed my path.

CHAPTER VII.
A CITY MISSIONARY.

BEFORE undertaking the Maryhill School, I had applied to be taken on as an agent in the Glasgow City Mission; and the night before I had to leave Maryhill, I received a letter from Rev. Thomas Caie, the superintendent of the said Mission, saying that the directors had kept their eyes on me ever since my application, and requesting, as they understood I was leaving the School, that I would appear before them the next morning, and have my qualifications for becoming a Missionary examined into. Praising God, I went off at once, passed the examination successfully, and was appointed to spend two hours that afternoon and the following Monday in visitation with two of the directors, calling at every house in a low district of the town, and conversing with all the characters encountered there as to their eternal welfare. I had also to preach a "trial" discourse in a Mission meeting, where a deputation of directors would be present, the following evening being Sunday; and on Wednesday evening they met again to hear their report and to accept or reject me.

All this had come upon me so unexpectedly, that I almost anticipated failure; but looking up for help I went through with it, and on the fifth day after leaving the School they called me before a meeting of directors, and informed me that I had passed my trials most successfully, and that the reports were so favorable that they had unanimously resolved to receive me at once as one of their City Missionaries. Deeply solemnized with the responsibilities of my new office, I left that meeting praising God for all His undeserved mercies, and seeing most clearly His gracious hand in all the way by which He had led me, and the trials by which He had prepared me for this sphere of service. Man proposes—God disposes.

I found the district a very degraded one. Many families said they had never been visited by any Minister; and many were lapsed professors of religion who had attended no church for ten, sixteen, or twenty years, and said they had never been called upon by any Christian visitor. In it were congregated many avowed infidels, Romanists, and drunkards,—living together, and associated for evil, but apparently without any effective counteracting influence. In many of its closes and courts sin and vice walked about openly—naked and not ashamed.

After nearly a year's hard work, I had only six or seven non-church-goers, who had been led to attend regularly there, besides about the same number who met on a week evening in the ground-floor of a house kindly granted for the purpose by a poor and industrious but ill-used Irishwoman. She supported her family by keeping a little shop, and selling coals. Her husband was a powerful man—a good worker, but a hard drinker; and, like too many others addicted to intemperance, he abused and beat her, and pawned and drank everything he could get hold of. She, amid many prayers and tears, bore everything patiently, and strove to bring up her only daughter in the fear of God. We exerted, by God's blessing, a good influence upon him through our meetings. He became a Total Abstainer, gave up his evil ways, and attended Church regularly with his wife. As his interest increased, he tried to bring others also to the meetings, and urged them to become Abstainers. His wife became a center of help and of good influence in all the district, as she kindly invited all and welcomed them to the meeting in her house, and my work grew every day more hopeful.

By and by Meetings and Classes were both too large for any house that was available for us in the whole of our district. We instituted a Bible Class, a Singing Class, a Communicants' Class, and a Total Abstinence Society; and, in addition to the usual meetings, we opened two prayer-meetings specially for the Calton division of the Glasgow Police—one at a suitable hour for the men on day duty, and another for those on night duty. The men got up a Mutual Improvement Society and Singing Class also amongst themselves, weekly, on another evening. My work now occupied every evening in the week; and I had two meetings every Sabbath. By God's blessing they all prospered, and gave evidence of such fruits as showed that the Lord was working there for good by our humble instrumentality.

The kind cowfeeder had to inform us—and he did it with much genuine sorrow—that at a given date he would require the hay-loft, which was our place of meeting; and as no other suitable house or hall could be got, the poor people and I feared the extinction of our work. At that very time however, a commodious block of buildings, that had been Church, Schools, Manse, etc., came into the market. My great-hearted friend, the late Thomas Binnie, persuaded Dr. Symingrton's congregation, Great Hamilton Street, in connection with which my Mission was carried on, to purchase the whole property. Its situation at the foot of Green Street gave it a control of the district where my work lay; and so the Church was given to me in which to conduct all my meetings, while the other Halls were adapted as Schools for poor girls and boys, where they were educated by a proper master, and were largely supplied with books, clothing, and sometimes even food, by the ladies of the congregation.

Availing myself of the increased facilities, my work was all reorganized. On Sabbath morning, at seven o'clock, I had one of the most deeply interesting and fruitful of all my Classes for the study of the Bible. It was attended by from seventy to a hundred of the very poorest young women and grown-up lads of the whole district. They had nothing to put on except their ordinary work-day clothes,—all without bonnets, some without shoes. Beautiful was it to mark how the poorest began to improve in personal appearance immediately after they came to our Class; how they gradually got shoes and one bit of clothing after another, to enable them to attend our other Meetings, and then to go to Church; and, above all, how eagerly they sought to bring others with them, taking a deep personal interest in all the work of the Mission. Long after they themselves could appear in excellent dress, many of them still continued to attend in their working clothes, and to bring other and poorer girls with them to that Morning Class, and thereby helped to improve and elevate their companions. My delight in that Bible Class was among the purest joys in all my life, and the results were amongst the most certain and precious of all my Ministry.

I had also a very large Bible Class—a sort of Bible-Reading—on Monday night, attended by all, of both sexes and of any age, who cared to come or had any interest in the Mission. Wednesday evening, again, was devoted to a prayer-meeting for all; and the attendance often more than half-filled the Church. There I usually took up some book of Holy Scripture and read and lectured right through, practically expounding and applying it. On Thursday I held a Communicants' Class, intended for the more careful instruction of all who wished to become full members of the Church. Our constant text-book was *Paterson on the Shorter Catechism* (Nelson and Sons), than which I have never seen a better compendium of the doctrines of Holy Scripture. Each being thus trained for a season, received from me, if found worthy, a letter to the Minister of any Protestant Church which he or she felt inclined to join. In this way great numbers became active and useful communicants in the surrounding congregations; and eight young lads of humble circumstances educated themselves for the Ministry of the Church—most of them getting their first lessons in Latin and Greek from my very poor stock of the same! Friday evening was occupied with a Singing Class, teaching Church music, and practising for our Sabbath meetings. On Saturday evening we held our Total Abstinence meeting, at which the members themselves took a principal part, in readings, addresses, recitations, singing hymns, etc.

Great good resulted from this Total Abstinence work. Many adults took and kept the pledge, thereby greatly increasing the comfort and happiness of their homes. Many were led to attend the Church on the Lord's Day, who had formerly spent it in rioting and drinking. But, above all, it trained the young to fear the very name of intoxicating drink, and to hate and keep far away from everything that led to intemperance.

I would add my testimony also against the use of tobacco, which injures and leads many astray, especially lads and young men, and which never can be required by any person in ordinary health. But I would not be understood to regard the evils that flow from it as deserving to be mentioned in comparison with the unutterable woes and miseries of intemperance.

To be protected, however, from suspicion and from evil, all the followers of our Lord Jesus should in self-denial (how small!) and in consecration to His service, be pledged Abstainers from both of these selfish indulgences, which are certainly injurious to many, which are no ornament to any character, and which can be no help in well-doing. Praise God for the many who are now so pledged!

CHAPTER VIII.
GLASGOW EXPERIENCES.

ON one occasion, it becoming known that we had arranged for a special Saturday afternoon Temperance demonstration, a deputation of Publicans complained beforehand to the Captain of the Police—that our meetings were interfering with their legitimate trade. The Captain, a pious Wesleyan, who was in full sympathy with us and our work, informed me of the complaints made, and intimated that his men would be present; but I was just to conduct the meeting as usual, and he would guarantee that strict justice would be done. The Publicans having announced amongst their sympathizers that the Police were to break up and prevent our meeting and take the conductors in charge, a very large crowd assembled, both friendly and unfriendly, for the Publicans and their hangers-on were there "to see the fun," and to help in "baiting" the Missionary. Punctually, I ascended the stone stair, accompanied by another Missionary who was also to deliver an address, and announced our opening hymn. As we sang, a company of Police appeared, and were quietly located here and there among the crowd, the sergeant himself taking his post close by the platform, whence the whole assembly could be scanned. Our enemies were jubilant, and signals were passed betwixt them and their friends, as if the time had come to provoke a row. Before the hymn was finished, Captain Baker himself, to the infinite surprise of friend and foe alike, joined us on the platform, devoutly listened to all that was said, and waited till the close. The Publicans could not for very shame leave, while he was there at their suggestion and request, though they had wit enough to perceive that his presence had frustrated all their sinister plans. They had to hear our addresses and prayers and hymns; they had to listen to the intimation of our future meetings. When all had quietly dispersed, the Captain warmly congratulated us on our large and well-conducted congregation, and hoped that great good would result from our efforts. This opposition also the Lord overruled to increase our influence, and to give point and publicity to our assaults upon the kingdom of Satan.

Though Intemperance was the main cause of poverty, suffering, misery, and vice in that district of Glasgow, I had also considerable opposition from Romanists and Infidels, many of whom met in clubs, where they drank together, and gloried in their wickedness and in leading other young men astray.

An Infidel, whose wife was a Roman Catholic, became unwell, and gradually sank under great suffering and agony. His blasphemies against

God were known and shuddered at by all the neighbors. His wife pled with me to visit him. She refused, at my suggestion, to call her own priest, so I accompanied her at last. The man refused to hear one word about spiritual things, and foamed with rage. He even spat at me, I mentioned the name of Jesus. "The natural receiveth not the things of the Spirit of God; for they are foolishness unto him!" There is a "wisdom" which is at best earthly, and *at worst* "sensual and devilish." I visited the poor man daily, but his enmity to God and his sufferings together seemed to drive him mad. Towards the end I pleaded with him even then to look to the Lord Jesus, and asked if I might pray with him? With all his remaining strength he shouted at me, "Pray for me to the devil!"

Reminding him how he had always denied that there was any devil, I suggested that he must surely believe in one now, else he would scarcely make such a request, even in mockery. In great rage he cried, "Tes, I believe there is a devil, and a God, and a just God too; but I have hated Him in life, and I hate Him in death!" With these awful words he wriggled into Eternity; but his shocking death produced a very serious impression for good, especially amongst young men, in the district where his character was known.

How different was the case of that Doctor who also had been an unbeliever as well as a drunkard! Highly educated, skilful, and gifted above most in his profession, he was taken into consultation for specially dangerous cases, whenever they could find him tolerably sober. After one of his excessive "bouts" he had a dreadful attack of *delirium tremens*. At one time wife and watchers had a fierce struggle to dash from his lips a draught of prussic acid; at another, they detected the silver-hafted lancet concealed in the band of his shirt, as he lay down, to bleed himself to death. His aunt came and pleaded with me to visit him. My heart bled for his poor young wife and two beautiful little children. Visiting him twice daily, and sometimes even more frequently, I found the way somehow into his heart, and he would do almost anything for me and longed for my visits. When again the fit of self-destruction seized him, they sent for me; he held out his hand eagerly, and grasping mine said, "Put all these people out of the room, remain you with me; I will be quiet, I will do everything you ask!"

I got them all to leave, but whispered to one in passing to "keep near the door."

Alone I sat beside him, my hand in his, and kept up a quiet conversation for several hours. After we had talked of everything that I could think of, and it was now far into the morning, I said, "If you had a Bible here, we might read a chapter, verse about."

He said dreamily, "There was once a Bible above yon press; if you can get up to it, you might find it there yet."

Getting it, dusting it, and laying it on a small table which I drew near to the sofa on which we sat, we read there and then a chapter together. After this I said; "Now, shall we pray?"

He replied heartily, "Yes."

I having removed the little table, we kneeled down together at the sofa; and after a solemn pause I whispered, "You pray first."

He replied, "I curse, I cannot pray; would you have me curse God to His face?"

I answered, "You promised to do all that I asked; you must pray, or try to pray, and let me hear that you cannot."

He said, "I cannot curse God on my knees; let me stand, and I will curse Him; I cannot pray."

I gently held him on his knees, saying, "Just try to pray, and let me hear you cannot."

Instantly he cried out, "O Lord, Thou knowest I cannot pray," and was going to say something dreadful as he strove to rise up. But I took up gently the words he had uttered as if they had been my own and continued the prayer, pleading for him and his dear ones as we knelt there together, till he showed that he was completely subdued and lying low at the feet of God. On rising from our knees he was manifestly greatly impressed, and I said, "Now, as I must be at College by daybreak and must return to my lodging for my books and an hour's rest, will do you one thing more for me before I go?"

"Yes," was his reply.

"Then," said I, "it is long since you had a refreshing sleep: now, will you lie down, and I will sit by you till you fall asleep?"

He lay down, and was soon fast asleep. After commending him to the care and blessing of the Lord, I quietly slipped out, and his wife returned to watch by his side. When I came back later in the day, after my Classes were over, he, on hearing my foot and voice, came to meet me, and clasping me in his arms, cried, "Thank God, I can pray now! I rose this morning refreshed from sleep, and prayed with my wife and children for the first time in my life; and now I shall do so every day, and serve God while I live, who hath dealt in so great mercy with me!"

After delightful conversation, he promised to go with me to Dr. Symington's church on Sabbath Day; there he took sittings beside me; at next half-yearly Communion he and his wife were received into membership, and their children were baptized; and from that day till his death he led a devoted and most useful Christian life. He now sleeps in Jesus; and I do believe I shall meet him in Glory as a trophy of redeeming grace and love!In my Mission district I was the witness of many joyful departures to be with Jesus,—I do not like to name them "deaths" at all. They left us rejoicing in the bright assurance that nothing present or to come "could ever separate them or us from the love of God which is in Christ Jesus our Lord." Many examples might be given; but I can find room for only one. John Sim, a dear little boy, was carried away by consumption. His child-heart seemed to be filled with joy about seeing Jesus. His simple prattle, mingled with deep questionings, arrested not only his young companions, but pierced the hearts of some careless sinners who heard him, and greatly refreshed the faith of God's dear people. It was the very pathos of song incarnated to hear the weak quaver of his dying voice sing out—

"I lay my sins on Jesus,
The spotless Lamb of God."

Shortly before his decease he said to his parents, "I am going soon to be with Jesus; but I sometimes fear that I may not see you there."

"Why so, my child?" said his weeping mother.

"Because," he answered, "if you were set upon going to Heaven and seeing Jesus there, you would pray about it, and sing about it; you would talk about Jesus to others, and tell them of that happy meeting with Him in Glory. All this my dear Sabbath School teacher taught me, and she will meet me there. Now why did not you, my father and mother, tell me all these things about Jesus, if you are going to meet Him too?" Their tears fell fast over their dying child; and he little knew, in his unthinking eighth year, what a message from God had pierced their souls through his innocent words.One day an aunt from the country visited his mother, and their talk had run in channels for which the child no longer felt any interest. On my sitting down beside him, he said, "Sit you down and talk with me about Jesus; I am tired hearing so much talk about everything else but Jesus; I am going soon to be with Him. Oh, do tell me everything you know or have ever heard about Jesus, the spotless Lamb of God!"At last the child literally longed to be away, not for rest, or freedom from pain—for of that he had very little—but, as he himself always put it, "to see Jesus." And, after all, that was the wisdom of the heart, however he learned it. Eternal life, here or hereafter, is just the vision of Jesus.

CHAPTER IX.
A FOREIGN MISSIONARY.

HAPPY in my work as I felt through these ten years, and successful by the blessing of God, yet I continually heard, and chiefly during my last years in the Divinity Hall, the wail of the perishing Heathen in the South Seas; and I saw that few were caring for them, while I well knew that many would be ready to take up my work in Calton, and carry it forward perhaps with more efficiency than myself. Without revealing the state of my mind to any person, this was the supreme subject of my daily meditation and prayer; and this also led me to enter upon those medical studies, in which I purposed taking the full course; but at the close of my third year, an incident occurred, which led me at once to offer myself for the Foreign Mission field.

The Reformed Presbyterian Church of Scotland, in which I had been brought up, had been advertising for another Missionary to join the Rev. John Inglis in his grand work on the New Hebrides. Dr. Bates, the excellent convener of the Heathen Missions Committee, was deeply grieved, because for two years their appeal had failed. At length, the Synod, after much prayer and consultation, felt the claims of the Heathen so gently pressed upon them by the Lord's repeated calls, that they resolved to cast lots, to discover whether God would thus select any Minister to be relieved from his home-charge, and designated as a Missionary to the South Seas. Each member of Synod, as I was informed, agreed to hand in, after solemn appeal to God, the names of the three best qualified in his esteem for such a work, and he who had the clear majority was to be loosed from his congregation, and to proceed to the Mission field—or the first and second highest, if two could be secured. Hearing this debate, and feeling an intense interest in these most unusual proceedings, I remember yet the hushed solemnity of the prayer before the names were handed in. I remember the strained silence that held the Assembly while the scrutineers retired to examine the papers; and I remember how tears blinded my eyes when they returned to announce that the result was so indecisive, that it was clear that the Lord had not in that way provided a Missionary. The cause was once again solemnly laid before God in prayer, and a cloud of sadness appeared to fall over all the Synod.

The Lord kept saying within me, "Since none better qualified can be got, rise and offer yourself!" Almost overpowering was the impulse to answer aloud, "Here am I, send me." But I was dreadfully afraid of mistaking my mere human emotions for the will of God. So I resolved to make it a subject of close deliberation and prayer for a few days longer, and to look at the proposal from every possible aspect. Besides, I was keenly solicitous about the effect upon the hundreds of young people and others, now attached to all my Classes and Meetings; and yet I felt a growing assurance that this was the call of God to His servant, and that He who was willing to employ me in the work abroad, was both able and willing to provide for the on-carrying of my work at home. My medical studies, as well as my literary and divinity training, had specially qualified me in some ways for the Foreign field, and from every aspect at which I could look the whole facts in the face, the voice within me sounded like a voice from God.

It was under good Dr. Bates of West Campbell Street that I had begun my career in Glasgow—receiving £25 per annum for district visitation in connection with his Congregation, along with instruction under Mr. Hislop and his staff in the Free Church Normal Seminary—and oh, how Dr. Bates did rejoice, and even weep for joy, when I called on him, and offered myself for the New Hebrides Mission! I returned to my lodging with a lighter heart than I had for sometime enjoyed, feeling that nothing so clears the vision, and lifts up the life, as a decision to move forward in what you know to be entirely the will of the Lord. I said to my fellow-student, Joseph Copeland, who had chummed with me all through our course at college, "I have been away signing my banishment" (a rather trifling way of talk for such an occasion). "I have offered myself as a Missionary for the New Hebrides."

After a long and silent meditation, in which he seemed lost in far-wandering thoughts, his answer was, "If they will accept of me, I am also resolved to go!"

I said, "Will you write the Convener to that effect, or let me do so?"

He replied, "You may."

A few minutes later his letter of offer was in the post-office. Next morning Dr. Bates called upon us, early, and after a long conversation, commended us and our future work to the Lord God in fervent prayer. At a meeting of the Foreign Missions Committee, held immediately thereafter, both were, after due deliberation, formally accepted, on condition that we passed successfully the usual examinations required of candidates for the Ministry. And for the next twelve months we were placed under a special committee for advice as to medical experience, acquaintance with the rudiments of trades, and anything else which might be thought useful to us in the Foreign field.

When it became known that I was preparing to go abroad as Missionary, nearly all were dead against the proposal, except Dr. Bates and my fellows-student. My dear father and mother, however, when I consulted them, characteristically replied, "that they had long since given me away to the Lord, and in this matter also would leave me to God's disposal." From other quarters we were besieged with the strongest opposition on all sides. Even Dr. Symington, one of my professors in divinity, and the beloved Minister in connection with whose congregation I had wrought so long as a City Missionary, and in whose Kirk Session I had for years sat as an Elder, repeatedly urged me to remain at home.

To his arguments I replied, "that my mind was finally resolved; that, though I loved my work and my people, yet I felt that I could leave them to the care of Jesus, who would soon provide them a better pastor than I; and that, with regard to my life amongst the Cannibals, as I had only once to die, I was content to leave the time and place and means in the hand of God who had already marvelously preserved me when visiting cholera patients and the fever-stricken poor; on that score I had positively no further concern, having left it all absolutely to the Lord, whom I sought to serve and honor, whether in life or by death."

The house connected with my Green Street Church was now offered to me for a Manse, and any reasonable salary that I cared to ask (as against the promised £120 per annum for the far-off and dangerous New Hebrides), on condition that I would remain at home. I cannot honestly say that such offers or opposing influences proved a heavy trial to me; they rather tended to confirm my determination that the path of duty was to go abroad.

Amongst many who sought to deter me, was one dear old Christian gentleman, whose crowning argument always was, "The cannibals! you will be eaten by cannibals!" At last I replied, "Mr. Dickson, you are advanced in years now, and your own prospect is soon to be laid in the grave, there to be eaten by worms, I confess to you, that if I can but live and die serving and honoring the Lord Jesus, it will make no difference to me whether I am eaten by cannibals or by worms; and in the Great Day my resurrection body will arise as fair as yours in the likeness of our risen Redeemer."

The old gentleman, raising his hands in a deprecating attitude, left the room exclaiming, "After that I have nothing more to say!"

My dear Green Street people grieved excessively at the thought of my leaving them, and daily pleaded with me to remain. Indeed, the opposition was so strong from nearly all, and many of them warm Christian friends, that I was sorely tempted to question whether I was carrying out the Divine will, or only some headstrong wish of my own. But conscience said louder and clearer every day, "Leave all these results with Jesus your Lord, who said, 'Go ye into all the world, preach the Gospel to every creature, and lo!

I am with you alway.'" These words kept ringing in my ears; these were our *marching orders*.

Some retorted upon me, "There are Heathen at home; let us seek and save, first of all, the lost ones perishing at our doors." This I felt to be most true, and an appalling fact; but I unfailingly observed that those who made this retort neglected these Home Heathen themselves; and so the objection, as from them, lost all its power.

On meeting, however, with so many obstructing influences, I again laid the whole matter before my dear parents, and their reply was to this effect:— "Heretofore we feared to bias you, but now we must tell you why we praise God for the decision to which you have been led. Your father's heart was set upon being a Minister, but other claims forced him to give it up! When you were given to them, your father and mother laid you upon the altar, their first-born, to be consecrated, if God saw fit, as a Missionary of the Cross; and it has been their constant prayer that you might be prepared, qualified, and led to this very decision; and we pray with all our heart that the Lord may accept your offering, long spare you, and give you many souls from the Heathen World for your hire." From that moment, every doubt as to my path of duty forever vanished. I saw the hand of God very visibly, not only preparing me for, but now leading me to, the Foreign Mission field.

Well did I know that the sympathy and prayers of my dear parents were warmly with me in all my studies and in all my Mission work; but for my education they could of course, give me no money help. All through, on the contrary, it was my pride and joy to help them, being the eldest in a family of eleven; though I here most gladly and gratefully record that all my brothers and sisters, as they grew up and began to earn a living, took their full share in this same blessed privilege. For we stuck to each other and to the old folks like burs, and had all things "in common," as a family in Christ—and I knew that never again, howsoever long they might be spared through the peaceful autumn of life, would the dear old father and mother lack any joy or comfort that the willing hands and loving hearts of all their children could singly or unitedly provide. For all this I did praise the Lord! It consoled me beyond description, in parting from them, probably forever, in this world at least.

CHAPTER X.
TO THE NEW HEBRIDES.

ON the first of December 1857—being then in my thirty-third year—the other Missionary-designate and I were "licensed" as preachers of the Gospel. Thereafter we spent four months in visiting and addressing nearly every Congregation and Sabbath School in the Reformed Presbyterian Church of Scotland, that the people might see us and know us, and thereby take a personal interest in our work. On the 23d March 1858, in Dr. Symington's church, Glasgow, in presence of a mighty crowd, and after a magnificent sermon on "Come over and help us," we were solemnly ordained as Ministers of the Gospel, and set apart as Missionaries to the New Hebrides. On the 16th April of the same year, we left the Tail of the Bank at Greenock, and set sail in the *Clutha* for the Foreign Mission field.

Our voyage to Melbourne was rather tedious, but ended prosperously, under Captain Broadfoot, a kindly, brave-hearted Scot, who did everything that was possible for our comfort. He himself led the singing on board at Worship, which was always charming to me, and was always regularly conducted—on deck when the weather was fair, below when it was rough. I was also permitted to conduct Bible Classes amongst both the crew and the passengers, at times and places approved of by the Captain—in which there was great joy.

Arriving at Melbourne, we were welcomed by Rev. Mr. Moor, Mr. and Mrs. Samuel Wilson, and Mr. Wright, all Reformed Presbyterians from Geelong. Mr. Wilson's two children, Jessie and Donald, had been under our care during the voyage; and my young wife and I went with them for a few days on a visit to Geelong, while Mr. Copeland remained on board the *Clutha* to look after our boxes and to watch for any opportunity of reaching our destination on the Islands. He heard that an American ship, the *Frances P. Sage*, was sailing from Melbourne to Penang; and the Captain agreed to land us on Aneityum, New Hebrides, with our two boats and fifty boxes, for £100. We got on board on the 12th August, but such a gale blew that we did not sail till the 17th. On the *Clutha* all was quiet, and good order prevailed; in the *F. P. Sage* all was noise and profanity. The Captain said he kept his second mate for the purpose of swearing at the men and knocking them about. The voyage was most disagreeable to all of us, but fortunately it lasted only twelve days. On the 29th we were close up to Aneityum; but the Captain refused to land us, even in his boats; some of us suspecting that his men were so badly used that had they got on shore they would never have returned to him! In any case he had beforehand secured his £100.

He lay off the island till a trader's boat pulled across to see what we wanted, and by it we sent a note to Dr. Geddie, one of the Missionaries there. Early next horning, Monday, he arrived in his boat, accompanied by Mr. Mathieson, a newly arrived Missionary from Nova Scotia; bringing also Captain Andersen in the small Mission schooner, the *John Knox*, and a large Mission boat called the *Columbia*, well manned with crews of able and willing Natives. Our fifty boxes were soon on board the *John Knox*, the *Columbia*, and our own boats—all being heavily loaded and built up, except those that had to be used in pulling the others ashore. Dr. Geddie, Mr. Mathieson, Mrs. Paton, and I were perched among the boxes on the *John Knox*, and had to hold on as best we could. On sheering off from the *F. P. Sage*, one of her davits caught and broke the mainmast of the little *John Knox* by the deck; and I saved my wife from being crushed to death by its fall, through managing to swing her instantaneously aside in an apparently impossible manner. It did graze Mr. Mathieson, but he was not hurt. The *John Knox*, already overloaded, was thus quite disabled; we were about ten miles at sea, and in imminent danger; but the captain of the *F. P. Sage* heartlessly sailed away, and left us to struggle with our fate.

We drifted steadily in the direction of Tanna, an island of cannibals, where our goods would have been plundered and all of us cooked and eaten. Dr. Geddie's boat, and mine had the *John Knox* in tow; and Mr. Copeland, with a crew of Natives, was struggling hard with his boat to pull the *Columbia* and her load towards Aneityum. As God mercifully ordered it, though we had a stiff trade wind to pull against, we had a comparatively calm sea; yet we drifted still to leeward, till Dr. Inglis going round to the harbor in his boat, as he had heard of our arrival, saw us far at sea, and hastened to our rescue. All the boats now, with their willing Native crews, got fastened to our schooner, and to our great joy she began to move ahead. After pulling for hours and hours, under the scorching rays of a tropical sun, we were all safely landed on shore at Aneityum, about six o'clock in the evening of 30th August, just four months and fourteen days since we sailed from Greenock. We got a hearty welcome from the Missionaries' wives, Mrs. Geddie, Mrs. Inglis, and Mrs. Mathieson, and from all our new friends the Christian Natives of Aneityum; and the great danger in which both life and property had been placed at the close of our voyage, made us praise God all the more that He had brought us to this quiet resting-place, around which lay the Islands of the New Hebrides, to which our eager hearts had looked forward, and into which we entered now in the name of the Lord.

Mr. Copeland, Mrs. Paton, and I went round the island to Dr. Inglis's Station, where we were most cordially received and entertained by his dear lady, and by the Christian Natives there. As he was making several additions to his house at that time, we received for the next few weeks our first practical and valuable training in Mission house-building, as well as in higher matters. Soon after, a meeting was called to consult about our settlement, and, by the advice and with the concurrence of all, Mr. and Mrs. Mathieson from Nova Scotia were located on the south side of Tanna, at Umairarekar, and Mrs. Paton and I at Port Resolution, on the same island. At first it was agreed that Mr. Copeland should be placed along with us; but owing to the weakly state of Mrs. Mathieson's health, it was afterwards resolved that, for a time at least, Mr. Copeland should live at either Station as seem most suitable or most requisite.

Dr. Inglis and a number of his most energetic Natives accompanied us to Umairarekar Tanna. There we purchased a site for Mission House and Church, and laid a stone foundation, and advanced as far as practicable the erection of a dwelling for Mr. and Mrs. Mathieson. Thence we proceeded to Port Resolution, Tanna, and similarly purchased a site, and advanced, to a forward stage, the house which Mrs. Paton and I were to occupy on our settlement there. Lime for plastering had to be burned in kilns from the coral rocks; and thatch, for roofing with sugar-cane leaf, had to be prepared by the Natives at both Stations before our return; for which, as for all else, a price was duly agreed upon, and was scrupulously paid. Unfortunately we learned, when too late, that both houses were too near the shore, exposed to unwholesome miasma, and productive of the dreaded fever and ague,— the most virulent and insidious enemy to all Europeans in those Southern Seas.

CHAPTER XI.
FIRST IMPRESSIONS OF HEATHENDOM.

MY first impressions drove me, I must confess, to the verge of utter dismay. On beholding these Natives in their paint and nakedness and misery, my heart was as full of horror as of pity. Had I given up my much-beloved work and my dear people in Glasgow, with so many delightful associations, to consecrate my life to these degraded creatures? Was it possible to teach them right and wrong, to Christianize, or even to civilize them? But that was only a passing feeling; I soon got as deeply interested in them, and in all that tended to advance them, and to lead them to the knowledge and love of Jesus, as ever I had been in my work at Glasgow. We were surprised and delighted at the remarkable change produced on the Natives of Aneityum through the instrumentality of Drs. Geddie and Inglis in so short a time; and we hoped, by prayerful perseverance in the use of similar means, to see the same work of God repeated on Tanna. Besides, the wonderful and blessed work done by Mrs. Inglis and Mrs. Geddie, at their Stations, filled our wives with the buoyant hope of being instruments in the hand of God to produce an equally beneficent change amongst the savage women of Tanna. Mrs. Paton had been left with Mrs. Inglis to learn all she could from her of Mission work on the Islands, till I returned with Dr. Inglis from the house-building operations on Tanna; during which period Mr. and Mrs. Mathieson were also being instructed by Dr. and Mrs. Geddie.

To the Tannese, Dr. Inglis and I were objects of curiosity and fear; they came crowding to gaze on our wooden and lime-plastered house; they chattered incessantly with each other, and left the scene day after day with undisguised and increasing wonderment. Possibly they thought us rather mad than wise!

Party after party of armed men going and coming in a state of great excitement, we were informed that war was on foot; but our Aneityumese Teachers were told to assure us that the Harbor people would only act on the defensive, and that no one would molest us at our work. One day two hostile tribes met near our Station; high words arose, and old feuds were revived. The Inland people withdrew; but the Harbor people, false to their promises, flew to arms and rushed past us in pursuit of their enemies. The discharge of muskets in the adjoining bush, and the horrid yells of the savages, soon informed us that they were engaged in deadly fights. Excitement and terror were on every countenance; armed men rushed about in every direction, with feathers in their twisted hair,—with faces painted red, black, and white, and some, one cheek black, the other red, others, the brow white, the chin blue—in fact, any color and on any part,—the more grotesque and savage-looking, the higher the art! Some of the women ran with their children to places of safety; but even then we saw other girls and women, on the shore close by, chewing sugar-cane and chaffering and laughing, as if their fathers and brothers had been engaged in a country dance, instead of a bloody conflict.

In the afternoon, as the sounds of the muskets and the yelling of the warriors came unpleasantly near to us, Dr. Inglis, leaning against a post for a little while in silent prayer, looked on us and said, "The walls of Jerusalem were built in troublous times, and why not the Mission House on Tanna? But let us rest for this day, and pray for these poor Heathen."

We retired to a Native house that had been temporarily granted to us for rest, and there pled before God for them all. The noise and the discharge of muskets gradually receded, as if the Inland people were retiring; and towards evening the people around us returned to their villages. We were afterwards informed that five or six men had been shot dead; that their bodies had been carried by the conquerors from the field of battle, and cooked and eaten that very night at a boiling spring near the head of the bay, less than a mile from the spot where my house was being built. We had also a more graphic illustration of the surroundings into which we had come, through Dr. Inglis's Aneityum boy, who accompanied us as cook. When our tea was wanted next morning, the boy could not be found. After a while of great anxiety on our part, he returned, saying, "Missi, this is a dark land. The people of this land do dark works. At the boiling spring they have cooked and feasted upon the slain. They have washed the blood into the water; they have bathed there, polluting everything. I cannot get pure water to make your tea. What shall I do?"

Dr. Inglis told him that he must try for water elsewhere, till the rains came and cleansed away the pollution; and that meanwhile, instead of tea, we would drink from the cocoa-nut, as they had often done before. The lad was quite relieved. It not a little astonished us, however, to see that his mind regarded their killing and eating each other as a thing scarcely to be noticed, but that it was horrible that they should spoil the water! How much are even our deepest instincts the creatures of mere circumstances! I, if trained like him, would probably have felt like him.

Next evening, as we sat talking about the people, and the dark scenes around us, the quiet of the night was broken by a wild wailing cry from the villages around, long-continued and unearthly. We were informed that one of the wounded men, carried home from the battle, had just died; and that they had strangled his widow to death, that her spirit might accompany him to the other world, and be his servant there, as she had been here. Now their dead bodies were laid side by side, ready to be buried in the sea. Our hearts sank to think of all this happening within ear-shot, and that we knew it not! Every new scene, every fresh incident, set more clearly before us the benighted condition and shocking cruelties of these Heathen people, and we longed to be able to speak to them of Jesus and the love of God. We eagerly tried to pick up every word of their language, that we might, in their own tongue, unfold to them the knowledge of the true God and of salvation from all these sins through Jesus Christ.

CHAPTER XII.
BREAKING GROUND ON TANNA.

OUR small Missionary schooner, the *John Knox*, having no accommodation for lady passengers, and little for anybody else except the discomfort of lying on deck, we took advantage of a trader to convey us from Aneityum to Tanna. The Captain kindly offered to take us and about thirty casks and boxes to Port Resolution for £5, which we gladly accepted. After a few hours' sailing we were all safely landed on Tanna on the 5th November, 1858. Dr. Geddie went for a fortnight to Umairarekar, now known as Kwamera, on the south side of Tanna, to assist in the settlement of Mr. and Mrs. Mathieson, and to help in making their house habitable and comfortable. Mr. Copeland, Mrs. Paton, and I were left at Port Resolution, to finish the building of our house there, and work our way into the good will of the Natives as best we could.

On landing, we found the people to be literally naked and painted Savages; they were at least as destitute of clothing as Adam and Eve after the fall, when they sewed fig-leaves for a girdle, and even more so, for the women wore only a tiny apron of grass, in some cases shaped like a skirt or girdle, the men an indescribable affair like a pouch or bag, and the children absolutely nothing whatever.

At first they came in crowds to look at us, and at everything we did or had. We knew nothing of their language; we could not speak a single word to them, nor they to us. We looked at them, they at us; we smiled and nodded, and made signs to each other; this was our first meeting and parting. One day I observed two men, the one lifting up one of our articles to the other, and saying, "Nungsi nari enu?"

I concluded that he was asking, "What is this?" Instantly, lifting a piece of wood, I said, "Nungsi nari enu?"

They smiled and spoke to each other. I understood them to be saying, "He has got hold of our language now." Then they told me their name for the thing which I had pointed to. I found that they understood my question, What is this? or, What is that? and that I could now get from them the name of every visible or tangible thing around us! We carefully noted down every name they gave us, spelling all phonetically, and also every strange sound we heard from them; thereafter, by painstaking comparison of different circumstances, we tried to ascertain their meanings, testing our own guess by again cross-questioning the Natives. One day I saw two men approaching, when one, who was a stranger, pointed to me with his finger, and said, "Se nangin?"

Concluding that he was asking my name, I pointed! to one of them with my finger, and looking at the other, inquired, "Se nangin?"

They smiled, and gave me their names. We were now able to get the names of persons and things, and so our ears got familiarized with the distinctive sounds of their language; and being always keenly on the alert, we made extraordinary progress in attempting bits of conversation and in reducing their speech for the first time to a written form—for the New Hebrideans had no literature, and not even the rudiments of an alphabet. I used to hire some of the more intelligent lads and men to sit and talk with us, and answer our questions about names and sounds; but they so often deceived us, and we, doubtless, misunderstood them so often, that this course was not satisfactory, till after we had gained some knowledge of their language and its construction, and they themselves had become interested in helping us. Amongst our most interesting helpers, and most trustworthy, were two aged chiefs—Nowa and Nouka—in many respects two of Nature's noblest gentlemen, kind at heart to all, and distinguished by a certain native dignity of bearing. But they were both under the leadership of the war-chief Miaki, a kind of devil-king over many villages and tribes.

The Tannese had hosts of stone idols, charms, and sacred objects, which they abjectly feared, and in which they devoutly believed. They were given up to countless superstitions, and firmly glued to their dark heathen practices. Their worship was entirely a service of fear, its aim being to propitiate this or that Evil Spirit, to prevent calamity or to secure revenge. They deified their chiefs, like the Romans of old, so that almost every village or tribe had its own Sacred Man, and some of them had many. They exercised an extraordinary influence for evil, these village or tribal priests, and were believed to have the disposal of life and death through their sacred ceremonies, not only in their own tribe, but over all the Islands. Sacred men and women, wizards and witches, received presents regularly to influence the gods, and to remove sickness, or to cause it by the *Nahak, i. e.* incantation over remains of food, or the skin of fruit, such as banana, which the person has eaten on whom they wish to operate. They also worshiped the spirits of departed ancestors and heroes, through their material idols of wood and stone, but chiefly of stone. They feared these spirits and sought their aid; especially seeking to propitiate those who presided over war and peace, famine and plenty, health and sickness, destruction and prosperity, life and death. Their whole worship was one of slavish fear; and, so far as ever I could learn, they had no idea of a God of mercy or grace.

But these very facts—that they did worship something, that they believed in spirits of ancestors and heroes, and that they cherished many legends regarding those whom they had never seen, and handed these down to their children—and the fact that they had ideas about the invisible world and its inhabitants, made it not so hard as some might suppose to convey to their minds, once their language and modes of thought were understood, some clear ideal of Jehovah God as the great uncreated Spirit Father, who Himself created and sustains all that is. It could not, however, be done offhand, or by a few airy lessons. The whole heart and soul and life had to be put into the enterprise. But it could be done—that we believed because they were men, not beasts; it had been done—that we saw in the converts on Aneityum; and our hearts rose to the task with quenchless hope!

CHAPTER XIII.
PIONEERS IN THE NEW HEBRIDES.

A GLANCE backwards over the story of the Gospel in the New Hebrides may help to bring my readers into touch with the events that are to follow. The ever-famous names of Williams and Harris are associated with the earliest efforts to introduce Christianity amongst this group of islands in the South Pacific Seas. John Williams and his young Missionary companion Harris, under the auspices of the London Missionary Society, landed on Erromanga on the 30th of November 1839. Alas, within a few minutes of their touching land, both were clubbed to death; and the savages proceeded to cook and feast upon their bodies. Thus were the New Hebrides baptized with the blood of Martyrs; and Christ thereby told the whole Christian world that He claimed these Islands as His own. His cross must yet be lifted up, where the blood of His saints has been poured forth in His name! The poor Heathen knew not that they had slain their best friends; but tears and prayers ascended for them from all Christian souls, wherever the story of the martyrdom on Erromanga was read or heard.

Again, therefore, in 1842, the London Missionary Society sent out Messrs. Turner and Nisbet to pierce this kingdom of Satan. They placed their standard on our chosen island of Tanna, the nearest to Erromanga. In less than seven months, however, their persecution by the savages became so dreadful, that we see them in a boat trying to escape by night with bare life. Out on that dangerous sea they would certainly have been lost, but the Ever-Merciful drove them back to land, and sent next morning a whaling vessel, which, contrary to custom, called there, and just in the nick of time. They, with all goods that could be rescued, were got safely on board, and sailed for Samoa. Say not their plans and prayers were baffled; for God heard and abundantly blessed them there, beyond all their dreams.

After these things, the London Missionary Society again and again placed Samoan Native Teachers on one or other island of the New Hebrides; but their unhealthiness, compared with the more wholesome Samoa or Rarotonga, so afflicted them with the dreaded ague and fever, besides what they endured from the inhospitable savages themselves, that no effective Mission work had been accomplished there till at last the Presbyterian Missionaries were led to enter upon the scene. Christianity had no foothold anywhere on the New Hebrides, unless it were in the memory and the blood of the Martyrs of Erromanga.

The Rev. John Geddie and his wife, from Nova Scotia, were landed on Aneityum, the most southerly island of the New Hebrides, in 1848; and the Rev. John Inglis and his wife, from Scotland, were landed on the other side of the same island, in 1852. An agent for the London Missionary Society, the Rev. T. Powell, accompanied Dr. Geddie for about a year, to advise as to his settlement and to assist in opening up the work. Marvelous as it may seem, the Natives on Aneityum, showed interest in the Missionaries from the very first, and listened to their teachings; so that in a few years Dr. Inglis and Dr. Geddie saw about 3500 savages throwing away their idols, renouncing their Heathen customs, and avowing themselves to be worshipers of the true Jehovah God. Slowly, yet progressively, they unlearned their Heathenism; surely and hopefully they learned Christianity and civilization. When these Missionaries "came to this Island, there were no Christians there; when they left it, there were no Heathens."

Further, these poor Aneityumese, having glimpses of the Word of God, determined to have a Holy Bible in their own mother tongue, wherein before no book or page ever had been written in the history of their race. The consecrated brain and hand of their Missionaries kept toiling day and night in translating the book of God; and the willing hands and feet of the Natives kept toiling through fifteen long but unwearying years, planting and preparing arrowroot to pay the £1200 required to be laid out in the printing and publishing of the book. Year after year the arrowroot, too sacred to be used for their daily food, was set apart as the Lord's portion; the Missionaries sent it to Australia and Scotland, where it was sold by private friends, and the whole proceeds consecrated to this purpose. On the completion of the great undertaking by the Bible Society, it was found that the Natives had earned as much as to pay every penny of the outlay; and their first Bibles went out to them, purchased with the consecrated toils of fifteen years!

Let those who lightly esteem their Bibles think on those things. Eight shillings for every leaf, or the labor and proceeds of fifteen years for the Bible entire, did not appear to these poor converted savages too much to pay for that Word of God, which had sent to them the Missionaries, which had revealed to them the grace of God in Christ, and which had opened their eyes to the wonders and glories of redeeming love!

CHAPTER XIV.
THE GREAT BEREAVEMENT.

MY first house on Tanna was on the old site occupied by Turner and Nisbet, near the shore, for obvious reasons, and only a few feet above tide-mark. So was that of Mr. Mathieson, handy for materials as goods being landed, and, as we imagined, close to the healthy breezes of the sea. Alas! we had to learn by sad experience, like our brethren in all untried Mission fields. The sites proved to be hot-beds for Fever and Ague, mine especially; and much of this might have been escaped by building on the higher ground, and in the sweep of the refreshing trade-winds. For all this, however, no one was to blame; everything was done for the best, according to the knowledge then possessed. Our house was sheltered behind by an abrupt hill about two hundred feet high, which gave the site a feeling of coziness. It was surrounded and much shaded, by beautiful breadfruit trees, and very large cocoa-nut trees; too largely beautiful, indeed, for they shut out many a healthy breeze that we sorely needed! There was a long swamp at the head of the bay, and, the ground at the other end on which our house stood being scarcely raised perceptibly higher, the malaria almost constantly enveloped us. Once, after a smart attack of the fever, an intelligent Chief said to me, "Missi, if you stay here, you will soon die! No Tanna man sleeps so low down as you do, in this damp weather, or he too would die. We sleep on the high ground, and the trade-wind keeps us well. You must go and sleep on the hill, and then you will have better health."

I at once resolved to remove my house to higher ground, at the earliest practicable moment; heavy though the undertaking would necessarily be, it seemed our only hope of being able to live on the island. Alas, for one of us, it was already too late!

My dear young wife, Mary Ann Robson, landed with me on Tanna on the 5th November 1858, in excellent health and full of all tender and holy hopes. On the 12th February 1859 God sent to us our first-born son; for two days or so both mother and child seemed to prosper, and our island-exile thrilled with joy! But the greatest of sorrows was treading hard upon the heels of that joy! My darling's strength showed no signs of rallying. She had an attack of ague and fever a few days before; on the third day or so thereafter, it returned, and attacked her every second day with increasing severity for a fortnight. Diarrhea ensued, and symptoms of pneumonia, with slight delirium at intervals; and then in a moment, altogether unexpectedly, she died on the 3d March. To crown my sorrows, and complete my loneliness, the dear baby-boy, whom we had named after her father, Peter Robert Robson, was taken from me after one week's sickness, on the 20th March. Let those who have ever passed through any similar darkness as of midnight feel for me; as for all others, it would be more than vain to try to paint my sorrows!

I knew then, when too late, that our work had been entered on too near the beginning of the rainy season. We were both, however, healthy and hearty; and I daily pushed on with the house, making things hourly more comfortable, in the hope that long lives were before us both, to be spent for Jesus in seeking the salvation of the perishing Heathen. In our mutual inexperience, and with our hearts aglow for the work of our lives, we incurred this risk which should never have been incurred; and I only refer to the matter thus, in the hope that others may take warning.

Stunned by that dreadful loss, in entering upon this field of labor to which the Lord had Himself so evidently led me, my reason seemed for a time almost to give way. Ague and fever, too, laid a depressing and weakening hand upon me, continuously recurring, and reaching oftentimes the very height of its worst burning stages. But I was never altogether forsaken. The ever-merciful Lord sustained me, to lay the precious dust of my beloved Ones in the same quiet grave, dug for them close by at the end of the house; in all of which last offices my own hands, despite breaking heart, had to take the principal share! I built the grave round and round with coral blocks, and covered the top with beautiful white coral, broken small as gravel; and that spot became my sacred and much-frequented shrine, during all the following months and years when I labored on for the salvation of these savage Islanders amidst difficulties, dangers, and deaths. Whensoever Tanna turns to the Lord, and is won for Christ, men in after-days will find the memory of that spot still green,—where with ceaseless prayers and tears I claimed that land for God in which I had "buried my dead" with faith and hope. But for Jesus, and the fellowship He vouchsafed me there, I must have gone mad and died beside that lonely grave!

Dr. Inglis, my brother Missionary on Aneityum, wrote to the Reformed Presbyterian Magazine:—"I trust all those who shed tears of sorrow on account of her early death will be enabled in the exercise of faith and resignation to say, 'The Will of the Lord be done; the Lord gave and the Lord hath taken away: blessed be the Name of the Lord!' I need not say how deeply we sympathize with her bereaved parents, as well as with her sorrowing husband. By her death the Mission has sustained a heavy loss. We were greatly pleased with Mrs. Paton during the period of our short intercourse with her. Her mind, naturally vigorous, had been cultivated by a superior education. She was full of Missionary spirit, and took a deep interest in the Native women. This was seen further, when she went to Tanna, where, in less than three months, she had collected a class of eight females, who came regularly to her to receive instruction. There was about her a maturity of thought, a solidity of character, a loftiness of aim and purpose, rarely found in one so young. Trained up in the fear of the Lord from childhood, like another Mary she had evidently chosen that good part, which is never taken away from those possessed of it. When she left this island, she had to all human appearance a long career of usefulness and happiness on Earth before her, but the Lord has appointed otherwise. She has gone, as we trust, to her rest and her reward. The Lord has said to her as He said to David, 'Thou didst well in that it was in thine heart to build a House for My Name.' Let us watch and pray, for our Lord cometh as a thief in the night."

Soon after her death, the good Bishop Selwyn called at Port Resolution, Tanna, in his Mission Ship. He came on shore to visit me, accompanied by the Rev. J. O. Patteson. They had met Mrs. Paton on Aneityum in the previous year soon after our arrival, and, as she was then the picture of perfect health, they also felt her loss very keenly. Standing with me beside the grave of mother and child, I weeping aloud on his one hand, and Patteson—afterward the Martyr Bishop of Kakupu—sobbing silently on the other, the godly Bishop Selwyn poured out his heart to God amidst sobs and tears, during which he laid his hands on my head, and invoked Heaven's richest consolations and blessings on me and my trying labors.

Sorrow and love constrain me to linger over her last words. She cried, "Oh, that my dear mother were here! She is a good woman, my mother, a jewel of a woman."

Then, observing Mr. Copeland near by, she said, "Oh, Mr. Copeland, I did not know you were there! You must not think that I regret coming here, and leaving my mother. If I had the same thing to do over again, I would do it with far more pleasure, yes, with all my heart. Oh no! I do not regret leaving home and friends, though at the time I felt it keenly."

Soon after this, looking up and putting her hand in mine, she said—

"J. C. wrote to our Janet saying, that young Christians under their first impressions thought they could do anything or make any sacrifice for Jesus, and he asked if she believed it, for he did not think they could, when tested; but Janet wrote back that she believed they could, and (added she with great emphasis) *I believe it is true!*"

In a moment, altogether unexpectedly, she fell asleep in Jesus, with these words on her lips. "Not lost, only gone before to be forever with the Lord"—my heart keeps saying or singing to itself from that hour till now.

It was very difficult to be resigned, left alone, and in sorrowful circumstance; but feeling immovably assured that my God and Father was too wise and loving to err in anything that He does or permits, I looked up to the Lord for help, and struggled on in His work. I do not pretend to see through the mystery of such visitations,—wherein God calls away the young, the promising, and those sorely needed for His service here; but this I do know and feel, that, in the light of such dispensations, it becomes us all to love and serve our blessed Lord Jesus so that we may be ready at His call for death and Eternity.

CHAPTER XV.
AT HOME WITH CANNIBALS.

IN the first letter, sent jointly by Mr. Copeland and myself from Tanna to the Church at home, the following statements occur:—

"We found the Tannese to be painted Savages, enveloped in all the superstition and wickedness of Heathenism. All the men and children go in a state of nudity. The older women wear grass skirts, and the young women and girls, grass or leaf aprons like Eve in Eden. They are exceedingly ignorant, vicious, and bigoted, and almost void of natural affection. Instead of the inhabitants of Port Resolution being improved by coming in contact with white men they are rendered much worse; for they have learned all their vices but none of their virtues,—if such are possessed by the pioneer traders among such races! The Sandal-wood Traders are as a class the most godless of men, whose cruelty and wickedness make us ashamed to own them as our countrymen. By them the poor defenseless Natives are oppressed and robbed on every hand; and if they offer the slightest resistance, they are ruthlessly silenced by the musket or revolver. Few months here pass without some of them being so shot, and, instead of their murderers feeling ashamed, they boast of how they despatch them. Such treatment keeps the Natives always burning under a desire for revenge, so that it is a wonder any white man is allowed to come among them. Indeed, all Traders here are able to maintain their position only by revolvers and rifles; but we hope a better state of affairs is at hand for Tanna."

The novelty of our being among them soon passed away, and they began to show their avarice and deceitfulness in every possible way. The Chiefs united and refused to give us the half of the small piece of land which had been purchased, on which to build our Mission House, and when we attempted to fence in the part they had left to us, they "tabooed" it, *i. e.* threatened our Teachers and us with death if we proceeded further with the work. This they did by placing certain reeds stuck into the ground here and there around our house, which our Aneityumese servants at once knew the meaning of, and warned us of our danger; so we left off making the fence, that we might if possible evade all offense. They then divided the few breadfruit and cocoa-nut trees on the ground amongst themselves, or demanded such payment for these trees as we did not possess, and threatened revenge on us if the trees were injured by any person. They now became so unreasonable and offensive, and our dangers so increased, as to make our residence amongst them extremely trying. At this time a vessel called; I bought from the Captain the things for payment which they demanded; on receiving it, they lifted the Taboo, and for a little season appeared to be friendly again. This was the third payment they had got for that site, and to yield was teaching them a cruel lesson; all this we felt and clearly saw, but they had by some means to be conciliated, if possible, and our lives had to be saved, if that could be done without dishonor to the Christian name.

After these events, a few weeks of dry weather began to tell against the growth of their yams and bananas. The drought was instantly ascribed to us and our God. The Natives far and near were summoned to consider the matter in public assembly. Next day, Nouka, the high chief, and Miaki, the war-chief, his nephew, came to inform us that two powerful Chiefs had openly declared in that assembly that if the Harbor people did not at once kill us or compel us to leave the island they would, unless the rain came plentifully in the meantime, summon all the Inland people and murder both our Chiefs and us. The friendly Chiefs said, "Pray to your Jehovah God for rain, and do not go far beyond your door for a time; we are all in greatest danger, and if war breaks out we fear we cannot protect you."

But this friendliness was all pretense; they themselves, being Sacred Men, professed to have the power of sending or withholding rain, and tried to fix the blame of their discomfiture on us. The rage of the poor ignorant Heathen was thereby fed against us. The Ever-Merciful, however, again interposed on our behalf. On the following Sabbath, just when we were assembling for worship, rain began to fall, and in great abundance. The whole inhabitants believed, apparently, that it was sent to save us in answer to our prayers; so they met again, and resolved to allow us to remain on Tanna. Alas! on the other hand, the continuous and heavy rains brought much sickness and fever in their train, and again their Sacred Men pointed to us as the cause. Hurricane winds also blew and injured their fruits and fruit-trees,—another opportunity for our enemies to lay the blame of everything upon the Missionaries and their Jehovah God! The trial and the danger daily grew, of living among a people so dreadfully benighted by superstition, and so easily swayed by prejudice and passion.

The Natives of Tanna were well-nigh constantly at war amongst themselves, every man doing that which was right in his own eyes, and almost every quarrel ending in an appeal to arms. Besides many battles far inland, one was fought beside our houses and several around the Harbor. In these conflicts many men were bruised with clubs and wounded with arrows, but few lives were lost, considering the savage uproar and frenzy of the scene. In one case, of which we obtained certain information, seven men were killed in an engagement; and, according to Tannese custom, the warriors and their friends feasted on them at the close of the fray, the widows of the slain being also strangled to death, and similarly disposed of.

Besides those who fell in war, the Natives living in our quarter had killed and feasted on eight persons, usually, in sacrificial rites.

It is said that the habitual Cannibal's desire for human flesh becomes so horrible that he has been known to disinter and feast upon those recently buried. Two cases of this revolting barbarism were reported as having occurred amongst the villagers living near us. On another occasion the great chief Nouka took seriously unwell, and his people sacrificed three women for his recovery! All such cruel and horrifying practises, however, they tried to conceal from us; and many must have perished in this way of whom we, though living at their doors, were never permitted to hear.

Amongst the Heathen, in the New Hebrides, and especially on Tanna, *woman* is the down-trodden slave of man. She is kept working hard, and bears all the heavier burdens, while he walks by her side with musket, club, or spear. If she offends him, he beats or abuses her at pleasure. A savage gave his poor wife a severe beating in front of our house and just before our eyes, while in vain we strove to prevent it. Such scenes were so common that no one thought of interfering. Even if the woman died in his hands, or immediately thereafter, neighbors, took little notice, if any at all. And their children were so little cared for, that my constant wonder was how any of them survived at all! As soon as they are able to knock about, they are left practically to care for themselves; hence the very small affection they show towards their parents, which results in the aged who are unable to work being neglected, starved to death, and sometimes even more directly and violently destroyed.

A Heathen boy's education consists in being taught to aim skilfully with the bow, throw the spear faultlessly at a mark, to wield powerfully the club and tomahawk, and to shoot well with musket and revolver when these can be obtained. He accompanies his father and brothers in all the wars and preparations for war, and is diligently initiated into all their cruelties and lusts, as the very prerequisite of his being regarded and acknowledged to be a man and a warrior. The girls have, with their mother and sisters, to toil and slave in the village plantations, to prepare all the materials for fencing these around, to bear every burden, and to be knocked about at will by the men and boys.

Oh, how sad and degraded is the position of Woman where the teaching of Christ is unknown, or disregarded though known! It is the Christ of the Bible, it is His Spirit entering into humanity, that has lifted Woman, and made her the helpmate and the friend of Man, not his toy or his slave.

CHAPTER XVI.
SUPERSTITIONS AND CRUELTIES.

ABOUT the time of my dear wife's death, our brother Missionary, Mr. Mathieson, also became exceedingly unwell. His delicate frame fast gave way, and brought with it weakness of the mind as well; and he was removed to Aneityum apparently in a dying condition. These sad visitations had a bad effect on the natives, owing to their wild superstitions about the cause of death and sickness. We had reason to fear that they would even interfere with the precious grave, over which we kept careful watch for a season; but God mercifully restrained them. Unfortunately, however, one of my Aneityumese Teachers who had gone round to Mr. Mathieson's Station took ill and died there, and this rekindled all their prejudices. He, poor fellow, before death said, "I shall not again return to Port Resolution, or see my dear Missi; but tell him that I die happy, for I love Jesus much, and I am going to Jesus!"

Hearing these things, the natives insolently demanded me to tell them the cause of his death, and of Mr. Mathieson's trouble, and of the other deaths. Other reasoning or explanation being to them useless, I turned the tables, and demanded them to tell me why all this trouble and death had overtaken us in their land, and whether they themselves were not the cause of it all? Strange to say, this simple question turned the whole current of their speculations. They held meeting after meeting to discuss it for several days, and returned the message, "We do not blame you, and you must not blame us, for causing these troubles and deaths; but we believe that a Bushman must have got hold of a portion of something we had eaten, and must have thrown it to the great Evil Spirit in the volcano, thereby bringing all these troubles and curses."

Another Chief vindicated himself and others thus:—"Karapanamun, the Aurumanu or great Evil Spirit of Tanna, whom we all fear and worship, is causing these troubles; for he knows that if we become worshipers of your Jehovah God, we cannot continue to fear him, or present him with the best of everything, as our forefathers have always done; he is angry at you and at us all."

The fear of the deaths and troubles being ascribed to them silenced their talk against us for a season; but very little made them either friends or foes, as the next event will too painfully show.

Nowhat, an old Chief of the highest rank from Aneityum, who spoke Tannese and was much respected by the natives all round the south side of

Tanna, came on a visit to our island. After returning home, he became very ill and died in a few days. The deluded Tannese, hearing of his death, ascribed it to me and the Worship, and resolved to burn our house and property, and either murder the whole Mission party, or compel us to leave the island. Nowhat's brother was sent from Aneityum to talk to the Tannese and conciliate them, but unfortunately he could not speak the language well; and the Aneityumese Teachers felt their lives to be at this time in such danger that they durst not accompany him as interpreters, while I, on the other hand, did not understand his language, nor he, mine. Within two days after landing, he had a severe attack of ague and fever; and, though the vessel he came in remained eight days, he was prostrated all the time, so that his well-intentioned visit did us much harm. The Tannese became furious. This was proof positive that we were the cause of all their sickness and death! Inland and all along the weather side of the island, when far enough away from us, they said that the natives were enjoying excellent health. Meeting after meeting was held; exciting speeches were delivered; and feasts were given, for which it was said that several women were sacrificed, cooked and eaten,—such being the bonds by which they entered into covenant with each other for life or death.

The inhabitants for miles around united in seeking our destruction, but God put it into even savage hearts to save us. Old Nowar, the Chief under whom we lived, and the Chief next under him, Arkurat, set themselves to rescue us. Along with Manuman and Sirawia they opposed every plan in the public assembly for taking our lives. Some of their people also remained friendly to us, and by the help of our Aneityumese Teachers, warned us of danger and protected our lives. Determined not to be baffled, a meeting of all our enemies on the island was summoned, and it was publicly resolved that a band of men be selected and enjoined to kill the whole of those friendly to the Mission, old Nowar among the rest, and not only to murder the Mission party, but also a trader who had lately landed to live there, that no one might be left to give information to the white men or bring punishment on the Islanders. Frenzy of excitement prevailed, and the blood-fiend seemed to override the whole assembly; when, under an impulse that surely came from the Lord of Pity, one great warrior Chief who had hitherto kept silent, rose, swung aloft a mighty club, and smashing it earthwards, cried aloud, "The man that kills Missi must first kill me,—the men that kill the Mission Teachers must first kill me and my people,—for we shall stand by them and defend them till death."

Instantaneously, another Chief thundered in with the same declaration; and the great assembly broke up in dismay. All the more remarkable was this deliverance, as these two Chiefs lived nearly four miles inland, and, as reputed disease makers and Sacred Men, were regarded as amongst our bitterest enemies. It had happened that, a brother of the former Chief having been wounded in battle, I had dressed his wounds and he recovered, for which perhaps he now favored us. But I do not put very much value on that consideration; for too clearly did our dear Lord Jesus interpose directly on our behalf that day. I and my defenseless company had spent it in anxious prayers and tears; and our hearts overflowed with gratitude to the Saviour who rescued us from the lions' jaws.

Leaving all consequences to the disposal of my Lord, I determined to make an unflinching stand against wife-beating and widow-strangling, feeling confident that even their natural conscience would be on my side, I accordingly pled with all who were in power to unite and put down these shocking and disgraceful customs. At length ten Chiefs entered into an agreement not to allow any more beating of wives or strangling of widows, and to forbid all common labor on the Lord's day; but alas, except for purposes of war or other wickedness, the influence of the Chiefs on Tanna was comparatively small. One Chief boldly declared, "If we did not beat our women, they would never work; they would not fear and obey us; but when we have beaten, and killed, and feasted on two or three, the rest are all very quiet and good for a long time to come!"

I tried to show him how cruel it was, besides that it made them unable for work, and that kindness would have a much better effect; but he promptly assured me that Tannese women "could not understand kindness." For the sake of teaching by example, my Aneityumese Teachers and I used to go a mile or two inland on the principal pathway, along with the Teachers' wives, and there cutting and carrying home a heavy load of firewood for myself and each of the men, while we gave only a small burden to each of the women. Meeting many Tanna-men by the way, I used to explain to them that this was how Christians helped and treated their wives and sisters, and then they loved their husbands and were strong to work at home; and that as men were made stronger, they were intended to bear the heavier burdens, and especially in all labors out of doors. Our habits and practises had thus as much to do as, perhaps more than, all our appeals, in leading them to glimpses of the life to which the Lord Jesus was calling them.

CHAPTER XVII.
STREAKS OF DAWN AMIDST DEEDS OF DARKNESS.

ANOTHER war-burst, that caused immense consternation, passed over with only two or three deaths; and I succeeded in obtaining the consent of twenty Chiefs to fight no more except on the defensive,—a covenant to which, for a considerable time, they strictly adhered, in the midst of fierce provocations. But to gain any such end, the masses of the people must be educated to the point of desiring it. The few cannot, in such circumstances, act up to it, without laying themselves open to be downtrodden and swept away by the savages around.

About this time, several men, afraid or ashamed by day, came to me regularly by night for conversation and instruction. Having seen the doors of the Mission House made fast and the windows blinded so that they could not be observed, they continued with me for many hours, asking all strange questions about the new Religion and its laws. I remember one Chief particularly, who came often, saying to me, "I would be an Awfuaki man (*i. e.* a Christian) were it not that all the rest would laugh at me; that I could not stand!"

"Almost persuaded"—before you blame him, remember how many in Christian lands and amid greater privileges live and die without ever passing beyond that stage.

The wife of one of those Chiefs died, and he resolved to imitate a Christian burial. Having purchased white calico from a Trader, he came to me for some tape which the Trader could not supply, and told me that he was going to dress the body as he had seen my dear wife's dressed, and lay her also in a similar grave. He declined my offer to attend the funeral and to pray with them, as in that case many of the villagers would not attend. He wanted all the people to be present, to see and to hear, as it was the first funeral of the kind ever celebrated among the Tannese; and my friend Nowar the Chief had promised to conduct a Service and offer prayer to Jehovah before all the Heathen. It moved me to many strange emotions, this Christian burial, conducted by a Heathen and in the presence of Heathens, with an appeal to the true and living God by a man as yet darkly groping among idols and superstitions. Many were the wondering questions from time to time addressed to me. The idea of a resurrection from the dead was that which most keenly interested these Natives, and called forth all their powers of inquiry and argument. Thus the waves of hope and fear swept alternately across our lives; but we embraced every possible opportunity of telling them the story of the life and death of Jesus, in the strong hope that God would spare us yet to bring the benighted Heathen to the knowledge of the true salvation, and to love and serve the only Saviour.

Confessedly, however, it was uphill, weary, and trying work. For one thing, these Tannese were terribly dishonest; and when there was any special sickness, or excitement from any cause, their bad feeling towards the Worship was displayed by the more insolent way in which they carried off whatever they could seize. When I opposed them, the club or tomahawk, the musket or *kawas* (*i. e.* killing-stone), being instantly raised, intimated that my life would be taken, if I resisted. Their skill in stealing on the sly was phenomenal! If an article fell, or was seen on the floor, a Tanna-man would neatly cover it with his foot, while looking you frankly in the face, and, having fixed it by his toes or by bending in his great toe like a thumb to hold it, would walk off with it, assuming the most innocent look in the world. In this way, a knife, a pair of scissors or any smaller article, would at once disappear. Another fellow would deftly stick something out of sight amongst the whipcord plaits of his hair, another would conceal it underneath his naked arm, while yet another would shamelessly lift what he coveted and openly carry it away.

With most of them, however, the shame was not in the theft, but in doing it so clumsily that they were discovered! Once, after continuous rain and a hot damp atmosphere, when the sun shone out I put my bedclothes on a rope to dry. I stood at hand watching, as also the wives of two Teachers, for things were mysteriously disappearing almost under our very eyes. Suddenly, Miaki, who with his war-companions had been watching us unobserved, came rushing to me breathless and alone, crying, "Missi, come in, quick, quick! I want to tell you something and to get your advice!"

He ran into my house, and I followed; but before he had got into his story, we heard the two women crying out, "Missi, Missi, come quick! Miaki's men are Stealing your sheets and blankets!"

I ran at once, but all were gone into the bush, and them my sheets and blankets. Miaki for a moment looked abashed, as I charged him with deceiving me just to give his men their opportunity. But he soon rose to the occasion. He wrought himself into a towering rage at them, flourished his huge club and smashed the bushes all around, shouting to me, "Thus will I smash these fellows, and compel them to return your clothes."

One dark night, I heard them amongst my fowls. These I had purchased from them for knives and calico; and they now stole them all away, dead or alive. Had I interfered, they would have gloried in the chance to club or shoot me in the dark, when no one could exactly say who had done the deed. Several of the few goats, which I had for milk, were also killed or driven away; indeed, all the injury that was possible was done to me, short of taking away my life, and that was now frequently attempted. Having no fires or fireplaces in my Mission House, such being not required there,— though sometimes a fire would have been invaluable for drying our bedclothes in the rainy season,—we had a house near by in which all our food was cooked, and there, under lock and key, we secured all our cooking utensils, pots, dishes, etc. One night that too was broken into, and everything was stolen. In consternation, I appealed to the Chief, telling him what had been done. He also flew into a great rage, and vowed vengeance on the thieves, saying that he would compel them to return everything. But, of course, nothing was returned; the thief could not be found! I, unable to live without something in which to boil water, at length offered a blanket to any one that would bring back my kettle. Miaki himself, after much professed difficulty, returned it *minus* the lid,—that, he said, probably fishing for a higher bribe, could not be got at any price, being at the other side of the island in a tribe over which he had no control! In the circumstances, I was glad to get kettle *minus* lid—realizing how life itself may depend on so small a luxury!

CHAPTER XVIII.
THE VISIT OF H. M. S. "CORDELIA."

ONE morning, the Tannese, rushing towards me in great excitement, cried, "Missi, Missi, there is a God, or a ship on fire, or something of fear, coming over the sea! We see no flames, but it smokes like a volcano. Is it a Spirit, a God, or a ship on fire? What is it? what is it?"

One party after another followed in quick succession, shouting the same questions in great alarm, to which I replied, "I cannot go at once; I must dress first in my best clothes; it will likely be one of Queen Victoria's Men-of-war, coming to ask of me if your conduct is good or bad, if you are stealing my property, or threatening my life, or how you are using me?"

They pled with me to go and see it; but I made much fuss about dressing, and getting ready to meet the great Chief on the vessel, and would not go with them. The two principal Chiefs now came running and asked, "Missi, will it be a ship of war?"

I called to them, "I think it will; but I have no time to speak to you now, I must get on my best clothes!"

They said, "Missi, only tell us, will he ask you if we have been stealing your things?"

I answered, "I expect he will."

They asked, "And will you tell him?"

I said, "I must tell him the truth; if he asks, I will tell him."

They then cried out, "Oh, Missi, tell him not! Everything shall be brought back to you at once, and no one will be allowed again to steal from you."

Then said I, "Be quick! Everything must be returned before he comes. Away, away! and let me get ready to meet the great Chief on the Man-of-war."

Hitherto, no thief could ever be found, and no Chief had power to cause anything to be restored to me; but now, in an incredibly brief space of time, one came running to the Mission House with a pot, another with a pan, another with a blanket, others with knives, forks, plates, and all sorts of stolen property. The Chiefs called me to receive these things, but I replied, "Lay them all down at the door, bring everything together quickly; I have no time to speak with you!"

I delayed my toilet, enjoying mischievously the magical effect of an approaching vessel that might bring penalty to thieves. At last the Chiefs, running in breathless haste, called out to me, "Missi, Missi, do tell us, is the stolen property all here?"

Of course I could not tell, but, running out, I looked on the promiscuous heap of my belongings, and said, "I don't see the lid of the kettle there yet!"

One Chief said, "No, Missi, for it is on the other side of the island; but tell him not, I have sent for it, and it will be here to-morrow."

I answered, "I am glad you have brought back so much; and now, if you three Chiefs, Nauka, Miaki, and Nowar, do not run away when he comes, he will not likely punish you; but, if you and your people run away, he will ask me why you are afraid, and I will be forced to tell him! Keep near me and you are all safe; only there must be no more stealing from me."

They said, "We are in black fear, but we will keep near you, and our bad conduct to you is done." The charm and joy of that morning are fresh to me still, when H. M. S. *Cordelia*, Captain Vernon, steamed into our lovely Harbor. The Commander, having heard rumor of my dangers on Tanna, kindly came on shore as soon as the ship cast anchor, with two boats, and a number of his officers and men, so far armed. He was dressed in splendid uniform, being a tall and handsome man, and he and his attendants made a grand and imposing show. On seeing Captain Vernon's boat nearing the shore, and the men glittering in gold lace and arms, Miaki the Chief left my side on the beach and rushed towards his village. I concluded that he had run for it through terror, but he had other and more civilized intentions in his Heathen head! Having obtained, from some trader or visitor in previous days, a soldier's old red coat, he had resolved to rise to the occasion and appear in his best before the Captain and his men. As I was shaking hands with them and welcoming them to Tanna, Miaki returned with the short red coat on, buttoned tightly round his otherwise naked body; and, surmounted by his ugly painted face and long whipcords of twisted hair, it completely spoiled any appearance that he might otherwise have had of savage freedom, and made him look a dirty and insignificant creature.

The Captain was talking to me, his men stood in order near by—to my eyes, oh how charming a glimpse of Home life!—when Miaki marched up and took his place most consequentially at my side. He felt himself the most important personage in the scene, and with an attempt at haughty dignity he began to survey the visitors. All eyes were fixed on the impudent little man, and the Captain asked, "What sort of a character is this?"

I replied, "This is Miaki, our great war Chief?"; and whispered to the Captain to be on his guard, as this man knew a little English, and might understand or misunderstand just enough to make it afterwards dangerous to me. The Captain only muttered, "The contemptible creature!" But such words were far enough beyond Miaki's vocabulary, so he looked on and grinned complacently. At last he said, "Missi, this great Chief whom Queen Victoria has sent to visit you in her Man-of-war, cannot go over the whole of this island so as to be seen by all our people; and I wish you to ask him if he will stand by a tree, and allow me to put a spear on the ground at his heel, and we will make a nick in it at the top of his head, and the spear will be sent round the island to let all the people see how tall this great man is!" They were delighted at the good Captain agreeing to their simple request; and that spear was exhibited to thousands, as the vessel, her Commander, officers, and men, were afterwards talked of round and round the island. Captain Vernon was extremely kind, and offered to do anything in his power for me, thus left alone on the island amongst such savages; but, as my main difficulties were connected with my spiritual work amongst them, rousing up their cruel prejudices, I did not see his kindness could effectually interpose. At his suggestion, however, I sent a general invitation to all the Chiefs within reach, to meet the Captain next morning at my house. True to their instincts of suspicion and fear, they despatched all their women and and children to the beach on the opposite side of the island, beyond reach of danger, and next morning my house was crowded with armed men, manifestly much afraid. Punctually at the hour appointed, 10 A.M., the Captain came on shore; and soon thereafter twenty Chiefs were seated with him in my house. He very kindly spent about an hour, giving them wise counsels and warning them against outrages on strangers, all calculated to secure our safety and advance the interests of our Mission work. He then invited all the Chiefs to go on board and see his vessel. They were taken to see the Armory, and the sight of the big guns running so easily on rails vastly astonished them. He then placed them round us on deck and showed them two shells discharged towards the ocean, at which, as they burst and fell far off, splash—splashing into the water, the terror of the Natives visibly increased. But, when he sent a large ball crashing through a cocoanut grove, breaking the trees like straws and cutting its way clear and swift, they were quite dumfounded and pled to be again set safely on shore. After receiving each some small gift, however, they were reconciled to the situation, and returned immensely interested in all that they had seen. Doubtless many a wild romance was spun by these savage heads, in trying to describe and hand down to others the wonders of the fire-god of the sea, and the Captain of the great white Queen. How easily it all lends itself to the service of poetry and myth!

CHAPTER XIX.
"NOBLE OLD ABRAHAM."

FEVER and ague had now attacked me fourteen times severely, with slighter recurring attacks almost continuously after my first three months on the island, and I now felt the necessity of taking the hint of the Tannese Chief before referred to—"Sleep on the higher ground." Having also received medical counsel to the same effect, though indeed experience was painfully sufficient testimony, I resolved to remove my house, and began to look about for a suitable site. There rose behind my present site, a hill about two hundred feet high, surrounded on all sides by a valley, and swept by the breezes of the trade-winds, being only separated from the ocean by a narrow neck of land. On this I had set my heart; there was room for a Mission House and a Church, for which indeed Nature seemed to have adapted it. I proceeded to buy up every claim by the Natives to any portion of the hill, paying each publicly and in turn, so that there might be no trouble afterwards. I then purchased from a Trader the deck planks of a shipwrecked vessel, with which to construct a house of two apartments, a bedroom and a small store-room adjoining it, to which I purposed to transfer and add the old house as soon as I was able.

Just at this juncture, the fever smote me again more severely than ever; my weakness after this attack was so great, that I felt as if I never could rally again. With the help of my faithful Aneityumese Teacher, Abraham, and his wife, however, I made what appeared my last effort to creep—I could not climb—up the hill to get a breath of wholesome air. When about two-thirds up the hill, I became so faint that I concluded I was dying. Lying down on the ground, sloped against the root of a tree to keep me from rolling to the bottom, I took farewell of old Abraham, of my Mission work, and of everything around! In this weak state I lay, watched over by my faithful companion, and fell into a quiet sleep. When consciousness returned, I felt a little stronger, and a faint gleam of hope and life came back to my soul.

Abraham and his devoted wife Nafatu lifted me and carried me to the top of the hill. There they laid me on cocoanut leaves on the ground, and erected over me a shade or screen of the same; and there the two faithful souls, inspired surely by something diviner even than mere human pity, gave me the cocoanut juice to drink and fed me with native food and kept me living—I know not for how long. Consciousness did, however, fully return. The trade-wind refreshed me day by day. The Tannese seemed to have given me up for dead; and providentially none of them looked near us for many days. Amazingly my strength returned, and I began planning about my new house on the hill. Afraid again to sleep at the old site, I slept under the tree, and sheltered by the cocoanut leaf screen, while preparing my new bedroom.

Here again, but for these faithful souls, the Aneityumese Teacher and his wife, I must have been baffled, and would have died in the effort. The planks of the wreck, and all other articles required, they fetched and carried; and it taxed my utmost strength to get them in some way planted together. But life depended on it. It was at length accomplished; and after that time I suffered comparatively little from anything like continuous attacks of fever and ague. That noble old soul, Abraham, stood by me as an angel of God in sickness and in danger; he went at my side wherever I had to go; he helped me willingly to the last inch of strength in all that I had to do; and it was perfectly manifest that he was doing all this not from mere human love, but for the sake of Jesus. That man had been a Cannibal in his Heathen days, but by the grace of God there he stood verily a new creature in Christ Jesus. Any trust, however sacred or valuable, could be absolutely reposed in him; and in trial or danger I was often refreshed by that old Teacher's prayers, as I used to be by the prayers of my saintly father in my childhood's home. No white man could have been more valuable helper to me in my perilous circumstances; and no person, white or black, could have shown more fearless and chivalrous devotion.

When I have read or heard the shallow objections of irreligious scribblers and talkers, hinting that there was no reality in conversions, and that Mission effort was but waste, oh, how my heart has yearned to plant them just one week on Tanna, with the "natural" man all around in the person of Cannibal and Heathen, and only the one "spiritual" man in the person of the converted Abraham, nursing them, feeding them, saving them "for the love of Jesus"—that I might just learn how many hours it took to convince them that Christ in man was a reality after all! All the skepticism of Europe would hide its head in foolish shame; and all its doubts would dissolve under one glance of the new light that Jesus, and Jesus alone, pours from the converted Cannibal's eye.

CHAPTER XX.
A TYPICAL SOUTH SEA TRADER.

THE prejudices and persecutions of Heathens were a sore enough trial, but sorer and more hopeless was the wicked and contaminating influence of, alas, my fellow-countrymen. One, for instance, a Captain Winchester, living with a native woman at the head of the bay as a Trader, a dissipated wretch, though a well-educated man, was angry forsooth at this state of peace! Apparently there was not the usual demand for barter for the fowls, pigs, etc., in which he traded. He developed at once a wonderful interest in their affairs, presented all the Chiefs around with powder, caps, and balls, and lent among them a number of flash-muskets. He urged them not to be afraid of war, as he would supply any amount of ammunition. I remonstrated, but he flatly told me that peace did not suit his purposes. Incited and encouraged thus, these poor Heathen people were goaded into a most unjust war on neighboring tribes. The Trader immediately demanded a high price for the weapons he had lent; the price of powder, caps, and balls rose exorbitantly with every fresh demand; his yards were crowded with poultry and pigs, which he readily disposed of to passing vessels; and he might have amassed great sums of money but for his vile dissipations. Captain Winchester, now glorying in the war, charged a large hog for a wine-glass full of powder, or three or four balls, or ten gun-caps; he was boastful of his "good luck" in getting rid of all his old muskets and filling his yards with pigs and fowls. Such is the infernal depth to which we can sink, when the misery and the ruin of many are thought to be more than atoned for by the wealth and prosperity of a few who trade in their doom!Miaki the war Chief had a young brother, Rarip by name, about eighteen years of age. When this war began he came to live with me at the Mission House. After it had raged some time, Miaki forced him to join the fighting men; but he escaped through the bush, and returned to me, saying, "Missi, I hate this fighting; it is not good to kill men; I will live with you!"

Again the war Chief came, and forced my dear young Rarip to join the hosts. Of course, I could only plead; I could not prevent him. This time, he placed him at his own side in the midst of his warriors. On coming in sight of the enemy, and hearing their first yells as they rushed from the bush, a bullet pierced young Rarip's breast, and he fell dead into the arms of Miaki. The body was carried home to his brother's village, with much wailing, and a messenger ran to tell me that Rarip was dead. On hasting thither, I found him quite dead, and the center of a tragic ceremonial. Around him, some sitting, others lying on the ground, were assembled all the women and girls, tearing their hair, wounding themselves with split bamboos and broken bottles, dashing themselves headlong to the earth, painting all black their faces, breasts, and arms, and wailing with loud lamentations! Men were also there, knocking their heads against the trees, gashing their bodies with knives till they ran with streaks of blood, and indulging in every kind of savage symbol of grief and anguish. My heart broke to see them, and to think that they knew not to look to our dear Lord Jesus for consolation.

I returned to the Mission House, and brought a white sheet and some tape, in which the body of dear young Rarip was wrapped and prepared for the grave. The Natives appeared to be gratified at this mark of respect; and all agreed that Rarip should have, under my direction, a Christian burial. The men prepared the grave in a spot selected near to his own house; I read the Word of God, and offered prayer to Jehovah, with a psalm of praise, amidst a scene of weeping and lamentation never to be forgotten; and the thought burned through my very soul—oh, when, when will the Tannese realize what I am now thinking and praying about, the life and immortality brought to light through Jesus?As the war still raged on, and many more were killed, vengeance threatened the miserable Trader. Miaki attacked him thus, "You led us into this war. You deceived us, and we began it. Rarip is dead, and many others. Your life shall yet go for his."Captain Winchester, heartless as a dog so long as pigs and fowls came to the yard at whatever cost to others' lives, now trembled like a coward for himself. He implored me to let him and his Mare wife sleep at my house for safety; but I refused to allow my Mission to be in any way identified with his crimes. The Natives from other islands, whom he kept and wrought like slaves, he now armed with muskets for his defence; but, having no faith in their protecting or even warning him, he implored me to send one of my Teachers, to assist his wife in watching till he snatched a few hours of sleep every day, and, if awake, he would sell his life as dearly as he could by aid of musket and revolver. The Teachers were both afraid and disinclined to go; and I could not honestly ask them to do so. His peril and terror became so real that by night he slept in his boat anchored out in the center of the bay, with his arms beside him, and a crew ready to start off at the approach of danger and lose everything; while by day he kept watch on shore, armed, and also ready to fly. Thus his miserable existence dragged on, keeping watch alternatively with his wife, till a trading vessel called and carried him off with all that he had rescued—for which deliverance we were unfeignedly thankful! The war, which he had wickedly instigated, lingered on for three months; and then, by a present given secretly to two leading Chiefs, I managed to bring it to a close. But feelings of revenge for the slain burned fiercely in many breasts; and young men had old feuds handed on to them by the recital of their fathers' deeds of blood.

CHAPTER XXI.
UNDER AX AND MUSKET.

ABOUT this time, our Sabbath audiences at the Mission numbered forty or so. Nowar and three or four more, and only they, seemed to love and serve Jesus. They were, however, changeable and doubtful, though they exerted a good influence on their villages, and were generally friendly to us and to the Worship.

One morning at daybreak I found my house surrounded by armed men, and a Chief intimated that they had assembled to take my life. Seeing that I was entirely in their hands, I knelt down and gave myself away body and soul to the Lord Jesus, for what seemed the last time on earth. Rising, I went out to them, and began calmly talking about their unkind treatment of me and contrasting it with all my conduct towards them. I also plainly showed them what would be the sad consequences, if they carried out their cruel purpose. At last some of the chiefs, who had attended the Worship, rose and said, "Our conduct has been bad; but now we will fight for you, and kill all those who hate you."

Grasping hold of their leader, I held him fast till he promised never to kill any one on my account, for Jesus taught us to love our enemies and always to return good for evil! During this scene, many of the armed slunk away into the bush, and those who remained entered into a bond to be friendly and to protect us. But again their Public Assembly resolved that we should be killed, because, as they said, they hated Jehovah and the Worship; for it made them afraid to do as they had always done. If I would give up visiting the villages, and praying and talking with them about Jehovah, they intimated that they would like me to stay and trade with them, as they liked the Traders but hated the Missionaries! I told them that the hope of being able to teach them the Worship of Jehovah alone kept me living amongst them; that I was there, not for gain or pleasure, but because I loved them, and pitied their estate, and sought their good continually by leading them to know and serve the only true God.

But my enemies seldom slackened their hateful designs against my life, however calmed or baffled for the moment. Within a few days of the above events, when Natives in large numbers were assembled at my house, a man furiously rushed on me with his ax; but a Kaserumini Chief snatched a spade with which I had been working, and dexterously defended me from instant death. Life in such circumstances led me to cling very near to the Lord Jesus; I knew not, for one brief hour, when or how attack might be made; and yet, with my trembling hand clasped in the Hand once nailed on Calvary, and now swaying the scepter of the Universe, calmness and peace and resignation abode in my soul.

Next day, a wild Chief followed me about for four hours with his loaded musket, and, though often directed towards me, God restrained his hand. I spoke kindly to him, and attended to my work as if he had not been there, fully persuaded that my God had placed me there, and would protect me till my allotted task was finished. Looking up in unceasing prayer to our dear Lord Jesus, I left all in His hands, and felt immortal till my work was done. Trials and hairbreadth escapes strengthened my faith, and seemed only to nerve me for more to follow; and they did tread swiftly upon each other's heels. Without that abiding consciousness of the presence and power of my dear Lord and Saviour, nothing else in all the world could have preserved me from losing my reason and perishing miserably. His words, "Lo, I am with you alway, even unto the end of the world," became to me so real that it would not have startled me to behold Him, as Stephen did, gazing down upon the scene. I felt His supporting power, as did St. Paul, when he cried, "I can do all things through Christ which strengthened me." It is the sober truth, and it comes back to me sweetly after twenty years, that I had my nearest and dearest glimpses of the face and smile of my blessed Lord in those dread moments when musket, club, or spear was being leveled at my life. Oh the bliss of living and enduring, as seeing "Him who is invisible!" One evening, I awoke three times to hear a Chief and his men trying to force the door of my house. Though armed with muskets, they had some sense of doing wrong, and were wholesomely afraid of a little retriever dog which had often stood betwixt me and death. God restrained them again; and next morning the report went all round the Harbor that those who tried to shoot me were "smitten weak with fear," and that shooting would not do. A plan was therefore deliberately set on foot to fire the premises, and club us if we attempted to escape. But our Aneityumese Teacher heard of it, and God helped us to frustrate their designs. When they knew their plots were revealed to us, they seemed to lose faith in themselves, and cast about to circumvent us in some more secret way, Their evil was overruled for good.

CHAPTER XXII.
A NATIVE SAINT AND MARTYR.

NAMUEI, one of my Aneityumese Teachers, was placed at our nearest village. There he had built a house for himself and his wife, and there he led amongst the Heathen a pure and humble Christian life. Almost every morning he came and reported on the state of affairs to me. Without books or a school, he yet instructed the Natives in Divine things, conducted the worship, and taught them much by his good example. His influence was increasing, when one morning a Sacred Man threw at him the *kawas* or killing-stone, a deadly weapon like a scythe stone in shape and thickness, usually round but sometimes angular, and from eighteen to twenty inches long. They throw it from a great distance and with fatal precision. The Teacher, with great agility, warded his head and received the deep cut from it in his left hand, reserving his right hand to guard against the club that was certain to follow swiftly. The Priest sprang upon him with his club and with savage yells. He evaded, yet also received, many blows; and, rushing out of their hands, actually reached the Mission House, bleeding, fainting, and pursued by howling murderers. I had been anxiously expecting him, and hearing the noise I ran out with all possible speed.

On seeing me, he sank down by a tree, and cried, "Missi, Missi, quick! and escape for your life! They are coming to kill you; they say they must kill us all to-day, and they have begun with me; for they hate Jehovah and the Worship!"

I hastened to the good Teacher where he lay; I bound up, washed, and dressed his wounds; and God, by the mystery of His own working, kept the infuriated Tannese watching at bay. Gradually they began to disappear into the bush, and we conveyed the dear Teacher to the Mission House. In three or four weeks, he so far recovered by careful nursing that he was able to walk about again. Some petitioned for him to return to the village; but I insisted, as a preliminary, that the Harbor Chiefs should unitedly punish him who had abused the Teacher; and this to test them, for he had only carried out their own wishes,—Nowar excepted, and perhaps one or two others. They made a pretense of atoning by presenting the Teacher with a pig and some yams as a peace-offering; but I said, "No! Such bad conduct must be punished, or we would leave their island by the first opportunity."

Now that Sacred Man, a Chief too, had gone on fighting with other tribes, till his followers had all died or been slain; and, after three weeks' palaver, the other Chiefs seized him, tied him with a rope, and sent me word to come and see him punished, as they did not want us after all to leave the island. I had to go, for fear of more bloody work, and after talk with them, followed by many fair promises, he was loosed.

All appearing friendly for some time, and willing to listen and learn, the Teacher earnestly desired to return to his post. I pled with him to remain at the Mission House till we felt more assured, but he replied, "Missi, when I see them thirsting for my blood, I just see myself when the Missionary first came to my island. I desired to murder him, as they now desire to kill me. Had he stayed away for such danger, I would have remained Heathen; but he came, and continued coming to teach us, till, by the grace of God, I was changed to what I am. Now the same God that changed me to this can change these poor Tannese to love and serve Him. I cannot stay away from them; but I will sleep at the Mission House, and do all I can by day to bring them to Jesus."

It was not in me to keep such a man, under such motives, from what he felt to be his post of duty. He returned to his village work, and for several weeks things appeared most encouraging. The inhabitants showed growing interest in us and our work, and less fear of the pretensions of their Heathen Priest, which, alas! fed his jealousy and anger. One morning during worship, when the good Teacher knelt in prayer, the same savage Priest sprang upon him with his great club and left him for dead, wounded and bleeding and unconscious. The people fled and left him in his blood, afraid of being mixed up with the murder. The Teacher, recovering a little, crawled to the Mission House, and reached it about midday in a dying condition. On seeing him, I ran to meet him, but he fell near the Teacher's house, saying, "Missi, I am dying! They will kill you also. Escape for your life."

Trying to console him, I sat down beside him, dressing his wounds and nursing him. He was quite resigned; he was looking up to Jesus, and rejoicing that he would soon be with Him in Glory. His pain and suffering were great but he bore all very quietly, as he said and kept saying, "For the sake of Jesus! For Jesu's sake!" He was constantly praying for his persecutors, "O Lord Jesus, forgive them, for they know not what they are doing. Oh, take not away all Thy servants from Tanna! Take not away Thy Worship from this dark island! O God, bring all the Tannese to love and follow Jesus!"

To him, Jesus was all and in all; and there were no bands in his death. He passed from us, in the assured hope of entering into the Glory of his Lord. Humble though he may appear in the world's esteem, I knew that a great man had fallen there in the service of Christ, and that he would take rank in the glorious Army of the Martyrs. I made for him a coffin, and dug his grave near the Mission House. With prayers, and many tears, we consigned his remains to the dust in the certainty of a happy resurrection. Even one such convert was surely a triumphant reward for the Missionaries, whom God had honored in bringing him to Jesus. May they have many like Namuri for their crown of joy and rejoicing in the great day!

CHAPTER XXIII.
BUILDING AND PRINTING FOR GOD.

FOR fully three months, all our available time, with all the native help which I could hire, was spent in erecting a building to serve for Church and School. It was fifty feet long, by twenty-one feet six inches broad. The studs were three feet apart, and all fixed by tenon and mortise into upper and lower wall plates. The beautiful roof of iron-wood and sugar-cane leaf was supported by three massive pillars of wood, sunk deeply into the ground. The roof extended about three feet over the wall plates, both to form a verandah and to carry the raindrops free beyond the walls. It was made of sugar-cane leaf and cocoanut leaves all around. The floor was laid with white coral, broken small, and covered with cocoanut leaf mats, such as those on which the Natives sat. Indeed, it was as comfortable a House of Prayer as any man need wish for in the tropics, though having only open spaces for doors and windows! I bought the heavy wood for it on Aneityum—price, fifty pairs of trousers for Natives; and these again were the gift of my Bible Class in Glasgow, all cut and sewed by their own hands. I gave also one hundred and thirty yards of cloth, along with other things, for other needful wood.

As we were preparing a foundation for the Church, a huge and singular-looking round stone was dug up, at sight of which the Tannese stood aghast. The eldest Chief said, "Missi, that stone was either brought there by Karapanamun (the Evil Spirit), or hid there by our great Chief who is dead. That is the Stone God to which our forefathers offered human sacrifices; these holes held the blood of the victim till drunk up by the Spirit. The Spirit of that stone eats up men and women and drinks their blood, as our fathers taught us. We are in greatest fear!"

A Sacred Man claimed possession, and was exceedingly desirous to carry it off; but I managed to keep it, and did everything in my power to show them the absurdity of these foolish notions. Idolatry had not indeed yet fallen throughout Tanna; but one cruel idol, at least, had to give way for the erection of God's House on that benighted land.

An ever-memorable event was the printing of my first book in Tannese. Thomas Binnie, Jun., Glasgow, gave me a printing-press and a font of type. Printing was one of the things I had never tried, but having now prepared a booklet in Tannese, I got my printing press into order, and began fingering the type. But book-printing turned out to be for me a much more difficult affair than house-building had been. Yet by dogged perseverance I succeeded at last. My biggest difficulty was how to arrange the pages properly! After many failures, I folded a piece of paper into the number of leaves wanted, cut the corners, folding them back, and numbering as they would be when correctly placed in the book; then folding all back without cutting up the sheet, I found now by these numbers how to arrange the pages in the frame or case for printing, as indicated on each side. And do you think me foolish, when I confess that I shouted in an ecstasy of joy when the first sheet came from the press all correct? It was about one o'clock in the morning. I was the only white man then on the island, and all the Natives had been fast asleep for hours! Yet I literally pitched my hat into the air, and danced like a schoolboy round and round that printing-press; till I began to think, Am I losing my reason? Would it not be like a Missionary to be upon my knees, adoring God for this first portion of His blessed Word ever printed in this new language? Friend, bear with me, and believe me—that was as true worship as ever was David's dancing before the Ark of his God! Nor think that I did not, over that first sheet of God's Word ever printed in the Tannese tongue, go upon my knees too, and then, and every day since, plead with the mighty Lord to carry the light and joy of His own Holy Bible into every dark heart and benighted home on Tanna!

Yet dangers darkened round me. One day, while toiling away at my house, the war Chief and his brother, and a large party of armed men, surrounded the plot where I was working. They all had muskets, besides their own native weapons. They watched me for some time in silence, and then every man leveled a musket straight at my head. Escape was impossible. Speech would only have increased my danger. My eyesight came and went for a few moments. I prayed to my Lord Jesus, either Himself to protect me or to take me home to His Glory. I tried to keep working on at my task, as if no one was near me. In that moment, as never before, the words came to me—"Whatsoever ye shall ask in My name, I will do it;" and I knew that I was safe. Retiring a little from their first position, no word having been spoken, they took up the same attitude somewhat farther off, and seemed to be urging one another to fire the first shot. But my dear Lord restrained them once again, and they withdrew, leaving me with a new reason for trusting Him with all that concerned me for Time and Eternity.

CHAPTER XXIV.
HEATHEN DANCE AND SHAM FIGHT.

THE Chief, Nowar Noukamara, usually known as Nowar, was my best and most-to-be-trusted friend. He influenced the Harbor Chiefs and their people for eight or ten miles around to get up a great feast in favor of the Worship of Jehovah. All were personally and specially invited, and it was the largest Assembly of any kind that I ever witnessed on the Islands.

When all was ready, Nowar sent a party of Chiefs to escort me and my Aneityumese Teachers to the feast. Fourteen Chiefs, in turn, made speeches to the assembled multitude; the drift of all being, that war and fighting be given up on Tanna,—that no more people be killed by Nahak, for witchcraft and sorcery were lies,—that Sacred Men no longer profess to make wind and rain, famine and plenty, disease and death,—that the dark Heathen talk of Tanna should cease,—that all here present should adopt the Worship of Jehovah as taught to them by the Missionary and the Aneityumese,—and that all the banished Tribes should be invited to their own lands to live in peace! These strange speeches did not draw forth a single opposing voice. The Tannese are born talkers, and can and will speechify on all occasions; but most of it means nothing, bears no fruit.

After these speeches, a scene followed which gradually assumed shape as an idolatrous ceremonial and greatly horrified me. It was in connection with the immense quantity of food that had been prepared for the feast, especially pigs and fowls. A great heap had been piled up for each Tribe represented, and a handsome portion also set apart for the Missionary and his Teachers. The ceremony was this, as nearly as I could follow it. One hundred or so of the leading men marched into the large clear space in the center of the assembled multitudes, and stood there facing each other in equal lines, with a man at either end closing up the passage between. At the middle they stood eight or ten feet apart, gradually nearing till they almost met at either end. Amid tremendous silence for a few moments, all stood hushed; then every man kneeled on his right knee, extended his right hand, and bent forward till his face nearly touched the ground. Thereon the man at the one end began muttering something, his voice rising ever louder as he rose to his feet, when it ended in a fearful yell as he stood erect. Next the two long lines of men, all in a body, went through the same ceremonial, rising gradually to their feet, with mutterings deepening into a howl, and heightening into a yell stood erect. Finally, the man at the other end went through the same hideous forms. All this was thrice deliberately repeated, each time with growing frenzy. And then, all standing on their feet, they united as with one voice in what sounded like music running mad up and down the scale—closing with a long, deep-toned, hollow howl as of souls in pain. With smiles of joy, the men then all shook hands with each other. Nowar and another Chief briefly spoke; and the food was then divided and exchanged, a principal man of each Tribe standing by to receive and watch his portion.

At this stage, Nowar and Nerwangi, as leaders, addressed the Teachers and the Missionary to this effect; "This feast is held to move all the Chiefs and People here to give up fighting, to become friends, and to worship your Jehovah God. We wish you to remain, and to teach us all good conduct. As an evidence of our sincerity, and of our love, we have prepared this pile of food for you."

In reply, I addressed the whole multitude, saying how pleased I was with their speeches and with the resolutions and promises which they all had made. I further urged them to stick fast by these, and that grand fruits would arise to their island, to themselves, and to their children.

Having finished a brief address, I then walked forward to the very middle of the circle, and laid down before them a bundle of stripes of red calico and pieces of white calico, a number of fish-hooks, knives, etc., etc., requesting the two Chiefs to divide my offering of goodwill among the Tribes assembled, and also the pile of food presented to us, as a token of my love and friendship to them all.

Not without some doubt, and under considerable trial, did I take this apparently unfriendly attitude of refusing to take their food. But I feared to seem even to approve of any act of devil-worship, or to confirm them in it, being there to discourage all such scenes, and to lead them to acknowledge only the true God. Yet all the time I felt this qualm,—that it might have been better to eat food with men who acknowledged some God and asked his blessing, than with those white Heathens at home, who asked the blessing of no God, nor thanked Him—in this worse than the dog which licks the hand that feeds it! Nowar and Nerwangi explained in great orations what I meant, and how I wished all to be divided amongst the assembled Tribes to show my love. With this, all seemed highly satisfied.

Heathen dances were now entered upon, their paint and feathers and ornaments adding to the wildness of the scene. The men seemed to dance in an inside ring, and the women in an outside ring, at a considerable distance from each other. Music was supplied by singing and clapping of hands. The order was perfect, and the figures highly intricate. But I have never been able to associate dancing with things lovely and of good report! After the dancing, all retired to the bush; and a kind of sham fight then followed on the public cleared ground. A host of painted savages rushed in and took possession with songs and shoutings. From the bush, on the opposite side, the chanting of women was heard in the distance, louder and louder as they approached. Snatching from a burning fire flaming sticks, they rushed on the men with these, beating them and throwing burning pieces of wood among them, till with deafening yells amongst themselves and amidst shouts of laughter from the crowd, they drove them from the space, and danced thereon and sang a song of victory. The dancing and fighting, the naked painted figures, and the constant yells and shoutings gave one a weird sensation, and suggested strange ideas of Hell broken loose.

The final scene approached, when the men assisted their women to fill all the allotted food into baskets to be carried home and eaten there; for the different Tribes do not sit down together and eat together as we would do; their coming together is for the purpose of exchanging and dividing the food presented. And now they broke into friendly confusion, and freely walked about mingling with each other; and a kind of savage rehearsal of Jonathan and David took place. They stripped themselves of their fantastic dresses, their handsomely woven and twisted grass skirts, leaf skirts, grass and leaf aprons; they gave away or exchanged all these, and their ornaments and bows and arrows, besides their less romantic calico and print dresses more recently acquired. The effusion and ceremonial of the gifts and exchanges seem to betoken a loving people; and so they were for the feast—but that laid not aside a single deadly feud, and streams of blood and cries of hate would soon efface all traces of this day.

CHAPTER XXV.
CANNIBALS AT WORK.

EARLY one morning, the savage yells of warring Tribes woke me from sleep. They had broken into a quarrel about a woman, and were fiercely engaged with their clubs. According to my custom, I rushed in amongst them, and, not without much difficulty, was blessed in separating them before deadly wounds had been given or received. On this occasion, the Chiefs of both Tribes, being very friendly to me, drove their people back from each other at my earnest appeals. Sitting down at length within earshot, they had it out in a wild scolding match, a contest of lung and tongue. Meanwhile I rested on a canoe midway betwixt them, in the hope of averting a renewal of hostilities. By and by an old Sacred Man, a Chief, called Sapa, with some touch of savage comedy in his breast, volunteered an episode which restored good humor to the scene. Leaping up, he came dancing and singing towards me, and there, to the amusement of all, reenacted the quarrel, and mimicked rather cleverly my attempt at separating the combatants. Smashing at the canoe with his club, he yelled and knocked down imaginary enemies; then, rushing first at one party and then at the other, he represented me as appealing and gesticulating and pushing them afar from each other, till he became quite exhausted. Thereon he came and planted himself in great glee beside me, and looked around as if to say, "You must laugh, for I have played." At this very juncture, a loud cry of "Sail O" broke upon our ears, and all parties leapt to their feet, and prepared for a new sensation; for in those climes, everything—war itself—is a smaller interest than a vessel from the Great Unknown Beyond sailing into your Harbor.

Not many days thereafter, a very horrible transaction occurred. Before daybreak, I heard shot after shot quickly discharged in the Harbor. One of my Teachers came running, and cried, "Missi, six or seven men have been shot dead this morning for a great feast. It is to reconcile Tribes that have been at war, and to allow a banished Tribe to return in peace."

I learned that the leading men had in council agreed upon this sacrifice, but the name of each victim was kept a secret till the last moment. The torture of suspense and uncertainty seemed to be borne by all as part of their appointed lot; nor did they prepare as if suspecting any dread assault. Before daylight, the Sacred Men allocated a murderer to the door of each house where a victim slept. A signal shot was fired; all rushed to their doors, and the doomed ones were shot and clubbed to death, as they attempted to escape. Their bodies were then borne to a sacred tree, and hung up there by the hands for a time as an offering to the gods. Being taken down, they were carried ceremoniously and laid out on the shore near my house, placed under a special guard.

Information had reached me that my Teachers and I were also destined victims for this same feast; and sure enough we espied a band of armed men, the killers, despatched towards òur premises. Instantaneously I had the Teachers and their wives and myself securely locked into the Mission House; and, cut off from all human hope, we set ourselves to pray to our dear Lord Jesus, either Himself to protect us or to take us to His glory. All through that morning and forenoon we heard them tramp-tramping round our house, whispering to each other, and hovering near window and door. They knew that there were a double-barreled fowling-piece and a revolver on the premises, though they never had seen me use them, and that may, under God, have held them back in dread. But the thought of using them did not enter our souls even in that awful time. I had gone to save, and not to destroy. It would be easier for me at any time to die, than to kill one of them. Our safety lay in our appeal to that blessed Lord who had placed us there, and to whom all power had been given in Heaven and on Earth. He that was with us was more than all that could be against us. This is strength;—this is peace:—to feel, in entering on every day, that all its duties and trials have been committed to the Lord Jesus,—that, come what may, He will use us for His glory and our own real good!

All through that dreadful morning, and far into the afternoon, we thus abode together, feeling conscious that we were united to this dear Lord Jesus; and we had sweet communion with Him, meditating on the wonders of His person and the hopes and glories of His kingdom. Oh, that all my readers may learn something of this in their own experience of the Lord! I can wish them nothing more precious. Towards sundown, constrained by the Invisible One, they withdrew from our Mission House, and left us once more in peace. They bore away the slain to be cooked, and distributed amongst the Tribes, and eaten in their feast of reconciliation; a covenant sealed in blood, and soon, alas, to be buried in blood again! For many days thereafter we had to take unusual care, and not unduly expose ourselves to danger; for dark characters were seen prowling about in the bush near at hand, and we knew that our life was the prize. We took what care we could, and God the Lord did the rest; or rather He did all—for His wisdom guided us, and His power baffled them.

CHAPTER XXVI.
THE DEFYING OF NAHAK.

SHORTLY thereafter war was again declared, by the Inland people attacking our Harbor people. It was an old quarrel; and the war was renewed and continued, long after the cause thereof had passed away. Going amongst them every day, I did my utmost to stop hostilities, setting the evils of war before them, and pleading with the leading men to renounce it. Thereon arose a characteristic incident of Island and Heathen life. One day I held a Service in the village where morning after morning their Tribes assembled, and declared that if they would believe in and follow the Jehovah God, He would deliver them from all their enemies and lead them into a happy life. There were present three Sacred Men, Chiefs, of whom the whole population lived in terror—brothers or cousins, heroes of traditional feats, professors of sorcery, and claiming the power of life and death, health and sickness, rain and drought, according to their will. On hearing me, these three stood up and declared they did not believe in Jehovah, nor did they need His help; for they had the power to kill my life by Nahak (*i.e.* sorcery or witchcraft), if only they could get possession of any piece of the fruit or food that I had eaten. This was an essential condition of their black art; hence the peel of a banana or an orange, and every broken scrap of food, is gathered up by the Natives, lest it should fall into the hands of the Sacred Men, and be used for Nahak. This superstition was the cause of most of the bloodshed and terror upon Tanna; and being thus challenged, I asked God's help, and determined to strike a blow against it.

A woman was standing near with a bunch of native fruit in her hand, like our plums, called quonquore. I asked her to be pleased to give me some; and she, holding out a bunch, said, "Take freely what you will!"

Calling the attention of all the Assembly to what I was doing, I took three fruits from the bunch, and taking a bite out of each, I gave them one after another to the three Sacred Men, and deliberately said in the hearing of all, "You have seen me eat of this fruit, you have seen me give the remainder to your Sacred Men; they have said they can kill me by Nahak, but I challenge them to do it if they can, without arrow or spear, club or musket; for I deny that they have any power against me, or against any one, by their Sorcery."

The challenge was accepted; the Natives looked terror-struck at the position in which I was placed! The ceremony of Nahak was usually performed in secret,—the Tannese fleeing in dread, as Europeans would from the touch of the plague; but I lingered and eagerly watched their ritual. As the three Chiefs arose, and drew near to one of the Sacred Trees, to begin their ceremonial, the Natives fled in terror, crying, "Missi, Iawé? Alas, Missi!"

But I held on at my post of observation. Amidst wavings and incantations, they rolled up the pieces of the fruit from which I had eaten, in certain leaves of this Sacred Tree, into a shape like a waxen candle; then they kindled a sacred fire near the root, and continued their mutterings, gradually burning a little more and a little more of the candle-shaped things, wheeling them round their heads, blowing upon them with their breaths, waving them in the air, and glancing wildly at me as if expecting my sudden destruction. Wondering whether after all they did not believe their own lie, for they seemed to be in dead earnest, I, more eager than ever to break the chains of such vile superstition, urged them again and again, crying, "Be quick! Stir up your gods to help you! I am not killed yet; I am perfectly well!"

At last they stood up and said, "We must delay till we have called all our Sacred Men. We will kill Missi before his next Sabbath comes round. Let all watch, for he will soon die and that without fail."

I replied, "Very good! I challenge all your Priests to unite and kill me by Sorcery or Nahak. If on Sabbath next I come again to your village in health, you will all admit that your gods have no power over me, and that I am protected by the true and living Jehovah God!"

Every day throughout the remainder of that week the Conchs were sounded; and over that side of the island all their Sacred Men were at work trying to kill me by their arts. Now and again messengers arrived from every quarter of the island, inquiring anxiously after my health, and wondering if I was not feeling sick, and great excitement prevailed amongst the poor deluded idolaters.

Sabbath dawned upon me peacefully, and I went to that village in more than my usual health and strength. Large numbers assembled, and when I appeared they looked at each other in terror, as if it could not really be I myself still spared and well. Entering into the public ground, I saluted them to this effect, "My love to you all, my friends! I have come again to talk to you about the Jehovah God and His Worship."

The three Sacred Men, on being asked, admitted that they had tried to kill me by Nahak, but had failed; and on being questioned, why they had failed; they gave the acute and subtle reply, that I also was myself a Sacred Man, and that my God being the stronger had protected me from their gods.

Addressing the multitude, I answered thus, "Yea, truly; my Jehovah God is stronger than your gods. He protected me, and helped me; for He is the only living and true God, the only God that can hear or answer any prayer from the children of men. Your gods cannot hear prayer, but my God can and will hear and answer you, if you will give heart and life to Him, and love and serve Him only. This is my God, and He is also your friend if you will hear and follow His voice."

Having said this, I sat down on the trunk of a fallen tree, and addressed them, "Come and sit down all around me, and I will talk to you about the love and mercy of my God, and teach you how to worship and please Him."

Two of the Sacred Men then sat down, and all the people gathered round and seated themselves very quietly. I tried to present to them ideas of sin, and of salvation through Jesus Christ, as revealed to us in the Holy Scriptures.

The third Sacred Man, the highest in rank, a man of great stature and uncommon strength, had meantime gone off for his warrior's spear, and returned brandishing it in the air and poising it at me. I said to the people, "Of course he can kill me with his spear, but he undertook to kill me by Nahak or Sorcery, and promised not to use against me any weapons of war; and if you let him kill me now, you will kill your friend, one who lives among you and only tries to do you good, as you all know so well. I know that if you kill me thus, my God will be angry and will punish you."

Thereon I seated myself calmly in the midst of the crowd, while he leaped about in rage, scolding his brothers and all who were present for listening to me. The other Sacred Men, however, took my side, and, as many of the people also were friendly to me and stood closely packed around me, he did not throw his spear. To allay the tumult and obviate further bloodshed, I offered to leave with my Teachers at once, and, in doing so, I ardently pled with them to live at peace. Though we got safely home, that old Sacred Man seemed still to hunger after my blood. For weeks thereafter, go where I would, he would suddenly appear on the path behind me, poising in his right hand that same Goliath spear. God only kept it from being thrown, and I, using every lawful precaution, had all the same to attend to my work, as if no enemy were there, leaving all other results in the hands of Jesus. This whole incident did, doubtless, shake the prejudices of many as to Sorcery; but few even of converted Natives ever get entirely clear of the dread of Nahak.

CHAPTER XXVII.
A PERILOUS PILGRIMAGE.

THE other Mission Station, on the southwest side of Tanna, had to be visited by me from time to time. Mr. and Mrs. Mathieson, there, were both in a weak state of health, having a tendency to consumption. On this account they visited Aneityum several times. They were earnestly devoted to their work, and were successful as far as health and the time allowed to them permitted. At this juncture, a message reached me that they were without European food, and a request to send them a little flour if possible. The war made the journey overland impossible. A strong wind and a high sea round the coast rendered it impracticable for my boat to go. The danger to life from the enemy was so great that I could not hire a crew. I pled therefore with Nowar and Manuman, and a few leading men, to take one of their best canoes, and themselves to accompany me. I had a large flat-bottomed pot with a close fitting lid, and that I pressed full of flour; and, tying the lid firmly down, I fastened it right in the center of the canoe, and as far above water-mark as possible. All else that was required we tied around our own persons. Sea and land being as they were, it was a perilous undertaking, which only dire necessity could have justified. They were all swimmers, but as I could not swim, the strongest man was placed behind me, to seize me and swim ashore, if a crash came.

Creeping round near the shore all the way, we had to keep just outside the great breakers on the coral reef, and were all drenched through and through with the foam of an angry surf. We arrived, however, in safety within two miles of our destination, where lived the friends of my canoe's company, but where a very dangerous sea was breaking on the reef. Here they all gave in, and protested that no further could they go; and truly their toil all the way with the paddles had been severe. I appealed to them, that the canoe would for certain be smashed if they tried to get on shore, that the provisions would be lost, and some of us probably drowned. But they turned to the shore, and remained for some time thus, watching the sea. At last their Captain cried, "Missi, hold on! There's a smaller wave coming; we'll ride in now."

My heart rose to the Lord in trembling prayer! The wave came rolling on; every paddle with all their united strength struck into the sea; and next moment our canoe was flying like a sea-gull on the crest of the wave towards the shore. Another instant, and the wave had broken on the reef with a mighty roar, and rushed passed us hissing in clouds of foam. My company were next seen swimming wildly about in the sea, Manuman the one-eyed Sacred Man alone holding on by the canoe, nearly full of water, with me still clinging to the seat of it, and the very next wave likely to devour us. In desperation, I sprang for the reef, and ran for a man half-wading, half-swimming to reach us; and God so ordered it, that just as the next wave broke against the silvery rock of coral, the man caught me and partly swam with me through its surf, partly carried me till I was set safely ashore. Praising God, I looked up and saw all the others as safe as myself, except Manuman, my friend, who was still holding on by the canoe in the face of wind and sea, and bringing it with him. Others ran and swam to his help. The paddles were picked up amid the surf. A powerful fellow came towards me with the pot of flour on his head, uninjured by water! The Chief who held on by the canoe got severely cut about the feet, and had been badly bruised and knocked about; but all the rest escaped without further harm, and everything that we had was saved. Amongst friends at last, they resolved to await a favorable wind and tide to return to their own homes. Singing in my heart unto God, I hired a man to carry the pot of flour, and soon arrived at the Mission Station.

Supplying the wants of our dear friends, Mr. and Mrs. Mathieson, whom we found as well as could be expected, we had to prepare, after a few hours of rest, to return to our own Station by walking overland through the night. I durst not remain longer away, lest my own house should be plundered and broken into. Though weak in health, my fellow-Missionaries were both full of hope, and zealous in their work, and this somewhat strange visit was a pleasant blink amidst our darkness. Before I had gone far on my return journey, the sun went down, and no Native could be hired to accompany me. They all told me that I would for certain be killed by the way. But I knew that it would be quite dark before I reached the hostile districts, and that the Heathen are great cowards in the dark and never leave their villages at night in the darkness, except in companies for fishing and suchlike tasks. I skirted along the sea-shore as fast as I could, walking and running alternately; and, when I got within hearing of voices, I slunk back into the bush till they had safely passed, and then groped my way back near the shore, that being my only guide to find a path.

Having made half the journey, I came to a dangerous path, almost perpendicular, up a great rock round the base of which the sea roared deep. With my heart lifted up to Jesus, I succeeded in climbing it, cautiously grasping roots, and resting by bushes, till I safely reached the top. There, to avoid a village, I had to keep crawling slowly along the brush near the sea, on the top of that great ledge of rock—a feat I could never have accomplished even in daylight without the excitement; but I felt that I was supported and guided in all that life-or-death journey by my dear Lord Jesus. I had to leave the shore, and follow up the bank of a very deep ravine to a place shallow enough for one to cross, and then through the bush away for the shore again. By holding too much to the right, I missed the point where I had intended to reach it. Small fires were now visible through the bush; I heard the voices of the people talking in one of our most Heathen villages.

Quietly drawing back, I now knew where I was, and easily found my way towards the shore; but on reaching the Great Rock, I could not in the darkness find the path down again. I groped about till I was tired. I feared that I might stumble over and be killed; or, if I delayed till daylight, that the savages would kill me. I knew that one part of the rock was steep-sloping, with little growth or none thereon, and I searched about to find it, resolved to commend myself to Jesus and slide down thereby, that I might again reach the shore and escape for my life. Thinking I had found this spot, I hurled down several stones and listened for their splash that I might judge whether it would be safe. But the distance was too far for me to hear or judge. At high tide the sea there was deep; but at low tide I could wade out of it and be safe. The darkness made it impossible for me to see anything. I let go my umbrella, shoving it down with considerable force, but neither did it send me back any news.

Feeling sure, however, that this was the place I sought, and knowing that to await the daylight would be certain death, I prayed to my Lord Jesus for help and protection, and resolved to let myself go. First, I fastened all my clothes as tightly as I could, so as not to catch on anything; then I lay down at the top on my back, feet foremost, holding my head downwards on my breast to keep it from striking on the rock; then, after one cry to my Saviour, having let myself down as far as possible by a branch, I at last let go, throwing my arms forward and trying to keep my feet well up. A giddy swirl, as if flying through the air, took possession of me; a few moments seemed an age; I rushed quickly down, and felt no obstruction till my feet struck into the sea below. Adoring and praising my dear Lord Jesus, who had ordered it so, I regained my feet; it was low tide, I had received no injury, I recovered my umbrella, and, wading through, I found the shore path easier and lighter than the bush had been. The vary darkness was my safety, preventing the Natives from rambling about. I saw no person to speak to, till I reached a village quite near to my own house, fifteen or twenty miles from where I had started; I here left the sea path and promised some young men a gift of fish-hooks to guide me the nearest way through the bush to my Mission Station, which they gladly and heartily did. I ran a narrow risk in approaching them; they thought me an enemy, and I arrested their muskets only by a loud cry—

"I am Missi! Don't shoot; my love to you, my friends!"

Praising God for His preserving care, I reached home, and had a long refreshing sleep. The natives, on hearing next day how I had come all the way in the dark exclaimed—

"Surely any of us would have been killed! Your Jehovah God alone thus protects you and brings you safely home."

With all my heart, I said, "Yes! and He will be your protector and helper too, if only you will obey and trust in Him."

Certainly that night put my faith to the test. Had it not been the assurance that I was engaged in His service, and that in every path of duty He would carry me through or dispose of me therein for His glory I could never have undertaken either journey. St. Paul's words are true to-day and forever—"I can do all things through Christ which strengthened me."

CHAPTER XXVIII.
THE PLAGUE OF MEASLES.

ABOUT this time I had a never-to-be-forgotten illustration of the infernal spirit that possessed some of the Traders towards these poor Natives. One morning, three or four vessels entered our Harbor and cast anchor in Port Resolution. The captains called on me, and one of them, with manifest delight, exclaimed, "We know how to bring down your proud Tannese now! We'll humble them before you!"

I answered, "Surely you don't mean to attack and destroy these poor people?"

He replied, not abashed but rejoicing, "We have sent the measles to humble them! That kills them by the score! Four young men have been landed at different ports, ill with measles, and these will soon thin their ranks."

Shocked above measure, I protested solemnly and denounced their conduct and spirit; but my remonstrances only called forth the shameless declaration, "Our watchword is,—Sweep these creatures away and let white men occupy the soil!"

Their malice was further illustrated thus: they induced Kapuku, a young Chief, to go off to one of their vessels, promising him a present. He was the friend and chief supporter of Mr. Mathieson and of his work. Having got him on board, they confined him in the hold amongst natives lying ill with measles. They gave him no food for about four-and-twenty hours; and then, without the promised present, they put him ashore far from his own home. Though weak and excited, he scrambled back to his tribe in great exhaustion and terror. He informed the Missionary that they had put him down amongst sick people, red and hot with fever, and that he feared their sickness was upon him. I am ashamed to say that these Sandal-wood and other Traders were our own degraded countrymen; and that they deliberately gloried in thus destroying the poor Heathen. A more fiendish spirit could scarcely be imagined; but most of them were horrible drunkards, and their traffic of every kind amongst these islands was, generally speaking, steeped in human blood.

The measles, thus introduced, became amongst our islanders the most deadly plague. It spread fearfully, and was accompanied by sore throat and diarrhea. In some villages, man, woman, and child were stricken, and none could give food or water to the rest. The misery, suffering, and terror were unexampled, the living being afraid sometimes even to bury the dead.

Thirteen of my own Mission party died of this disease; and, so terror-stricken were the few who survived, that when the little Mission schooner *John Knox* returned to Tanna, they all packed up and left for their own Aneityum, except my own dear old Abraham.

At first, thinking that all were on the wing, he also had packed his chattels, and was standing beside the others ready to leave with them. I drew near to him, and said, "Abraham, they are all going; are you also going to leave me here alone on Tanna, to fight the battles of the Lord?"

He asked, "Missi, will you remain?"

I replied, "Yes; but Abraham, the danger to life is now so great that I dare not plead with you to remain, for we may both be slain. Still, I cannot leave the Lord's work now."

The noble old Chief looked at the box and his bundles, and, musingly, said, "Missi, our danger is very great now."

I answered, "Yes; I once thought you would not leave me alone to it; but, as the vessel is going to your own land, I cannot ask you to remain and face it with me!"

He again said, "Missi, would you like me to remain alone with you, seeing my wife is dead and in her grave here?"

I replied, "Yes, I would like you to remain; but, considering the circumstances in which we will be left alone, I cannot plead with you to do so."

He answered, "Then, Missi, I remain with you of my own free choice, and with all my heart. We will live and die together in the work of the Lord. I will never leave you while you are spared on Tanna."

So saying, and with a light that gave the fore-gleam of a Martyr's glory to his dark face, he shouldered his box and bundles back to his own house; and thereafter, Abraham was my dear companion and constant friend, and my fellow-sufferer in all that remains still to be related of our Mission life on Tanna.

Before this plague of measles was brought amongst us I had sailed round in the *John Knox* to Black Beach on the opposite side of Tanna, and prepared the way for settling Teachers. And they were placed soon after by Mr. Copeland and myself with encouraging hopes of success, and with the prospect of erecting there a Station for Mr. and Mrs. Johnson, the newly arrived Missionaries from Nova Scotia. But this dreadful imported epidemic blasted all our dreams. They devoted themselves from the very first, and assisted me in every way to alleviate the dread sufferings of the

Natives. We carried medicine, food, and even water, to the surrounding villages every day, few of themselves being able to render us much assistance. Nearly all who took our medicine and followed instructions as to food, etc., recovered; but vast numbers of them would listen to no counsels, and rushed into experiments which made the attack fatal all around. When the trouble was at its height, for instance, they would plunge into the sea, and seek relief; they found it an almost instant death. Others would dig a hole into the earth, the length of the body and about two feet deep; therein they laid themselves down, the cold earth feeling agreeable to their fevered skins; and when the earth around them grew heated, they got friends to dig a few inches deeper, again and again, seeking a cooler and cooler couch. In this ghastly effort many of them died, literally in their own graves, and were buried where they lay! It need not be surprising, though we did everything in our power to relieve and save them, that the natives associated us with the white men who had so dreadfully afflicted them, and that their blind thirst for revenge did not draw fine distinctions between the Traders and the Missionaries. Both were whites—that was enough.

Before leaving this terrible plague of measles, I may record my belief that it swept away, with accompanying sore throat and diarrhea, a third of the entire population of Tanna; nay? in certain localities more than a third perished. The living declared themselves unable to bury the dead, and great want and suffering ensued. The Teacher and his wife and child, placed by us at Black Beach, were also taken away; and his companion, the other Teacher there, embraced the first opportunity to leave along with his wife for his own island, else his life would have been taken in revenge. Yet, from all accounts afterwards received, I do not think the measles were more fatal on Tanna than on the other Islands of the group. They appear to have carried off even a larger proportion on Aniwa—the future scene of many sorrows but of greater triumphs.

CHAPTER XXIX.
ATTACKED WITH CLUBS.

THE 1st January 1861 was a New Year's Day ever to be remembered. Mr. and Mrs. Johnston, Abraham, and I, had spent nearly the whole time in a kind of solemn yet happy festival. Anew in a holy covenant before God, we unitedly consecrated our lives and our all to the Lord Jesus, giving ourselves away to His blessed service for the conversion of the Heathen on the New Hebrides. After evening Family Worship, Mr. and Mrs. Johnston left my room to go to their own house, only some ten feet distant; but he returned to inform me that there were two men at the window, armed with huge clubs, and having black painted faces. Going out to them and asking them, what they wanted, they replied, "Medicine for a sick boy."

With difficulty I persuaded them to come in and get it. At once, it flashed upon me, from their agitation and their disguise of paint, that they had come to murder us. Mr. Johnston had also accompanied us into the house. Keeping my eye constantly fixed on them, I prepared the medicine and offered it. They refused to receive it, and each man grasped his killing-stone. I faced them firmly and said, "You see that Mr. Johnston is now leaving, and you too must leave this room for to-night. To-morrow, you can bring the boy or come for the medicine."

Seizing their clubs, as if for action, they showed unwillingness to withdraw, but I walked deliberately forward and made as if to push them out, when both turned and began to leave.

Mr. Johnston had gone in front of them and was safely out. But he bent down to lift a little kitten that had escaped at the open door; and at that moment one of the savages, jerking in behind, aimed a blow with his huge club, in avoiding which Mr. Johnston fell with a scream to the ground. Both men sprang towards him, but our two faithful dogs ferociously leapt in their faces and saved his life. Rushing out, but not fully aware of what had occurred, I saw Mr. Johnston trying to raise himself, and heard him cry, "Take care these men have tried to kill me, and they will kill you!"

Facing them sternly I demanded, "What is it that you want? He does not understand your language. What do you want? Speak with me."

Both men, thereon, raised their great clubs and made to strike me; but quick as lightning these two dogs sprang at their faces and baffled their blows. One dog was badly bruised, and the ground received the other blow that would have launched me into Eternity. The best dog was a little cross-bred retriever with terrier blood in him, splendid for warning us of approaching dangers, and which had already been the means of saving my life several times. Seeing how matters stood, I now hounded both dogs furiously upon them, and the two savages fled. I shouted after them, "Remember, Jehovah God sees you and will punish you for trying to murder His servants!"

In their flight, a large body of men, who had come eight or ten miles to assist in the murder and plunder, came slipping here and there from the bush and joined them, fleeing too. Verily, "the wicked flee, when no man pursueth." David's experience and assurance came home to us, that evening, as very real:—"God is our refuge and our strength...therefore we will not fear."

I, now accustomed to such scenes on Tanna, retired to rest and slept soundly; but my dear fellow-laborer, as I afterwards learned, could not sleep for one moment. His pallor and excitement continued next day, indeed for several days; and after that, though he was naturally lively and cheerful, I never saw him smile again.

For that morning, 1st January 1861, the following entry was found in his Journal: "To-day, with a heavy heart and a feeling of dread, I know not why, I set out on my accustomed wanderings amongst the sick. I hastened back to get the Teacher and carry Mr. Paton to the scene of distress. I carried a bucket of water in one hand and medicine in the other; and so we spent a portion of this day endeavoring to alleviate their sufferings, and our work had a happy effect also on the minds of others." In another entry, on 22d December, he wrote: "Measles are making fearful havoc amongst the poor Tannese. As we pass through the villages, mournful scenes meet the eye; young and old prostrated on the ground, showing all these painful symptoms which accompany loathsome and malignant diseases. In some villages few are left able to prepare food, or to carry drink to the suffering and dying. How pitiful to see the sufferers destitute of every comfort, attention, and remedy that would ameliorate their suffering or remove their disease! As I think of the tender manner in which we are nursed in sickness, the many remedies employed to give relief, with the comforts and attention bestowed upon us, my heart sickens, and I say, Oh my ingratitude and the ingratitude of Christian people!"

Having, as above recorded, consecrated our lives anew to God on the first day of January, I was, up till the 16th of the month, accompanied by Mr. Johnston and sometimes also by Mrs. Johnston on my rounds in the villages amongst the sick, and they greatly helped me. But by an unhappy accident I was laid aside when most sorely needed. When adzing a tree for housebuilding I observed that Mahanan, the war Chief's brother, had been keeping too near me, and that he carried a tomahawk in his hand; and, in trying both to do my work and to keep an eye on him, I struck my ankle severely with the adze. He moved off quickly, saying, "I did not do that," but doubtless rejoicing at what had happened. The bone was badly hurt, and several of the blood-vessels cut. Dressing it as well as I could, and keeping it constantly soaked in cold water, I had to exercise the greatest care. In this condition, amidst great sufferings, I was sometimes carried to the villages to administer medicine to the sick, and to plead and pray with the dying.

On such occasions, in this mode of transit even, the conversations that I had with dear Mr. Johnston were most solemn and greatly refreshing. He had, however, scarcely ever slept since the 1st of January, and during the night of the 16th he sent for my bottle of laudanum. Being severely attacked with ague and fever, I could not go to him, but sent the bottle, specifying the proper quantity for a dose, but that he quite understood already. He took a dose for himself, and gave one also to his wife, as she too suffered from sleeplessness. This he repeated three nights in succession, and both of them obtained a long, sound and refreshing sleep. He came to my bedside, where I lay in the ague-fever, and said with great animation, amongst other things, "I have had such a blessed sleep, and feel so refreshed! What kindness in God to provide such remedies for suffering man!"

At midday his dear wife came to me crying, "Mr. Johnston has fallen asleep, so deep that I cannot awake him."

My fever had reached the worst stage, but I struggled to my feet got to his bedside, and found him in a state of coma, with his teeth fixed in tetanus. With great difficulty we succeeded in slightly rousing him; with a knife, spoon, and pieces of wood, we forced his teeth open, so as to administer an emetic with good effects, and also other needful medicines. For twelve hours, we had to keep him awake by repeated cold dashes in the face, by ammonia, and by vigorously moving him about. He then began to speak freely; and next day he rose and walked about a little. For the two following days, he was sometimes better and sometimes worse; but we managed to keep him up till the morning of the 21st, when he again fell into a state of coma, from which we failed to rouse him. At two o'clock in the afternoon he fell asleep—another Martyr for the testimony of Jesus in those dark and trying Isles, leaving his young wife in indescribable sorrow, which she strove to bear with Christian resignation. Having made his coffin and dug his grave, we two alone at sunset laid him to rest beside my own dear wife and child, close by the Mission House.

CHAPTER XXX.
KOWIA.

ANOTHER tragedy followed, with, however, much of the light of Heaven amid its blackness, in the story of Kowia, a Tannese Chief of the highest rank. Going to Aneityum in youth, he had there become a true Christian. He married an Aneityumese Christian woman, with whom he lived very happily and had two beautiful children. Some time before the measles reached our island he returned to live with me as a Teacher and to help forward our work on Tanna. He proved himself to be a decided Christian; he was a real Chief amongst them, dignified in his whole conduct, and every way a valuable helper to me. Everything was tried by his own people to induce him to leave me and to renounce the Worship, offering him every honor and bribe in their power. Failing these, they threatened to take away all his lands, and to deprive him of Chieftainship, but he answered "Take all! I shall still stand by Missi and the Worship of Jehovah."

From threats they passed to galling insults, all which he bore patiently for Jesu's sake. But one day a party of his people came and sold some fowls, and an impudent fellow lifted them after they had been bought and offered to sell them again to me. Kowia shouted, "Don't purchase these, Missi; I have just bought them for you, and paid for them!"

Thereon the fellow began to mock at him. Kowia, gazing round on all present, and then on me, rose like a lion awaking out of sleep, and with flashing eyes exclaimed, "Missi, they think that because I am now a Christian I have become a coward! a woman! to bear every abuse and insult they can heap upon me. But I will show them for once that I am no coward, that I am still their Chief, and that Christianity does not take away but gives us courage and nerve."

Springing at one man, he wrenched in a moment the mighty club from his hands, and swinging it in air above his head like a toy, he cried, "Come any of you, come all against your Chief! My Jehovah God makes my heart and arms strong. He will help me in this battle as He helps me in other things, for He inspires me to show you that Christians are no cowards, though they are men of peace. Come on, and you will yet know that I am Kowia your Chief."

All fled as he approached them; and he cried, "Where are the cowards now?" and handed back to the warrior his club. After this they left him at peace.

He lived at the Mission House, with his wife and children, and was a great help and comfort to Abraham and myself. He was allowed to go more freely and fearlessly amongst the people than any of the rest of our Mission staff. The ague and fever on me at Mr. Johnston's death so increased and reduced me to such weakness that I had become insensible, while Abraham and Kowia alone attended to me. On returning to consciousness I heard as in a dream Kowia lamenting over me, and pleading that I might recover, so as to hear and speak with him before he died. Opening my eyes and looking at him, I heard him say, "Missi, all our Aneityumese are sick. Missi Johnson is dead. You are very sick, and I am weak and dying. Alas, when I too am dead, who will climb the trees and get you a cocoanut to drink? And who will bathe your lips and brow?"

Here he broke down into deep and long weeping, and then resumed, "Missi, the Tanna-men hate us all on account of the Worship of Jehovah; and I now fear He is going to take away all His servants from this land, and leave my people to the Evil One and his service!"

I was too weak to speak, so he went on, bursting into a soliloquy of prayer: "O Lord Jesus, Missi Johnston is dead; Thou hast taken him away from this land. Missi Johnston the woman and Missi Paton are very ill; I am sick, and Thy servants the Aneityumese are all sick and dying. O Lord, our Father in Heaven, art Thou going to take away all Thy servants, and Thy Worship from this dark land? What meanest Thou to do, O Lord? The Tannese hate Thee and Thy Worship and Thy servants; but surely, O Lord, Thou canst not forsake Tanna and leave our people to die in the darkness! Oh, make the hearts of this people soft to Thy Word and sweet to Thy Worship; teach them to fear and love Jesus; and oh, restore and spare Missi, dear Missi Paton, that Tanna may be saved!"

Touched to the very fountains of my life by such prayers, from a man once a Cannibal, I began under the breath of God's blessing to revive.

A few days thereafter, Kowia came again to me, and rousing me out of sleep, cried, "Missi, I am very weak; I am dying. I come to bid you farewell, and go away to die. I am nearing death now, and I will soon see Jesus."

I spoke what words of consolation and cheer I could muster, but he answered, "Missi, since you became ill my dear wife and children are dead and buried. Most of our Aneityumese are dead, and I am dying. If I remain on the hill, and die here at the Mission House, there are none left to help Abraham to carry me down to the grave where my wife and children are laid. I wish to lie beside them, that we may rise together in the Great Day when Jesus comes. I am happy, looking unto Jesus! One thing only deeply grieves me now; I fear God is taking us all away from Tanna, and will leave my poor people dark and benighted as before, for they hate Jesus and the

Worship of Jehovah. O Missi, pray for them, and pray for me once more before I go!"

He knelt down at my side, and we prayed for each other and for Tanna. I then urged him to remain at the Mission House, but he replied, "O Missi, you do not know how near to death I am! I am just going, and will soon be with Jesus, and see my wife and children now. While a little strength is left, I will lean on Abraham's arm, and go down to the graves of my dear ones and fall asleep there, and Abraham will dig a quiet bed and lay me beside them. Farewell, Missi, I am very near death now; we will meet again in Jesus and with Jesus!"

With many tears he dragged himself away; and my heart-strings seemed all tied round that noble simple soul, and felt like breaking one by one as he left me there on my bed of fever all alone. Abraham sustained him, tottering to the place of graves; there he lay down, and immediately gave up the ghost and slept in Jesus; and there the faithful Abraham buried him beside his wife and children. Thus died a man who had been a cannibal Chief, but by the grace of God and the love of Jesus, changed, transfigured into a character of light and beauty. I lost, in losing him, one of my best friends and most courageous helpers; but I knew that day, and I know now, that there is one soul at least from Tanna to sing the glories of Jesus in Heaven—and, oh, the rapture when I meet him there!

CHAPTER XXXI.
MARTYRDOM OF THE GORDONS.

MAY 1861 brought with it a sorrowful and tragic event, which fell as the very shadow of doom across our path; I mean the martyrdom of the Gordons on Erromanga. Rev. G. N. Gordon was a native of Prince Edward Island, Nova Scotia, and was born in 1822. He was educated at the Free Church College, Halifax, and placed as Missionary on Erromanga in June 1857. Much troubled and opposed by the Sandal-wooders, he had yet acquired the language and was making progress by inroads on Heathenism. A considerable number of young men and women embraced the Christian Faith, lived at the Mission House, and devotedly helped him and his excellent wife in all their work. But the hurricanes and the measles, already referred to, caused great mortality in Erromanga also; and the degraded Traders, who had introduced the plague, in order to save themselves from revenge, stimulated the superstitions of the Heathen, and charged the Missionaries there too with causing sickness and all other calamities. The Sandal-wooders hated him for fearlessly denouncing and exposing their hideous atrocities.

When Mr. Copeland and I placed the Native Teachers at Black Beach, Tanna, we ran across to Erromanga in the *John Knox*, taking a harmonium to Mrs. Gordon, just come by their order from Sydney. When it was opened out at the Mission House, and Mrs. Gordon began playing on it and singing sweet hymns, the native women were in ecstasies. They at once proposed to go off to the bush and cut each a burden of long grass, to thatch the printing-office which Mr. Gordon was building in order to print the Scriptures in their own tongue, if only Mrs. Gordon would play to them at night and teach them to sing God's praises. They joyfully did so, and then spent a happy evening singing those hymns. Next day being Sabbath, we had a delightful season there, about thirty attending Church and listening eagerly. The young men and women living at the Mission House were being trained to become Teachers; they were reading a small book in their own language, telling them the story of Joseph; and the work every way seemed most hopeful. The Mission House had been removed a mile or so up a hill, partly for Mrs. Gordon's health, and partly to escape the annoying and contaminating influence of the Sandal-wooders on the Christian Natives.

On the 20th May 1861 he was still working at the roofing of the printing-office, and had sent his lads to bring each a load of the long grass to finish the thatching. Meantime a party of Erromangans from a district called

Bunk-Hill, under a Chief named Lovu, had been watching him. They had been to the Mission House inquiring and they had seen him send away his Christian lads. They then hid in the bush and sent two of their men to the Missionary to ask for calico. On a piece of wood he wrote a note to Mrs. Gordon to give them two yards each. They asked him to go with them to the Mission House, as they needed medicine for a sick boy, and Lovu their Chief wanted to see him. He tied up in a napkin a meal of food, which had been brought to him but not eaten, and started to go with them. He requested the native Narubulet to go on before with his companion, but they insisted upon his going in front. In crossing a streamlet, which I visited shortly afterwards, his foot slipped. A blow was aimed at him with a tomahawk, which he caught; the other man struck, but his weapon was also caught. One of the tomahawks was then wrenched out of his grasp. Next moment a blow on the spine laid the dear Missionary low, and a second on the neck almost severed the head from the body. The other Natives then rushed from their ambush, and began dancing round him with frantic shoutings. Mrs. Gordon hearing the noise, came out and stood in front of the Mission House, looking in the direction of her husband's working place, and wondering what had happened. Ouben, one of the party, who had run towards the Station the moment that Mr. Gordon fell, now approached her. A merciful clump of trees had hid from her eyes all that had occurred, and she said to Ouben, "What's the cause of that noise?"

He replied, "Oh, nothing! only the boys amusing themselves!"

Saying, "Where are the boys?" she turned round. Ouben slipped stealthily behind her, sank his tomahawk into her back, and with another blow almost severed her head!

Such was the fate of those two devoted servants of the Lord; loving in their lives, and in their deaths not divided—their spirits, wearing the crown of martyrdom, entered Glory together to be welcomed by Williams and Harris, whose blood was shed near the same now hallowed spot for the name and cause of Jesus. They had labored four years on Erromanga, amidst trials and dangers manifold, and had not been without tokens of blessing in the Lord's work. Never more earnest or devoted Missionaries lived and died in the Heathen field.

CHAPTER XXXII.
SHADOWS DEEPENING ON TANNA.

IMMEDIATELY thereafter, a Sandal-wood Trader brought in his boat a party of Erromangans by night to Tanna. They assembled our Harbor Chiefs and people, and urged them to kill us and Mr. and Mrs. Mathieson and the Teachers, or allow them to do so, as they had killed Mr. and Mrs. Gordon. Then they proposed to go to Aneityum and kill the Missionaries there, as the Aneityumese Natives had burned their Church, and thus they would sweep away the Worship and the servants of Jehovah from all the New Hebrides. Our Chiefs, however, refused, restrained by the Merciful One, and the Erromangans returned to their own island in a sulky mood.

Notwithstanding this refusal, as if they wished to reserve the murder and plunder for themselves, our Mission House was next day thronged with armed men, some from Inland, others from Mr. Mathieson's Station. They loudly praised the Erromangans! The leader said again and again in my hearing, "The men of Erromanga killed Missi Williams long ago. We killed the Rarotongan and Samoan Teachers. We fought Missi Turner and Missi Nisbet, and drove them from our island. We killed the Aneityumese Teachers on Aniwa, and one of Missi Paton's Teachers too. We killed several white men, and no Man-of-war punished us. Let us talk over this, about killing Missi Paton and the Aneityumese, till we see if any Man-of-war comes to punish the Erromangans. If not, let us unite, let us kill these Missionaries, let us drive the Worship of Jehovah from our land!"

An Inland Chief said or rather shouted in my hearing, "My love to the Erromangans! They are strong and brave men, the Erromangans. They have killed their Missi and his wife, while we only talk about it. They have destroyed the Worship and driven away Jehovah!"

I stood amongst them and protested, "God will yet punish the Erromangans for such wicked deeds. God has heard all your bad talk, and will punish it in His own time and way."

But they shouted me down, amidst great excitement, with the cry, "Our love to the Erromangans! Our love to the Erromangans!"

After I left them, Abraham heard them say, "Miaki is lazy. Let us meet in every village, and talk with each other. Let us all agree to kill Missi and the Aneityumese for the first of our Chiefs that dies."

The night after the visit of the Erromangan boat, and the sad news of Mr. and Mrs. Gordon's death, the Tannese met on their village dancing-grounds and held high festival in praise of the Erromangans. Our best friend, old Nowar the Chief, who had worn shirt and kilt for some time and had come regularly to the Worship, relapsed once more; he painted his face, threw off his clothing, resumed his bow and arrows and his tomahawk, of which he boasted that it had killed very many men and at least one woman! On my shaming him for professing to worship Jehovah and yet uniting with the Heathen in rejoicing over the murder of His servants on Erromanga, he replied to this effect, "Truly, Missi, they have done well. If the people of Erromanga are severely punished for this by the Man-of-war, we will all hear of it; and our people will then fear to kill you and the other Missionaries, so as to destroy the Worship of Jehovah. Now, they say, the Erromangans killed Missi Williams and the Samoan, Rarotongan, and Aneityumese Teachers, besides other white men, and no Man-of-war has punished either them or us. If they are not punished for what has been done on Erromanga, nothing else can keep them here from killing you and me and all who worship at the Mission House!"

I answered, "Nowar, let us all be strong to love and serve Jehovah Jesus. If it be for our good and His glory, He will protect us; if not, He will take us to be with Himself. We will not be killed by their bad talk. Besides, what avails it to us, when dead and gone, if even a Man-of-war should come and punish our murderers?"

He shrugged his shoulders, answering, "Missi, by and by you will see. Mind, I tell you the truth. I know our Tannese people. How is it that Jehovah did not protect the Gordons and the Erromangan worshipers? If the Erromangans are not punished, neither will our Tannese be punished, though they murder all Jehovah's people!"

I felt for Nowar's struggling faith, just trembling on the verge of Cannibalism yet, and knowing so little of the true Jehovah.

Groups of Natives assembled suspiciously near us and sat whispering together. They urged old Abraham to return to Aneityum by the very first opportunity, as our lives were certain to be taken, but he replied, "I will not leave Missi."

Abraham and I were thrown much into each other's company, and he stood by me in every danger. We conducted Family Prayers alternately; and that evening he said during the prayer in Tannese, in which language alone we understood each other:—

"O Lord, our Heavenly Father, they have murdered Thy servants on Erromanga. They have banished the Aneityumese from dark Tanna. And now they want to kill Missi Paton and me! Our great King, protect us, and make their hearts soft and sweet to Thy Worship. Or, if they are permitted to kill us, do not Thou hate us, but wash us in the blood of Thy dear Son Jesus Christ. He came down to Earth and shed His blood for sinners; through Him forgive us our sins and take us to Heaven—that good place where Missi Gordon the man and Missi Gordon the woman and all thy dear servants now are singing Thy praise and seeing Thy face. Our Lord, our hearts are pained just now, and we weep over the death of Thy dear servants; but make our hearts good and strong for Thy cause, and take thou away all our fears. Make us two and all Thy servants strong for Thee and for Thy Worship; and if they kill us two, let us die together in Thy good work, like Thy servants Missi Gordon the man and Missi Gordon the woman."

In this manner his great simple soul poured itself out to God; and my heart melted within me as it had never done under any prayer poured from the lips of cultured Christian men!

Under the strain of these events, Miaki came to our house, and attacked me in hearing of his men to this effect, "You and the Worship are the cause of all the sickness and death now taking place on Tanna! The Erromanga men killed Missi Gordon the man and also the woman, and they are all well long ago. The Worship is killing us all; and the Inland people will kill us for keeping you and the Worship here; for we love the conduct of Tanna, but we hate the Worship. We must kill you and it, and we shall all be well again."

I tried to reason firmly and kindly with them, showing them that their own conduct was destroying them, and that our presence and the Worship could only be a blessing to them in every way, if only they would accept of it and give up their evil ways. I referred to a poor girl, whom Miaka and his men had stolen and abused—that they knew such conduct to be bad, and that God would certainly punish them for it.

He replied, "Such is the conduct of Tanna. Our fathers loved and followed it, we love and follow it, and if the Worship condemns it, we will kill you and destroy the Worship."

I said, "The Word of the Holy God condemns all bad conduct, and I must obey my God in trying to lead you to give it up, and to love and serve His Son Jesus our Saviour. If I refuse to obey my God, He will punish me."

He declared that his heart was good, that his conduct was good, but that he hated the teaching of the Worship. He had a party of men staying with him from the other side of the island, and he sent back a present of four large fat hogs to their Chiefs, with a message as to the killing of the Mathiesons. If that were done, his hands would be strengthened in dealing with us.

To know what was best to be done, in such trying circumstances, was an abiding perplexity. To have left altogether, when so surrounded by perils and enemies, at first seemed the wisest course, and was the repeated advice of many friends. But again, I had acquired the language, and had gained a considerable Influence amongst the Natives, and there were a number warmly attached both to himself and to the Worship. To have left would have been to lose all, which to me was heartrending; therefore, risking all with Jesus, I held on while the hope of being spared longer had not absolutely and entirely vanished.

The following quotation from a letter of the late A. Clark, Esq., J. P., Auckland, New Zealand, will show what Bishop Selwyn thought of my standing fast on Tanna at the post of duty, and he knew what he was writing about. These are the words:—"'Talk of bravery! talk of heroism! The man who leads a forlorn hope is a coward in comparison with him, who, on Tanna, thus alone, without a sustaining look or cheering word from one of his own race, regards it as his duty to hold on in the face of such dangers. We read of the soldier, found after the lapse of ages among the ruins of Herculaneum, who stood firm at his post amid the fiery rain destroying all around him, thus manifesting the rigidity of the discipline among those armies of Ancient Rome which conquered the World. Mr. Paton was subjected to no such iron law. He might with honor, when offered to him, have sought a temporary asylum in Auckland, where he would have been heartily received. But he was moved by higher considerations. He chose to remain, and God knows whether at this moment he is in the land of the living!' When the Bishop told us that he declined leaving Tanna by H. M. S. *Pelorus,* he added, 'And I like him all the better for so doing!'"

For my part I feel quite confident that, in like circumstances, that noble Bishop of God would have done the same. I, born in the bosom of the Scottish Covenant descended from those who suffered persecution for Christ's honor, would have been unworthy of them and of my Lord had I deserted my post for danger only. Yet not to me, but to the Lord who sustained me, be all the praise and the glory.

CHAPTER XXXIII.
THE VISIT OF THE COMMODORE.

AT that time, though my life was daily attempted, a dear lad, named Katasian, was coming six miles regularly to the Worship and to receive frequent instruction. One day, when engaged in teaching him, I caught a man stealing the blind from my window. On trying to prevent him, he aimed his great club at me, but I seized the heavy end of it with both my hands as it swung past my head, and held on with all my might. What a prayer went up from me to God at that dread moment! The man, astonished and abashed at my kind words and appeal, slunk away and left me in peace. God never took away from me the consciousness that it was still right for me to be kind and forgiving, and to hope that I might lead them to love and imitate Jesus.

For some time, Nouka and his wife and daughter—a handsome girl, his only child—and Miaki's principal wife and her two sons, and nine Chiefs attended Worship regularly at the Mission House, on Sabbaths and on the afternoon of every Wednesday. In ail, about sixty persons somewhat regularly waited on our ministrations at this time; and amidst all perils I was encouraged, and my heart was full of hope. Yet one evening when feeling more consoled and hopeful than ever before, a musket was discharged at my very door, and I was constrained to realize that we were in the midst of death. Father, our times are in Thy hand!

In my Mission School, I offered as a prize a red shirt for the first Chief who knew the whole Alphabet without a mistake. It was won by an Inikahi Chief, who was once a terror to the whole community. Afterwards, when trying to teach the A B C to others, he proceeded in something like this graphic style: "A is a man's legs with the body cut off; B is like two eyes; C is a three-quarters moon; D is like one eye; E is a man with one club under his feet and another over his head; F is a man with a large club and a smaller one," etc., etc.; L was like a man's foot; Q was the talk of the dove, etc. Then he would say, "Remember these things; you will soon get hold of the letters and be able to read. I have taught my little child, who can scarcely walk, the names of them all. They are not hard to hold, but soft and easy. You will soon learn to read the book, if you try it with all your heart!"

But Miaki was still our evil genius, and every incident seemed to be used by him for one settled purpose of hate. A Kaserumini Chief, for instance, and seven men took away a young girl in a canoe to Aniwa, to be sold to friends there for tobacco leaf, which the Aniwans cultivated extensively. They also prepared to take revenge there for a child's death, killed in their belief by the sorcery of an Aniwan. When within sight of the shore, the canoes were upset and all were said to have been devoured by sharks, excepting only one canoe out of six. This one returned to Tanna and reported that there were two white Traders living on Aniwa, that they had plenty of ammunition and tobacco, but that they would not come to Tanna as long as a Missionary lived there. Under this fresh incitement, a party of Miaki's men came to my house, praising the Erromangans for the murder of their Missionaries and threatening me.

Even the friendly Nowar said, "Miaki will make a great wind and sink any Man-of-war that comes here. We will take the Man-of-war and kill all that are on board. If you and Abraham do not leave us we will kill you both, for we must have the Traders and the powder."

Just as they were assuming a threatening attitude, other Natives came running with the cry, "Missi, the *John Knox* is coming into the Harbor, and two great ships of fire, Men-of-war, behind her, coming very fast!"

I retorted upon Nowar and the hostile company, "Now is your time! Make all possible haste! Let Miaki raise his great wind now; get all your men ready; I will tell them that you mean to fight, and you will find them always ready!"

Miaki's men fled away in unconcealed terror; but Nowar came to me and said "Missi, I know that my talk is all lies, but if I speak the truth, they will kill me!"

I answered, "Trust in Jehovah, the same God who sent these vessels now, to protect us from being murdered." But Nowar always wavered.

And now from all parts of the island those who were most friendly flocked to us. They were clamorous to have Miaki and some others of our enemies punished by the Man-of-war in presence of the Natives; and then they would be strong to speak in our defense and to lead the Tannese to worship Jehovah.

Commodore Seymour, Captain Hume, and Dr. Geddie came on shore. After inquiring into everything, the Commodore urged me to leave at once, and very kindly offered to remove me to Aneityum, or Auckland, or any place of safety that I preferred. Again, however, I hesitated to leave my dear benighted Tannese, knowing that both Stations would be instantly broken up, that all the influence gained would be thrown away, that the Church would lose all that had been expended, and above all, that those friendly to us would be left to persecution and destruction. For a long time I had seldom taken off my clothes at night, needing to be constantly on the alert to start at a moment's notice; yet, while hope burned within my soul I could not withdraw, so I resolved to risk all with my dear Lord Jesus, and remained at my post. At my request, however, they met and talked with all the leaders who could be assembled at the Mission House. The Natives declared frankly that they liked me, but did not like the Worship. The Commodore reminded them that they had invited me to land among them, and had pledged their word more than once to protect me; he argued with them that as they had no fault to find with me, but only with the Worship, which could do them only good, they must bind themselves to protect my life. Miaki and others promised, and gave him their hand to do so. Lathella, an Aneityumese Chief, who was with Dr. Geddie, interpreted for him and them, Dr. Geddie explaining fully to Lathella in Aneityumese what the Commodore said in English, and Lathella explaining all to the Tannese in their own tongue.

At last old Mouka spoke out for all and said, "Captain Paddan and all the Traders tell us that the Worship causes all our sickness and death. They will not trade with us, nor sell us tobacco, pipes, powder, balls, caps, and muskets, till we kill our Missi like the Erromangans, but after that they will send a Trader to live among us and give us plenty of all these things. We love Missi. But when the Traders tell us that the Worship makes us sick, and when they bribe us with tobacco and powder to kill him or drive him away, some believe them and our hearts do bad conduct to Missi. Let Missi remain here, and we will try to do good conduct to Missi; but you must tell Queen 'Toria of her people's bad treatment of us, and that she must prevent her Traders from killing us with their measles, and from telling us lies to make us do bad conduct to Missi! If they come to us and talk as before, our hearts are very dark and may again lead us to bad conduct to Missi."

After this little parley, the Commodore invited us all on board, along with the Chiefs. They saw about three hundred brave marines ranked up on deck, and heard a great cannon discharged. For all such efforts to impress them and open their eyes, I felt profoundly grateful; but too clearly I knew and saw that only the grace of God could lastingly change them! They were soon back to their old arguments, and were heard saying to one another, "If no punishment is inflicted on the Erromangans for murdering the Missi there, we fear the bad conduct of the Tannese will continue."

No punishment was inflicted at Erromanga, and the Tannese were soon as bold and wicked as ever. For instance, while the Man-of-war lay in the Harbor, Nowar kept himself closely concealed; but no sooner had she sailed than the cowardly fellow came out, laughing at the others, and protesting that he was under no promise and was free to act as he pleased! Yet in the hour of danger he generally proved to be our friend; such was his vacillating character. Nor was Miaki very seriously impressed. Mr. Mathieson shortly thereafter sent his boat round to me, being again short of European food. On his crew leaving her to deliver their message to me, some of Miaki's men at once jumped into the boat and started off round the island in search of kava. I went to Miaki, to ask that the boat might be brought back soon, but on seeing me he ran for his club and aimed to strike me. I managed to seize it, and to hold on, pleading with God and talking with Miaki, till by interference of some friendly Natives his wrath was assuaged a little. Returning home, I sent food overland to keep the Mathiesons going till the boat returned, which she did in about eight days. Thus light and shadow pursued each other, the light brightening for a moment, but upon the whole the shadows deepening.

CHAPTER XXXIV.
THE WAR CHIEFS IN COUNCIL.

A TIME of great excitement amongst the Natives now prevailed. War, war, nothing but war was spoken of! Preparations for war were being made in all the villages far and near. Fear sat on every face, and armed bands kept watching each other, as if uncertain where the war was to begin or by whom. All work was suspended, and that war spirit was let loose which rouses the worst passions of human nature. Again we found ourselves the center of conflict, one party set for killing us or driving us away; the other wishing to retain us, while all old bitter grievances were also dragged into their speeches.

Miaki and Nouka said, "If you will keep Missi and his Worship, take him with you to your own land, for we will not have him to live at the Harbor."

Ian, the great Inland Chief, rose in wrath and said, "On whose lands does the Missi live, yours or ours? Who fight against the Worship and all good, who are the thieves and murderers, who tell the lies, you or we? We wish peace, but you will have war. We like Missi and the Worship, but you hate them and say, 'Take him to your own land!' It is our land on which he now lives; it is his own land which he bought from you, but which our fathers sold Missi Turner long ago. The land was not yours to sell; it was really ours. Your fathers stole it from us long ago by war; but we would not have asked it back, had you not asked us to take Missi away. Now we will defend him on it, and he will teach us and our people in our own land!" So meeting after meeting broke into fiery speech, and separated with many threats.

To the next great meeting I was invited, but did not go, contenting myself with a message pleading that they should live at peace and on no account go to war with each other. But Ian himself came for me. I said, "Ian, I have told you my whole heart. Go not to that meeting. I will rather leave the island or die, than see you going to war about me!"

He answered, "Missi, come with me, come now!"

I replied, "Ian, you are surely not taking me away to kill me? If you are, my God will punish it."

His only reply was, "Follow me, follow me quickly."

I felt constrained to go. He strode on before me till we reached the great village of his ancestors. His followers, armed largely with muskets as well as native weapons, filled one half the Village Square or dancing-ground. Miaki,

Nouka, and their whole party sat in manifest terror upon the other half. Marching into the center, he stood with me by his side, and proudly looking round, exclaimed, "Missi, these are my men and your friends! We are met to defend you and the Worship." Then pointing across to the other side, he cried aloud, "These are your enemies and ours! The enemies of the Worship, the disturbers of the peace on Tanna! Missi, say the word, and the muskets of my men will sweep all opposition away, and the Worship will spread and we will all be strong for it on Tanna. We will not shoot without your leave; but if you refuse they will kill you and persecute us and our children, and banish Jehovah's Worship from our land."

I said, "I love all of you alike. I am here to teach you how to turn away from all wickedness, to worship and serve Jehovah, and to live in peace. How can I approve of any person being killed for me or for the Worship? My God would be angry at me and punish me, if I did!"

He replied, "Then, Missi, you will be murdered and the Worship destroyed."

I then stood forth in the middle before them all and cried, "You may shoot or murder me, but I am your best friend. I am not afraid to die. You will only send me the sooner to my Jehovah God, whom I love and serve, and to my dear Saviour Jesus Christ, who died for me and for you, and who sent me here to tell you all His love. If you will only love and serve Him and give up your bad conduct, you will be happy. But if you kill me, His messenger, rest assured that He will in His own time and way punish you. This is my word to you all; my love to you all!"

So saying, I turned to leave; and Ian strode suddenly away and stood at the head of his men, crying, "Missi, they will kill you! they will kill us, and you will be to blame!"

Miaki and Nouka, full of deceit, now cried out, "Missi's word is good! Let us all obey it. Let us all worship."

An old man, Sirawia, one of Ian's under-chiefs, then said, "Miaki and Nouka say that the land on which Missi lives was theirs; though they sold it to him and he has paid them for it, they all know that it was ours, and is yet ours by right; but if they let Missi live on it in peace, we will all live at peace, and worship Jehovah. And if not, we will surely claim it again."

Miaki and his party hereon went off to their plantations, and brought a large present of food to Ian and his men as a peace-offering. This they accepted; and the next day Ian and his men brought Miaki a return present and said, "You know that Missi lives on our land? Take our present, be friends, and let him live quietly and teach us all. Yesterday you said his word was good; obey it now, else we will punish you and defend the Missi."

Miaki accepted the token, and gave good promises for the future. Ian then came to the hill-top near our house, by which passed the public path, and cried aloud in the hearing of all, "Abraham, tell Missi that you and he now live on our land. This path is the march betwixt Miaki and us. We have this day bought back the land of our fathers by a great price to prevent war. Take of our breadfruits and also of our cocoanuts what you require, for you are our friends and living on our land, and we will protect you and the Worship!"

CHAPTER XXXV.
UNDER KNIFE AND TOMAHAWK.

CHAFED at the upsetting of all their plans and full of revenge, Nouka and Miaki and their allies declared publicly that they were now going to kill Ian by sorcery, *i. e.* by Nahak, more feared by the poor Tannese than the field of battle. Strange to say, Ian became sick shortly after the Sacred Men had made the declaration about their Nahak-sorcery. I attended him, and for a time he recovered, and appeared very grateful. But he soon fell sick again. I sent him and the Chief next under him a blanket each; I also gave shirts and calico to a number of his leading men. They wore them and seemed grateful and pleased. Ian, however, gradually sank and got worse. He had every symptom of being poisoned, a thing easily accomplished, as they know and use many deadly poisons. His sufferings were very great, which prevented me from ascribing his collapse to mere superstitious terror. I did all that could be done; but all thought him dying, and of course by sorcery. His people were angry at me for not consenting before to their shooting of Miaki; and Miaki's people were now rejoicing that Ian was being killed by Nahak.

One night, his brother and a party came for me to go and see Ian, but I declined to go till the morning for fear of the fever and ague. On reaching his village, I saw many people about, and feared that I had been led into a snare; but I at once entered into his house to talk and pray with him, as he appeared to be dying. After prayer, I discovered that I was left alone with him, and that all the people had retired from the village; and I knew that, according to their custom, this meant mischief. Ian said, "Come near me, and sit by my bedside to talk with me, Missi."

I did so, and while speaking to him he lay as if lost in a swoon of silent meditation. Suddenly he drew from the sugar-cane leaf thatch close to his bed a large butcher-like knife, and instantly feeling the edge of it with his other hand, he pointed it to within a few inches of my heart and held it quivering there, all atremble with excitement. I durst neither move nor speak, except that my heart kept praying to the Lord to spare me, or if my time was come to take me home to Glory with Himself. There passed a few moments of awful suspense. My sight went and came. Not a word had been spoken, except to Jesus; and then Ian wheeled the knife around, thrust it into the sugar-cane leaf, and cried to me, "Go, go quickly!"

Next moment I was on the road. Not a living soul was to be seen about the village. I understood then that it had been agreed that Ian was to kill me, and that they had all withdrawn so as not to witness it, that when the Man-of-war came to inquire about me, Ian would be dead, and no punishment could overtake the murderer. I walked quietly till quite free of the village, lest some hid in their houses might observe me. Thereafter, fearing that they, finding I had escaped, might overtake and murder me, I ran for my life a weary four miles till I reached the Mission House, faint yet praising God for such a deliverance. Poor Ian died soon after, and his people strangled one of his wives and hanged another, and took out the three bodies together in a canoe and sank them in the sea.

Miaki was jubilant over having killed his enemy by Nahak; but the Inland people now assembled in thousands to help Sirawia and his brother to avenge that death on Miaki, Nouka, and Karewick. These, on the other hand, boasted that they would kill all their enemies by Nahak-sorcery, and would call up a hurricane to destroy their houses, fruit-trees, and plantations. Immediately after Miaki's threat about bringing a storm, one of their great hurricanes actually smote that side of the island and laid everything waste. His enemies were greatly enraged, and many of the injured people united with them in demanding revenge on Miaki. Hitherto I had done everything in my power to prevent war, but now it seemed inevitable, and both parties sent word that if Abraham and I kept to the Mission House no one would harm us. We had little faith in any of their promises, but there was no alternative for us.

On the following Saturday, 18th January 1862, the war began. Musket after musket was discharged quite near us, and the bush all around rang with the yell of their war-cry, which if once heard will never be forgotten. It came nearer and nearer, for Miaki fled, and his people took shelter behind and around our house. We were placed in the heart of danger, and the balls flew thick all around us. In the afternoon Ian's brother and his party retired, and Miaki quickly sent messengers and presents to the Inikahimini and Kaserumini districts, to assemble all their people and help him "to fight Missi and the Tannese who were friends of the Worship." He said, "Let us cook his body and Abraham's, and distribute them to every village on this side of the island!"

Yet all the while Miaki assured me that he had sent a friendly message. The war went on, and poor Nowar the Chief protected us, till he had a spear broken into his right knee. The enemy would have carried him off to feast on his body; but his young men, shouting wildly his name and battle-cry, rushed in with great impetuosity and carried their wounded Chief home in triumph. The Inland people now discharged muskets at my house and beat against the walls with their clubs. They smashed in the door and window of our storeroom, broke open boxes and casks, tore my books to pieces and scattered them about, and carried off everything for which they cared, including my boat, mast, oars, and sails. They broke into Abraham's house and plundered it; after which they made a rush at the bedroom, into which we were locked, firing muskets, yelling, and trying to break it in. A Chief, professing to be sorry for us, called me to the window, but on seeing me he sent a tomahawk through it crying, "Come on, let us kill him now!"

I replied, "My Jehovah God will punish you; a Man-of-war will come and punish you, if you kill Abraham, his wife, or me."

He retorted, "It's all lies about a Man-of-war! They did not punish the Erromangans. They are afraid of us. Come on, let us kill them!"

He raised his tomahawk and aimed to strike my forehead, many muskets were uplifted as if to shoot, so I raised a revolver in my right hand and pointed it at them. The Rev. Joseph Copeland had left it with me on a former visit. I did not wish it, but he insisted upon leaving it, saying that the very knowledge that I had such a weapon might save my life. Truly, on this occasion it did so. Though it was harmless they fell back quickly. My immediate assailant dropped to the ground, crying, "Missi has got a short musket! He will shoot you all!"

After lying flat on the ground for a little, they all got up and ran to the nearest bush, where they continued yelling about and showing their muskets. Towards nightfall they left, loaded with the plunder of the store and of Abraham's house. So God once more graciously protected us from falling into their cruel hands.

In the evening, after they left, I went to Miaki and Nouka. Miaki, with a sneer, said, "Missi, where was Jehovah to-day? There was no Jehovah to-day to protect you. It's all lies about Jehovah. They will come and kill you, and Abraham, and his wife, and cut your bodies into pieces to be cooked and eaten in every village upon Tanna."

I said, "Surely, when you had planned all this, and brought them to kill us and steal all our property, Jehovah did protect us, or we would not have been here!"

He replied, "There was no Jehovah to-day! We have no fear of any Man-of-war. They dare not punish us. They durst not punish the Erromangans for murdering the Gordons. They will talk to us and say we must not do so again, and give us a present. That is all. We fear nothing. The talk of all Tanna is that we will kill you and seize all your property tomorrow."

I warned him that the punishment of a Man-of-war can only reach the body and the land, but that Jehovah's punishment reached both body and soul in Time and in Eternity.

He replied, "Who fears Jehovah? He was not here to protect you to-day!"

"Yes," I said, "my Jehovah God is here now. He hears all we say, sees all we do, and will punish the wicked and protect His own people."

After this, a number of the people sat down around me, and I prayed with them. But I left with a very heavy heart, feeling that Miaki was evidently bent on our destruction.

CHAPTER XXXVI.
THE BEGINNING OF THE END.

I SENT Abraham to consult Nowar, who had defended us till disabled by a spear in the right knee. He sent a canoe by Abraham, advising me to take some of my goods in it to his house by night, and he would try to protect them and us. The risk was so great we could only take a very little. Enemies were on every hand to cut off our flight, and Miaki, the worst of all, whose village had to be passed in going to Nowar's. In the darkness of the Mission House, we durst not light a candle for fear of some one seeing and shooting us. Not one of Nowar's men durst come to help us. But in the end it made no difference, for Nowar and his men kept what was taken there, as their portion of the plunder. Abraham, his wife, and I waited anxiously for the morning light. Miaki, the false and cruel, came to assure us that the Heathen would not return that day. Yet, as daylight came in, Miaki himself stood and blew a great conch not far from our house. I ran out to see why this trumpet-shell had been blown, and found it was the signal for a great company of howling armed savages to rush down the hill on the other side of the bay and make straight for the Mission House. We had not a moment to lose. To have remained would have been certain death to us all, and also to Matthew, a Teacher just arrived from Mr. Mathieson's Station. Though I am by conviction a strong Calvinist, I am no Fatalist. I held on while one gleam of hope remained. Escape for life was now the only path of duty. I called the Teachers, locked the door, and made quickly for Nowar's village. There was not a moment left to carry anything with us. In the issue, Abraham and his wife and I lost all our earthly goods, and all our clothing except what we had on. My Bible, the few translations which I had made into Tannese, and a light pair of blankets I carried with me.

We durst not choose the usual path along the beach, for there our enemies would have quickly overtaken us. We entered the bush in the hope of getting away unobserved. But a cousin of Miaki, evidently secreted to watch us, sprang from behind a breadfruit tree, and swinging his tomahawk, aimed it at my brow with a fiendish look. Avoiding it I turned upon him and said in a firm bold voice, "If you dare to strike me, my Jehovah God will punish you. He is here to defend me now!"

The man, trembling, looked all round as if to see the God who was my defender, and the tomahawk gradually lowered at his side. With my eye fixed upon him, I gradually moved backwards in the track of the Teachers, and God mercifully restrained him from following me.

On reaching Nowar's village unobserved, we found the people terror-stricken, crying, rushing about in despair at such a host of armed savages approaching. I urged them to ply their axes, cut down trees, and blockade the path. For a little they wrought vigorously at this; but when, so far as eye could reach, they saw the shore covered with armed men rushing on towards their village, they were overwhelmed with fear, they threw away their axes and weapons of war, they cast themselves headlong on the ground, and they knocked themselves against the trees as if to court death before it came. They cried, "Missi, it's of no use! We will all be killed and eaten to-day! See what a host are coming against us."

Mothers snatched up little children and ran to hide in the bush. Others waded as far as they could into the sea with them, holding their heads above the water. The whole village collapsed in a condition of indescribable terror. Nowar, lame with his wounded knee, got a canoe turned upside-down and sat upon it where he could see the whole approaching multitude. He said, "Missi, sit down beside me, and pray to our Jehovah God, for if He does not send deliverance now, we are all dead men. They will kill us all on your account, and that quickly. Pray, and I will watch!"

They had gone to the Mission House and broken in the door, and finding that we had escaped, they rushed on to Nowar's village. For, as they began to plunder the bedroom, Nouka said, "Leave everything. Missi will come back for his valuable things at night, and then we will get them and him also!"

So he nailed up the door, and they all marched for Nowar's. We prayed as one can only pray when in the jaws of death and on the brink of Eternity. We felt that God was near, and omnipotent to do what seemed best in His sight. When the savages were about three hundred yards off, at the foot of a hill leading up to the village, Nowar touched my knee, saying. "Missi, Jehovah is hearing! They are all standing still."

Had they come on they would have met with no opposition, for the people were scattered in terror. On gazing shorewards, and round the Harbor, as far as we could see, was a dense host of warriors, but all were standing still, and apparently absolute silence prevailed. We saw a messenger or herald running along the approaching multitude, delivering some tidings as he passed, and then disappearing in the bush. To our amazement, the host began to turn, and slowly marched back in great silence, and entered the remote bush at the head of the Harbor. Nowar and his people were in ecstasies, crying out, "Jehovah has heard Missi's prayer! Jehovah has protected us and turned them away back."

About midday, Nouka and Miaki sent their cousin Jonas, who had always been friendly to me, to say that I might return to my house in safety, as they were now carrying the war inland. Jonas had spent some years on Samoa, and been much with Traders in Sydney, and spoke English well; but we felt they were deceiving us. Next night, Abraham ventured to creep near the Mission House, to test whether we might return, and save some valuable things, and get a change of clothing. The house appeared to stand as when they nailed up the door. But a large party of Miaki's allies at once enclosed Abraham, and, after asking many questions about me, they let him go since I was not there. Had I gone there they would certainly that night have killed me. Again, at midnight Abraham and his wife and Matthew went to the Mission House, and found Nouka, Miaki, and Karewick near by, concealed in the bush among the reeds. Once more they enclosed them, thinking I was there too, but Nouka, finding that I was not, cried out, "Don't kill them just now! Wait till Missi comes."

Hearing this, Matthew slipped into the bush and escaped. Abraham's wife waded into the sea, and they allowed her to get away. Abraham was allowed to go to the Mission House, but he too crept into the bush, and after an anxious waiting they all came back to me in safety. We now gave up all hope of recovering anything from the house.

Towards morning, when Miaki and his men saw that I was not coming back to deliver myself into their hands, they broke up my house and stole all they could carry away. They tore my books, and scattered them about. They took away the type of my printing-press, to be made into bullets for their muskets. For similar uses they melted down the zinc lining of my boxes, and everything else that could be melted. What they could not take away, they destroyed.

As the night advanced, Nowar declared that I must leave his village before morning, else he and his people would be killed for protecting me. He advised me, as the sea was good, to try for Mr. Mathieson's Station; but he objected to my taking away any of my property—he would soon follow with it himself! But how to sail? Miaki had stolen my boat, mast, sails, and oars, as also an excellent canoe made for me and paid for by me on Aneityum; and he had threatened to shoot any person that assisted me to launch either the one or the other. The danger still increasing, Nowar said, "You cannot remain longer in my house! My son will guide you to the large chestnut tree in my plantation in the bush. Climb up into it, and remain there till the moon rises."

Being entirely at the mercy of such doubtful and vacillating friends, I, though perplexed, felt it best to obey. I climbed into the tree, and was left there alone in the bush. The hours I spent there live all before me as if it were but of yesterday. I heard the frequent discharging of muskets, and the yells of the savages. Yet I sat there among the branches, as safe in the arms of Jesus. Never, in all my sorrows, did my Lord draw nearer to me, and speak more soothingly in my soul, than when the moonlight flickered among these chestnut leaves, and the night air played on my throbbing brow, as I told all my heart to Jesus. Alone, yet not alone! If it be to glorify my God, I will not grudge to spend many nights alone in such a tree, to feel again my Saviour's spiritual presence, to enjoy His consoling fellowship. If thus thrown back upon your own soul, alone, all, all alone, in the midnight, in the bush, in the very embrace of death itself, have you a Friend that will not fail you then?

CHAPTER XXXVII.
FIVE HOURS IN A CANOE.

GLADLY would I have lingered there for one night of comparative peace! But Nowar sent his son to call me down from the tree, and to guide me to the shore where he himself was, as it was now time to take to sea in the canoe. Pleading for my Lord's continuing presence, I had to obey. My life and the lives of my Aneityumese now hung upon a very slender thread; the risk was almost equally great from our friends so-called, or from our enemies. Had I been a stranger to Jesus and to prayer, my reason would verily have given way, but my comfort and joy sprang out of these words, "I will never leave thee, nor forsake thee; lo, I am with you alway!" Pleading these promises, I followed my guide. We reached the beach, just inside the Harbor, at a beautiful white sandy bay on Nowar's ground, from which our canoe was to start. A good number of the Natives had assembled there to see us off. Arkurat, having got a large roll of calico for the loan of his canoe, hid it away, and then refused the canoe, saying that if he had to escape with his family he would require it. He demanded an ax, a sail for his canoe, and a pair of blankets. As Koris had the ax and another had the quilt, I gave the quilt to him for a sail, and the ax and blankets for the canoe, in fact, these few relics of our earthly all at Nowar's were coveted by the savages and endangered our lives, and it was as well to get rid of them altogether. He cruelly proposed a small canoe for two; but I had hired the canoe for five, and insisted upon getting it, as he had been well paid for it. As he only laughed and mocked us, I prepared to start and travel overland to Mr. Mathieson's Station. He then said, "My wrath is over! You may take it and go."

We launched it, but now he refused to let us go till daylight. He had always been one of my best friends, but now appeared bent on a quarrel, so I had to exercise much patience with him and them. Having launched it, he said I had hired the canoe but not the paddles. I protested, "Surely you know we hired the paddles too. What could we do without paddles?"

But Arkurat lay down and pretended to have fallen asleep, snoring on the sand, and could not be awaked. I appealed to Nowar, who only said, "That is his conduct, Missi, our conduct!"

I replied, "As he has got the blankets which I saved to keep me from ague and fever, and I have nothing left now but the clothes I have on, surely you will give me paddles."

Nowar gave me one. Returning to the village, friends gave me one each till I got other three. Now Arkurat started up, and refused to let us go. A Chief and one of his men, who lived on the other side of the island near to where we were going, and who was hired by me to go with us and help in paddling the canoe, drew back also and refused to go. Again I offered to leave the canoe, and walk overland if possible, when Faimungo, the Chief who had refused to go with us, came forward and said, "Missi, they are all deceiving you! The sea is so rough, you cannot go by it; and if you should get round the weather point, Miaki has men appointed to shoot you as you pass the Black Rocks, while by land all the paths are guarded by armed men. I tell you the truth, having heard all their talk. Miaki and Karewick say they hate the Worship, and will kill you. They killed your goats, and stole all your property yesterday. Farewell!"

The Teachers, the boy, and I now resolved to enter the canoe and attempt it, as the only gleam of hope left to us. My party of five embarked in our frail canoe; Abraham first, I next, Matthew after me, the boy at the steering paddle, and Abraham's wife sitting in the bottom, where she might hold on while it continued to float. For a mile or more we got away nicely under the lee of the island, but when we turned to go south for Mr. Mathieson's Station, we met the full force of wind and sea, every wave breaking over and almost swamping our canoe. The Native lad at the helm paddle stood up crying, "Missi, this is the conduct of the sea! It swallows up all who seek its help."

I answered, "We do not seek help from it, but from Jehovah Jesus."

Our danger became very great, as the sea broke over and lashed around us. My faithful Aneityumese, overcome with terror, threw down their paddles, and Abraham said, "Missi, we are all drowned now! We are food for the sharks. We might as well be eaten by the Tannese as by fishes; but God will give us life with Jesus in heaven!"

I seized the paddle nearest me; I ordered Abraham to seize another within his reach; I enjoined Matthew to bail the canoe for life, and the lad to keep firm in his seat, and I cried, "Stand to your post, and let us return! Abraham, where is now your faith in Jesus? Remember, He is Ruler on sea as on land. Abraham, pray and ply your paddle! Keep up stroke for stroke with me, as our lives depend on it. Our God can protect us. Matthew, bail with all your might. Don't look round on the sea and fear. Let us pray to God and ply our paddles, and He will save us yet!"

Dear old Abraham said, "Thank you for that, Missi. I will be strong. I pray to God and ply my paddle. God will save us!"

With much labor, and amid deadly perils, we got the canoe turned; and after four hours of a terrible struggle, we succeeded, towards daylight as the tide turned, in again reaching smooth water. With God's blessing we at last reached the shore, exactly where we had left it five hours ago!

Now drenched and weary, with the skin of our hands sticking to the paddles, we left the canoe on the reef and waded ashore. Many Natives were there, and looked sullen and disappointed at our return. Katasian, the lad who had been with us, instantly fled for his own land; and the Natives reported that he was murdered soon after. Utterly exhausted, I lay down on the sand and immediately fell into a deep sleep. By and by I felt someone pulling from under my head the native bag in which I carried my Bible and the Tannese translations—the all that had been saved by me from the wreck! Grasping the bag, I sprang to my feet, and the man ran away. My Teachers had also a hedging knife, a useless revolver, and a fowling-piece, the sight of which, though they had been under the salt water for hours, God used to restrain the savages. Calling my Aneityumese near, we now, in united prayer and kneeling on the sands, committed each other unto the Lord God, being prepared for the last and worst.

CHAPTER XXXVIII.
A RACE FOR LIFE.

As I sat meditating on the issues, Faimungo, the friendly Inland Chief, again appeared to warn us of our danger, now very greatly increased by our being driven back from the sea. All Nowar's men had fled, and were hid in the bush and in rocks along the shore; while Miaki was holding a meeting not half a mile away, and preparing to fall upon us. Faimungo said, "Farewell, Missi, I am going home. I don't wish to see the work and the murders of this morning."

He was Nowar's son-in-law. He had always been truthful and kindly with me. His home was about half-way across the island, on the road that we wanted to go, and under sudden impulse I said, "Faimungo, will you let us follow you? Will you show us the path? When the Mission Ship arrives, I will give you three good axes, blankets, knives, fish-hooks, and many things you prize."

The late hurricanes had so destroyed and altered the paths, that only Natives who knew them well could follow them. He trembled much and said, "Missi, you will be killed. Miaki and Karewick will shoot you. I dare not let you follow. I have only about twenty men, and your following might endanger us all."

I urged him to leave at once, and we would follow of our own accord. I would not ask him to protect us; but if he betrayed us and helped the enemy to kill us, I assured him that our God would punish him. If he spared us, he would be rewarded well; and if we were killed against his wishes, God would not be angry at him. He said, "Seven men are with me now, and thirteen are to follow. I will not now send for them. They are with Miaki and Nouka. I will go; but if you follow, you will be killed on the way. You may follow me as far as you can."

Off he started to Nowar's, and got a large load of my stolen property, blankets, sheets, etc., which had fallen to his lot. He called his seven men, who had also shared in the plunder, and, to avoid Miaki's men, they ran away under a large cocoanut grove skirting the shore, calling, "Be quick! Follow and keep as near to us as you can."

Though Nowar had got a box of my rice and appropriated many things from the plunder of the Mission House besides the goods entrusted to his care, and got two of my goats killed and cooked for himself and his people, yet now he would not give a particle of food to my starving Aneityumese or myself, but hurried us off, saying, "I will eat all your rice and keep all that has been left with me, in payment for my lame knee and for my people fighting for you!"

My three Aneityumese and I started after Faimungo and his men. We could place no confidence in any of them; but, feeling that we were in the Lord's hands, it appeared to be our only hope of escaping instant death. We got away unobserved by the enemies. We met several small parties of friends in the Harbor, apparently glad to see us trying to get away. But about four miles on our way, we met a large party of Miaki's men, all armed, and watching as outposts. Some were for shooting us, but others hesitated. Every musket was, however, raised and leveled at me. Faimungo poised his great spear and said, "No, you shall not kill Missi to-day. He is with me." Having made this flourish, he strode off after his own men, and my Aneityumese followed, leaving me face to face with a ring of leveled muskets.

Sirawia, who was in command of this party, and who once, like Nowar, had been my friend, said to me, Judas like, "My love to you, Missi." But he also shouted after Faimungo, "Your conduct is bad in taking the Missi away; leave him to us to be killed!" I then turned upon him, saying, "Sirawia, I love you all. You must know that I sought only your good. I gave you medicine and food when you and your people were sick and dying under measles; I gave you the very clothing you wear. Am I not your friend? Have we not often drunk tea and eaten together in my house? Can you stand there and see your friend shot? If you do, my God will punish you severely."

He then whispered something to his company which I did not hear; and, though their muskets were still raised, I saw in their eyes that he had restrained them. I therefore began gradually to move backwards, still keeping my eyes fixed on them, till the bush hid them from my view, whereon I turned and ran after my party, and God kept the enemy from following. We trusted in Jehovah Jesus, and pressed on in flight.

A second hostile party encountered us, and with great difficulty we also got away from them. Soon thereafter a friendly company crossed our path. We learned from them that the enemies had slaughtered other two of Manuman's men, and burned several villages with fire. Another party of the enemy encountered us, and were eager for our lives. But this time Faimungo withstood them firmly, his men encircled us, and he said, "I am not afraid now, Missi; I am feeling stronger near my own land!"

CHAPTER XXXIX.
FAINT YET PURSUING.

HURRYING still onwards, we came to that village on their high ground called Aneai, *i. e.* Heaven. The sun was oppressively hot, the path almost unshaded, and our whole party very exhausted, especially Faimungo, carrying his load of stolen goods. So here he sat down on the village dancing-ground for a smoke, saying, "Missi, I am near my own land now. We can rest with safety."

In a few minutes, however, he started up, he and his men, in wild excitement. Over a mountain, behind the village and above it, there came the shoutings, and anon the tramp, tramp of a multitude making rapidly towards us. Faimungo got up and planted his back against a tree. I stood beside him, and the Aneityumese woman and the two men stood near me, while his men seemed prepared to flee. At full speed a large body of the tallest and most powerful men that I had seen on Tanna came rushing on and filled the dancing-ground. They were all armed, and flushed with their success in war. A messenger had informed them of our escape, probably from Miaki, and they had crossed the country to intercept us.

Faimungo was much afraid, and said, "Missi, go on in that path, you and your Aneityumese; and I will follow when I have had a smoke and a talk with these men."

I replied, "No, I will stand by your side till you go; and if I am killed, it will be by your side, I will not leave you."

He implored us to go on, but that I knew would be certain death. They began urging one another to kill us, but I looked round them as calmly as possible, saying, "My Jehovah God will punish you here and hereafter, if you kill me or any of His servants."

A killing-stone, thrown by one of the savages, grazed poor old Abraham's cheek, and the dear soul gave such a look at me, and then upwards, as if to say, "Missi, I was nearly away to Jesus." A club was also raised to follow the blow of the killing-stone, but God baffled the aim. They encircled us in a deadly ring, and one kept urging another to strike the first blow, or fire the first shot. My heart rose up to the Lord Jesus; I saw Him watching all the scene. In that awful hour I beheld His own words, as if carved in letters of fire upon the clouds of Heaven: "Seek, and ye shall find. Whatsoever ye shall ask in My name, that will I do, that the Father may be glorified in the Son." I could understand how Stephen and John saw the glorified Saviour as they gazed up through suffering and persecution to the Heavenly Throne!

Yet I never could say that on such occasions I was entirely without fear. Nay, I have felt my reason reeling, my sight coming and going, and my knees smiting together when thus brought close to a violent death, but mostly under the solemn thought of being ushered into Eternity and appearing before God. Still, I was never left without hearing that promise in all its consoling and supporting power coming up through the darkness and the anguish, "Lo, I am with you alway;" And with Paul I could say, even in this dread moment and crisis of being, "I am persuaded that neither death nor life,.. nor any other creature, shall be able to separate us from the love of God which is in Christ Jesus our Lord."

Faimungo and others now urged us to go on in the path. I said, "Faimungo, why are we to leave you? My God heard your promise not to betray me. He knows now what is in your heart and in mine. I will not leave you; and if I am to die, I will die by your side."

He replied, "Now, I go on before; Missi, keep close to me."

His men had gone, and I persuaded my Aneityumese to follow them. At last, with a bound, Faimungo started after them. I followed, keeping as near him as I could, pleading with Jesus to protect me or to take me home to Glory. The host of armed men also ran along on each side with their weapons ready; but leaving everything to Jesus, I ran on as if they were my escort, or as if I saw them not. If any reader wonders how they were restrained, much more would I, unless I believed that the same Hand that restrained the lions from touching Daniel held back these Savages from hurting me! We came to a stream crossing our path. With a bound all my party cleared it, ran up the bank opposite, and disappeared in the bush. "Faint yet pursuing," I also tried the leap, but I struck the bank and slid back on my hands and knees towards the stream. At this moment I heard a crash above my head amongst the branches of an overhanging tree, and I knew that a *Kawas* had been thrown, and that that branch had saved me. Praising my God, I scrambled up on the other side, and followed the track of my party into the bush. The savages gazed after me for a little in silence, but no one crossed the stream; and I saw them separate into two, one portion returning to the village and another pressing inland. With what gratitude did I recognize the Invisible One who brought their counsels to confusion.

I found my party resting in the bush, and amazed to see me escaped alive from men who were thirsting for my blood. Faimungo and his men received me with demonstrations of joy, perhaps feeling a little ashamed of their own cowardice. He now ascended the mountain and kept away from the common path to avoid other Native bands. At every village enemies to the Worship were ready to shoot us. But I kept close to our guide, knowing that the fear of shooting him would prevent their shooting at me, as he was the most influential Chief in all that section of the island.

One party said, "Miaki and Karewick said that Missi made the sickness and the hurricanes, and we ought to kill him."

Faimungo replied, "They lie about Missi! It is our own bad conduct that makes us sick."

They answered, "We don't know who makes the sickness, but our fathers have taught us to kill all Foreign men."

Faimungo, clutching club and spear, exclaimed, standing betwixt them and us, "You won't kill Missi to-day!"

Faimungo now sent his own men home by a near path, and guided us himself till we were close upon the shore. There sitting down, he said, "Missi, I have now fulfilled my promise. I am so tired, I am so afraid, I dare not go farther. My love to you all. Now go on quickly! Three of my men will go with you to the next rocks. Go quickly! Farewell."

These men went on a little, and then said, "Missi, we dare not go! Faimungo is at war with the people of the next land. You must keep straight along this path." So they turned and ran back to their own village.

To us this district was especially perilous. Many years ago the Aneityumese had joined in a war against the Tannese of this tribe, and the thirst for revenge yet existed in their hearts, handed down from sire to son. Most providentially the men were absent on a war expedition, and we saw only three lads and a great number of women and children, who ran off to the bush in terror. In the evening the enraged savages of another district assaulted the people of the shore villages for allowing us to pass, and, though sparing their lives, broke in pieces their weapons of war—a very grievous penalty.

In the next district, as we hasted along the shore, two young men came running after us, poising their quivering spears. I took the useless revolver out of my little native basket, and raising it cried, "Beware! Lay down your spears at once on the sand, and carry my basket to the next landing at the Black Rocks."

They threw their spears on the sand, lifted the bag, and ran on before us to the rocks which formed the march betwixt them and their enemies. Laying it down, they said appealingly, "Missi, let us return to our home!" And how they did run, fearing the pursuit of their foes.

In the next land we saw none. After that we saw crowds all along, some friendly, others unfriendly, but they let us pass on, and with the blessing of Almighty God we drew dear to Mr. Mathieson's Station in safety. Here a man gave me a cocoanut for each of our party, which we greatly required, having tasted nothing all that day, and very little for several days before. We were so weak that only the struggle for life enabled us to keep our feet; yet my poor Aneityumese never complained and never halted, not even the woman. The danger and excitement kept us up in the race for life; and by the blessing of God we were now approaching the Mission House, praising God for His wonderful deliverances.

Hearing of our coming, Mr. Mathieson came running to meet me. They had heard of our leaving my own Station, and they thought I was dead! They were themselves both very weak; their only child had just been laid in the grave, and they were in great grief and in greater peril. We praised the Lord for permitting us to meet; we prayed for support, guidance, and protection; and resolved now, in all events, to stand by each other till the last.

CHAPTER XL.
WAITING AT KWAMERA.

BEFORE I left the Harbor I wrote and left with Nowar letters to be given to the Captains of any vessels which called, for the first, and the next, and the next, telling them of our great danger, that Mr. Mathieson was almost without food, and that I would reward them handsomely if they would call at the Station and remove any of us who might be spared thence to Aneityum. Two or three vessels called, and, as I afterwards learned, got my letters; but, while buying my stolen property from the Natives for tobacco, powder, and balls, they took no further notice of my appeals, and sailed past Mr. Mathieson's, straight on to Aneityum. "The tender mercies of the wicked are cruel!"

Let me now cull the leading events from my Journal, that intervened betwixt this date and the break-up of the Mission on Tanna—at least for a season—though, blessed be God! I have lived to see the light rekindled by my dear friends Mr. and Mrs. Watt, and shining more brightly and hopefully than ever. The candle was quenched, but the candlestick was not removed!

On the 23d January, 1862, Mr. Mathieson sent for Taura, Kati, and Kapuku, his three principal Chiefs, to induce them to promise protection till a vessel called to take us away. They appeared friendly, and promised to do their best. Alas! the promises of the Tannese Chiefs had too often proved to be vain.

On Friday, 24th January, report reached our Station that Miaki and his party, hearing that a friendly Chief had concealed two of Manuman's young men, compelled him to produce them and club them to death before their eyes. Also, that they surrounded Manuman's party on a mountain, and hemmed them in there, dying of starvation, and trying to survive on the carcasses of the dead and on bark and roots. Also, that Miaki had united all the Chiefs, friends and foes alike, in a bond of blood, to kill every one pertaining to the whole Mission on Tanna. Jesus reigns!

On Sunday, the 26th January, thirty persons came to worship at the Mission House. Thereafter, at great risk, we had Worship at three of the nearest and most friendly villages. Amidst all our perils and trials we preached the Gospel to about one hundred and sixteen persons. It was verily a sowing time of tears; but, despite all that followed, who shall say that it was vain! Twenty years have passed, and now when I am writing this, there is a Church of God singing the praises of Jesus in that very district of

Tanna. On leaving the second village, a young lad affectionately took my hand to lead me to the next village; but a sulky, down-browed savage, carrying a ponderous club, also insisted upon accompanying us. I led the way, guided by the lad. Mr. Mathieson got the man to go before him, while he himself followed, constantly watching. Coming to a place where another path branched off from ours, I asked which path we took, and, on turning to the left as instructed by the lad, the savage, getting close behind me, swung his huge club over his shoulder to strike me on the head. Mr. Mathieson, springing forward, caught the club from behind with a great cry to me; and I, wheeling instantly, had hold of the club also, and betwixt us we wrested it out of his hands. The poor creature, craven at heart however bloodthirsty, implored us not to kill him. I raised the club threateningly, and caused him to march in front of us till we reached the next village fence. In terror lest these villagers should kill him, he gladly received back his club, as well as the boy his bow and arrows, and they were lost in the bush in a moment.

At the village from which this man and boy had come, one savage brought his musket while we were conducting Worship, and sat sullen and scowling at us all the time. Mocking questions were also shouted at us, such as, "Who made the rains, winds, and hurricanes? Who caused all the disease? Who killed Missi Mathieson's child?" They sneered and scoffed at our answers, and in this Taura the Chief joined the rest.

On the 27th, at daylight, a vessel was seen in the offing, as if to tantalize us. The Captain had been at the Harbor, and had received my letter from Nowar. I hoisted a flag to induce him to send or come on shore, but he sailed off for Aneityum, bearing the plunder of my poor Mission House, purchased for ammunition and tobacco for the Natives. He left the news at Aneityum that I had been driven from my Station some time ago, and was believed to have been murdered.

On the 29th of January, the young Chief Kapuku came and handed to Mr. Mathieson his own and his father's war-gods and household idols. They consisted chiefly of a basket of small and peculiar stones, much worn and shining with use. He said, "While many are trying to kill you and drive the Worship of Jehovah from this island, I give up my gods, and will send away all Heathen idols from my land."

On the 31st, we learned that a party of Miaki's men were going about Mr. Mathieson's district inciting the people to kill us. Faimungo also came to inform us that Maiki was exerting all his artifice to get us and the Worship destroyed. Manuman even sent, from inland, Raki, his adopted son, to tell me of the fearful sufferings that he and his people were now passing through, and that some were killed almost every day. Raki's wife was a

Chief's daughter, who, when the war began, returned to her father's care. The savages of Miaki went to her own father's house and compelled him to give her up as an enemy. She was clubbed and feasted on.

On Sabbath, 2d February, thirty-two people attended the Morning Service. I addressed them on the Deluge, its causes and lessons. I showed them a doll, explaining that such carved and painted images could not hear our prayers or help us in our need, that the living Jehovah God only could hear and help. They were much interested, and after Worship carefully examined the doll. Mr. Mathieson and I, committing ourselves to Jesus, went inland and conducted Worship at seven villages, listened to by about one hundred people in all. Nearly all appeared friendly. The people of one village had been incited to kill us on our return; but God guided us to return by another way, and so we escaped.

During the day, on 3d February, a company of Miaki's men came to the Mission House, and forced Mrs. Mathieson to show them through the premises. Providentially, I had bolted myself that morning into a closet room, and was engrossed with writing. They went through every room in the house and did not see me, concluding I had gone inland. They discharged a musket into our Teacher's house, but afterwards left quietly, greatly disappointed at not finding me. My heart still rose in praise to God for another such deliverance, neither by man nor of man's planning!

CHAPTER XLI.
THE LAST AWFUL NIGHT.

WORN out with long watching and many fatigues, I lay down that night early, and fell into a deep sleep. About ten o'clock the savages again surrounded the Mission House. My faithful dog Clutha, clinging still to me amid the wreck of all else on earth, sprang quietly upon me, pulled at my clothes, and awoke me, showing danger in her eye glancing at me through the shadows. I silently awoke Mr. and Mrs. Mathieson, who had also fallen asleep. We committed ourselves in hushed prayer to God and watched them, knowing that they could not see us. Immediately a glare of light fell into the room! Men passed with flaming torches; and first they set fire to the Church all round, and then to a reed fence connecting the Church and the dwelling-house. In a few minutes the house, too, would be in flames, and armed savages waiting to kill us on attempting an escape!

Taking my harmless revolver in the left hand and a little American tomahawk in the right, I pleaded with Mr. Mathieson to let me out and instantly to again lock the door on himself and wife. He very reluctantly did so, holding me back and saying, "Stop here and let us die together! You will never return!"

I said, "Be quick! Leave that to God. In a few minutes our house will be in flames, and then nothing can save us."

He did let me out, and locked the door again quickly from the inside; and, while his wife and he prayed and watched for me from within, I ran to the burning reed fence, cut it from top to bottom, and tore it up and threw it back into the flames, so that the fire could not by it be carried to our dwelling-house. I saw on the ground shadows, as if something were falling around me, and started back. Seven or eight savages had surrounded me, and raised their great clubs in air. I heard a shout—"Kill him! Kill him!" One savage tried to seize hold of me, but, leaping from his clutch, I drew the revolver from my pocket and leveled it as for use, my heart going up in prayer to my God. I said, "Dare to strike me, and my Jehovah God will punish you. He protects us, and will punish you for burning His Church, for hatred to His Worship and people, and for all your bad conduct. We love you all; and for doing you good only, you want to kill us. But our God is here now to protect us and to punish you."

They yelled in rage, and urged each other to strike the first blow, but the Invisible One restrained them. I stood invulnerable beneath His invisible shield, and succeeded in rolling back the tide of flame from our dwelling-house.

At this dread moment occurred an incident, which my readers may explain as they like, but which I trace directly to the interposition of my God. A rushing and roaring sound came from the South, like the noise of a mighty engine or of muttering thunder. Every head was instinctively turned in that direction, and they knew, from previous hard experience, that it was one of their awful tornadoes of wind and rain. Now, mark, the wind bore the flames away from our dwelling-house; had it come in the opposite direction, no power on earth could have saved us from being all consumed! It made the work of destroying the Church only that of a few minutes; but it brought with it a heavy and murky cloud, which poured out a perfect torrent of tropical rain. Now, mark again, the flames of the burning Church were thereby cut off from extending to and seizing upon the reeds and the bush; and, besides, it had become almost impossible now to set fire to our dwelling-house. The stars in their courses were fighting against Sisera!

The mighty roaring of the wind, the black cloud pouring down unceasing torrents, and the whole surroundings, awed those savages into silence. Some began to withdraw from the scene, all lowered their weapons of war, and several, terror-struck, exclaimed, "That is Jehovah's rain! Truly their Jehovah God is fighting for them and helping them. Let us away!" A panic seized upon them; they threw away their remaining torches; in a few moments they had all disappeared in the bush; and I was left alone, praising God for His marvelous works. "O taste and see that God is good! Blessed is the man that trusteth in Him!"

Returning to the door of the Mission House, I cried, "Open and let me in. I am now all alone."

Mr. Mathieson let me in, and exclaimed, "If ever, in time of need, God sent help and protection to His servants in answer to prayer, He has done so to-night! Blessed be His holy Name!"

In fear and in joy we united our praises. Truly our Jesus has all power, not less in the elements of Nature than in the savage hearts of the Tannese. Precious Jesus! Often since have I wept over His love and mercy in that deliverance, and prayed that every moment of my remaining life may be consecrated to the service of my precious Friend and Saviour!

CHAPTER XLII.
"SAIL O! SAIL O!"

ALL through the remainder of that night I lay wide awake keeping watch, my noble little dog lying near me with ears alert. Early in the morning friends came weeping around us. Our enemies were loudly rejoicing. It had been finally resolved to kill us at once, to plunder our house and then to burn it. The noise of the shouting was distinctly heard as they neared the Mission premises, and our weeping, friendly Natives looked terror-struck, and seemed anxious to flee for the bush. But just when the excitement rose to the highest pitch, we heard, or dreamed that we heard, a cry higher still, "Sail O!"

We were by this time beginning to distrust almost our very senses; but again and again that cry came rolling up from the shore, and was repeated from crowd to crowd all along the beach, "Sail O! Sail O!"

The shouts of those approaching us gradually ceased, and the whole multitude seemed to have melted away from our view. I feared some cruel deception, and at first peered out very cautiously to spy the land. But yonder in very truth a vessel came sailing into view. It was the *Blue Bell* Captain Hastings. I set fire to the reeds on the side of the hill to attract his attention. I put a black shawl as a flag on one end of the Mission House and a white sheet on the other.

This was one of the vessels that had been to Port Resolution, and had sailed past to Aneityum some time ago. I afterwards saw the mate and some of the men wearing my shirts, which they had bought from the Tannese on their former visit. At the earnest request of Messrs. Geddie and Copeland, Mr. Underwood, the owner, had sent Captain Hastings to Tanna to rescue us if yet alive. For this purpose he had brought twenty armed men from Aneityum, who came on shore in two boats in charge of the mate, the notorious Ross Lewin. He returned to the ship with a boat-load of Mr. Mathieson's things, leaving ten of the Natives to help us to pack more and carry them down to the beach, especially what the Missionary thought most valuable.

The two boats were now loaded and ready to start. It was about two o'clock in the afternoon, when a strange and painful trial befell us. Poor dear Mr. Mathieson, apparently unhinged, locked himself all alone into what had been his study, telling Mrs. Mathieson and me to go, for he had resolved to remain and die on Tanna. We tried to show him the inconsistency of praying to God to protect us or grant us means of escape, and then refuse to accept a rescue sent to us in our last extremity. We argued that it was surely better to live and work for Jesus than to die as a self-made martyr, who, in God's sight, was guilty of self-murder. His wife wept aloud and pleaded with him, but all in vain! He refused to leave or to unlock his door. I then said, "It is now getting dark. Your wife must go with the vessel, but I will not leave you alone. I shall send a note explaining why I am forced to remain; and as it is certain that we shall be murdered whenever the vessel leaves, I tell you God will charge you with the guilt of our murder." At this he relented, unlocked the door, and accompanied us to the boats, in which we all immediately left.

Meantime, having lost several hours, the vessel had drifted leeward; darkness suddenly settled upon us, and when we were out at sea we lost sight of her and she of us. After tumbling about for some hours in a heavy sea, and unable to find her, those in charge of the boats came near for consultation, and, if possible, to save the lives of all. We advised that they should steer for Port Resolution by the flame of the volcano—a never failing lighthouse, seen fifty miles away—and there await the vessel. The boats were to keep within hearing of each other by constant calling; but this was soon lost to the ear, though on arriving in the bay we found they had got to anchor before us. There we sat in the boats and waited for the coming day.

As the light appeared, we anchored as far out as possible, beyond the reach of musket shots; and there without water or food we sat under a tropical sun till midday came, and still there was no sign of the vessel. The mate at last put all the passengers and the poorest seamen into one boat and left her to swing at anchor, while, with a strong crew in the other, he started off in search of the vessel.

In the afternoon, Nowar and Miaki came off in a canoe to visit us. Nowar had on a shirt, but Miaki was naked and frowning. He urged me to go and see the Mission House, but as we had seen a body of men near it I refused to go. Miaki declared that everything remained as I had left it, but we knew that he lied. Old Abraham and a party had slipped on shore in a canoe, and had found the windows smashed and everything gone except my books, which were scattered about and torn in pieces. They learned that Miaki had sold everything that he could sell to the Traders. The mate and men of the *Blue Bell* had on my very clothes. They boasted that they had bought them for a few figs of tobacco and for powder, caps, and balls. But they would not return a single shirt to me, though I was without a change. We had all been without food since the morning before, so Nowar brought us off a cocoanut each, and two very small roasted yams for the ladies. Those, however, only seemed to make our thirst the more severe, and we spent a trying day in that boat under a burning sun.

Nowar informed me that only a few nights before this, Miaki and his followers went inland to a village where last year they had killed ten men. Having secretly placed a savage at the door of every house, at a given signal they yelled, and when the terrified inmates tried to escape, they killed almost every man, woman, and child. Some fled into the bush, others rushed to the shore. A number of men got into a canoe to escape, but hearing women and children crying after them they returned, and taking those they could with them, they killed the rest, lest they should fall alive into Miaki's hands. These are surely "they who through fear of death are all their lifetime subject to bondage." The Chief and nearly his whole village were cut off in one night! The dark places of the Earth are "full of the habitations of horrid cruelty." To have actually lived amongst the Heathen and seen their life gives a man a new appreciation of the power and blessings of the Gospel, even where its influence is only very imperfectly allowed to guide and restrain the passions of men. Oh, what it will be when all men in all nations love and serve the glorious Redeemer!

CHAPTER XLIII.
FAREWELL TO TANNA.

ABOUT five o'clock in the evening the vessel hove in sight. Before dark we were all on board, and were sailing for Aneityum. Though both Mr. and Mrs. Mathieson had become very weak, they stood the voyage wonderfully. Next day we were safely landed. We had offered Captain Hastings £20 to take us to Aneityum, but he declined any fare. However, we divided it amongst the mate and crew, for they had every one shown great kindness to us on the voyage.

After arriving on Aneityum, Mrs. Mathieson gradually sank under consumption, and fell asleep in Jesus on 11th March, 1862, and was interred there in the full assurance of a glorious resurrection. Mr. Mathieson, becoming more and more depressed after her death, went over to Mr. Creagh's Station, on Mare, and there died on 14th June, 1862, still trusting in Jesus, and assured that he would soon be with Him in Glory.

After their death I was the only one left alive, in all the New Hebrides Mission north of Aneityum, to tell the story of those pioneer years, during which were sown the seeds of what is now fast becoming a glorious harvest. Twenty-five years ago, all these dear brethren and sisters who were associated with me in the work of the Mission were called home to Glory, to cast their crowns at the feet of Jesus and enjoy the bliss of the redeemed; while I am privileged still to toil and pray for the salvation of the poor Islanders, and plead the cause of the Mission both in the Colonies and at home, in which work the Lord has graciously given me undreamt-of success. My constant desire and prayer are that I may be spared to see at least one Missionary on every island of the group, or trained Native Teachers under the superintendence of a Missionary, to unfold the riches of redeeming love and to lead the poor Islanders to Jesus for salvation.

What could be taken in three boats was saved out of the wreck of Mr. Mathieson's property; but my earthly all perished, except the Bible and the translations into Tannese. Along with the goods pertaining to the Mission, the property which I had to leave behind would be under-estimated at £600, besides the value of the Mission House, etc. Often since have I thought that the Lord stripped me thus bare of all these interests that I might with undistracted mind devote my entire energy to the special work soon to be carved out for me, and of which at this moment neither I nor any one had ever dreamed. At any rate, the loss of my little Earthly All, though doubtless costing me several pangs, was not an abiding sorrow like that which sprang from the thought that the Lord's work was now broken up at both Stations, and that the Gospel was for the time driven from Tanna.

In the darkest moment I never doubted that ultimately the victory there, as elsewhere, would be on the side of Jesus, believing that the whole Earth would yet be filled with the glory of the Lord. But I sometimes sorely feared that I might never live to see or hear of that happy day! By the goodness of the Ever-merciful One I have lived to see and hear of a Gospel Church on Tanna, and to read about my dear fellow-Missionaries, Mr. and Mrs. Watt, celebrating the Holy Supper to a Native Congregation of Tannese, amid the very scenes and people where the seeds of faith and hope were planted not only in tears, but tears of blood,—"in deaths oft."

My own intention was to remain on Aneityum, go on with my work of translating the Gospels, and watch the earliest opportunity, as God opened up my way, to return to Tanna, I had, however, got very weak and thin; my health was undoubtedly much shaken by the continued trials and dangers through which we had passed; and therefore, as Dr. and Mrs. Inglis were at home carrying the New Testament through the press in the language of Aneityum, and as Tanna was closed for a season—Dr. Geddie, the Rev. Joseph Copeland, and Mr. Mathieson all urged me to go to Australia by a vessel then in the Harbor and leaving in a few days. My commission was to awaken an interest among the Presbyterian Churches of our Colonies in this New Hebrides Mission which lay at their doors, up till this time sustained by Scotland and Nova Scotia alone. And further, and very specially, to raise money there, if possible, to purchase a new Mission Ship for the work of God in the New Hebrides,—a clamant necessity which would save all future Missionaries some of the more terrible of the privations and risks of which a few examples have in these pages already been recorded.

With regrets, and yet with unquenchable hope for these Islands, I embarked for Australia. But I had only spoken to one man in Sydney; all the doors to influence had therefore to be unlocked; and I had no helper, no leader, but the Spirit of my Lord.

Oftentimes, while passing through the perils and defeats of my first four years in the Mission field on Tanna, I wondered, and perhaps the reader hereof has wondered, why God permitted such things. But on looking back now, I already clearly perceive, and the reader of my future pages will, I think, perceive, that the Lord was thereby preparing me for doing, and providing me materials wherewith to accomplish, the best work of all my life, namely, the kindling of the heart of Australian Presbyterianism with a living affection for these Islanders of their own Southern Seas—the binding of all their children into a happy league of shareholders, first in one Mission Ship, and finally in a larger and more commodious Steam-Auxiliary; and, last of all, in being the instrument under God of sending out Missionary after Missionary to the New Hebrides, to claim another island and still another for Jesus. That work, and all that may spring from it in Time and Eternity, never could have been accomplished by me, but for first the sufferings and then the story of my Tanna days!

Never for one moment have I had occasion to regret the step then taken. The Lord has so used me, during the five-and-twenty years that have passed over me since my farewell to Tanna, as to stamp the event with His own most gracious approval. Oh, to see a Missionary, and Christian Teachers, planted on every island of the New Hebrides! For this I labor, and wait, and pray. To help on the fulfillment thereof is the sacred work of my life, under God. When I see that accomplished, or in a fair way of being so, through the organization that will provide the money and call forth the men, I can lay down my head as peacefully and gratefully as ever warrior did, with the shout of victory in his ears—"Lord, now lettest Thou Thy servant depart in peace!"

(For "Good News from Tanna," see Supplementary Chapter by the Editor, p.393.)

CHAPTER XLIV.
THE FLOATING OF THE "DAYSPRING."

RESCUED from Tanna by the *Blue Bell* in the Spring of 1869, I was landed on Aneityum, leaving behind me all that I owned on Earth, save the clothes upon my back, my precious Bible, and a few translations that I had made from it into the Tannese language. The Missionaries on Aneitymn united in urging me to go to Australia in the interests of our Mission. A Mission Ship was sorely needed—was absolutely required—to prevent the needless sacrifice of devoted lives. More Missionaries were called for, and must somehow be brought into the field, unless the hope of claiming these fair Islands for Jesus was to be forever abandoned.

With unaffected reluctance, I at last felt constrained to undertake this unwelcome but apparently inevitable task. It meant the leaving of my dear Islanders for a season; but it embraced within it the hope of returning to them again, with perhaps every power of blessing amongst them tenfold increased.

A *Sandal-wooder*, then lying at Aneityum, was to sail in a few days direct for Sydney. My passage was secured for £10. And, as if to make me realize how bare the Lord had stripped me in my late trials, the first thing that occupied me on board was the making with my own hands, from a piece of cloth obtained on Aneityum, another shirt for the voyage, to change with that which I wore—the only one that had been left to me.

The Captain proved to be a profane and brutal fellow. And how my heart bled for some poor Islanders whom he had on board! They knew not a word of English, and no one in the vessel knew a sound of their language. They were made to work, and to understand what was expected of them, only by hard knocks and blows, being pushed and pulled hither and thither. They were kept quite naked on the voyage up; but, when nearing Sydney, each received two yards of calico to be twisted as a kilt around his loins. A most pathetic spectacle it was to watch these poor Natives,—when they had leisure to sit on deck,—gazing, gazing, intently and imploringly, upon the face of the Sun! This they did every day, and at all hours, and I wept much to look on them, and not be able to tell them of the Son of God, the Light of the world, for I knew no word of their language. Perhaps they were worshipers of the Sun; and perhaps, amid all their misery, oh, *perhaps*, some ray of truth from the great Father of Lights may have streamed into those darkened souls!

When we arrived at Sydney the Inspecting Officer of the Government, coming on board, asked how these Islanders came to be there. The Captain impudently replied that they were "passengers." No further question was put. No other evidence was sought. Yet all who knew anything of our South-Sea Island Traders were perfectly aware that the moral certainty was that these Natives were there practically as Slaves. They would be privately disposed of by the Captain to the highest bidder; and that, forsooth, is to be called the *Labor* Traffic,—*Free* Labor! I will, to my dying breath, denounce and curse this *Kanaka* traffic as the worst of Slavery.

As we came to anchorage, about midnight, in Sydney Harbor, I anxiously paced the deck, gazing towards the gas-lighted city, and pleading with God to open up my way, and give success in the work before me, on which the salvation of thousands of the Heathen might depend. Still I saw them perishing, still heard their wailing cry on the Islands behind me. At the same time, I knew not a soul in that great city; though I had a note of introduction to one person, which, as experience proved, I would have been better without.

That friend, however, did his best. He kindly called with me on a number of Ministers and others. They heard my story, sympathized with me, shook hands, and wished me success; but, strangely enough, something "very special" prevented every one of them from giving me access to his pulpit or Sabbath School. At length I felt so disappointed, so miserable, that I wished I had been in my grave with my dear departed, and my brethren on the Islands, who had fallen around me, in order that the work on which so much now appeared to depend might have been entrusted to some one better fitted to accomplish it. The heart seemed to keep repeating, "All these things are against thee."

Finding out at last the Rev. A. Buzacott, then retired, but formerly the successful and honored representative of the London Missionary Society on Rarotonga, considerable light was let in upon the mystery of my last week's experiences. He informed me that the highly-esteemed friend, who had kindly been introducing me all round, was at that moment immersed in a keen Newspaper war with Presbyterians and Independents. This made it painfully manifest that, in order to succeed, I must strike out a new course for myself, and one clear from all local entanglement.

Paying a fortnight in advance, I withdrew even from the lodging I had taken, and turned to the Lord more absolutely for guidance. He brought me into contact with good and generous-souled servants of His, the open-hearted Mr. and Mrs. Foss. Though entire strangers, they kindly invited me to be their guest while in Sydney, assuring me that I would meet with many Ministers and other Christians at their house who could help me in my work. God had opened the door; I entered with a grateful heart; they will not miss their recompense.

A letter and appeal had been already printed on behalf of our Mission. I now re-cast and reprinted it, adding a postscript, and appending my own name and address. This was widely circulated among Ministers and others engaged in Christian work; and by this means, and by letters in the newspapers, I did everything in my power to make our Mission known. But one week had passed, and no response came. One Lord's Day had gone by, and no pulpit had been opened to me. I was perplexed beyond measure how to get access to Congregations and Sabbath Schools; though a something deep in my soul assured me, that if once my lips were opened, the Word of the Lord would not return void.

On my second Sabbath in Sydney I wandered out with a great yearning at heart to get telling my message to any soul that would listen. It was the afternoon; and children were flocking into a Church that I passed. I followed them—that yearning growing stronger every moment. My God so ordered it that I was guided thus to the Chalmers Presbyterian Church. The Minister, the Rev. Mr. M'Skimming, addressed the children. At the close I went up and pleaded with him to allow me ten minutes to speak to them. After a little hesitation, and having consulted together, they gave me fifteen minutes. Becoming deeply interested, the good man invited me to preach to his Congregation in the evening. This was duly intimated in the Sabbath School; and thus my little boat was at last launched—surely by the hand of the dear Lord, with the help of His little children.

CHAPTER XLV.
A SHIPPING COMPANY FOR JESUS.

THE kindly minister of Chalmers church, now very deeply interested, offered to spend the next day in introducing me to his clerical brethren. For his sake, I was most cordially received by them all, but especially by Dr. Dunmore Lang, who greatly helped me; and now access was granted me to almost every church and Sabbath School, both Presbyterian and Independent. In Sabbath Schools, I got a collection in connection with my address, and distributed, with the sanction of superintendents, collecting cards amongst the children, to be returned through the Teachers within a specified date. In congregations, I received for the Mission the surplus over and above the ordinary collection when I preached on Sabbaths, and the full collection at all week-night meetings for which I could arrange.

I now appealed to a few of the most friendly ministers to form themselves into an honorary committee of advice; and, at my earnest request, they got J. Goodlet, Esq., an excellent elder, to become honorary treasurer, and to take charge of all funds raised for the Mission ship. For the public knew nothing of me; but all knew my good treasurer and these faithful ministers, and had confidence in the work. They knew that every penny went direct to the Mission; and they saw that my one object was to promote God's glory in the conversion of the heathen. Our dear Lord Jesus thus opened up my way; and now I had invitations from more schools and congregations than I knew how to overtake—the response in money being also gratifying beyond almost all expectation.

It was now that I began a little plan of interesting the children, that attracted them from the first, and has since had an amazing development. I made them shareholders in the new Mission Ship—each child receiving a printed form, in acknowledgment of the number of shares, at sixpence each, of which he was the owner. Thousands of these shares were taken out, were shown about amongst families, and were greatly prized. The Ship was to be their very own! They were to be a great Shipping Company for Jesus. In hundreds of homes these receipt-forms have been preserved; and their owners, now in middle years, are training their children of to-day to give their pennies to support the white-winged Angel of the Seas, that bears the Gospel and the Missionary to the Heathen Isles.

Let no one think me ungrateful to my good Treasurer and his wife, to Dr. and Mrs. Moon, and to other dear friends who generously helped me, when I trace step by step how the Lord Himself opened up my way. The Angel of His Presence went before me, and wonderfully moved His people to contribute in answer to my poor appeals. I had indeed to make all my own arrangements and correspond regarding all engagements and details,—to me, always a slow and laborious writer, a very burdensome task. But it was all necessary in order to the fulfillment of the Lord's purposes; and, to one who realizes that he is a fellow-laborer with Jesus, every yoke that He lays on becomes easy and every burden light.

Having done all that could at that time be accomplished in New South Wales, and as rapidly as possible—my Committee gave me a Letter of Commendation to Victoria. But there I had no difficulty. The Ministers had heard of our work in Sydney. They received me most cordially, and at my request formed themselves into a Committee of Advice. Our dear friend, James M'Bain, Esq., now Sir James, became Honorary Treasurer. All moneys from this Colony, raised by my pleading for the Ship, were entrusted to him; and, ultimately, the acknowledging of every individual sum cost much time and labor. Dr. Cairns, and many others now gone to their rest, along with two or three honored Ministers yet living, formed my Committee. The Lord richly reward them all in that Day!

As in New South Wales, I made, chiefly by correspondence, all my own engagements, and arranged for Churches and Sabbath Schools as best I could. Few in the other Denominations of Victoria gave any help, but the Presbyterians rose to our appeal as with one heart. God moved them by one impulse; and Ministers, Superintendents, Teachers, and Children, heartily embraced the scheme as their own. I addressed three or four meetings every Sabbath, and one or more every week-day; and thus traveled over the length and breadth of Victoria, Tasmania, and South Australia. Wheresoever a few of the Lord's people could be gathered together, thither I gladly went, and told the story of our Mission, setting forth its needs and claims.

The contributions and collections were nearly all in very small sums, I recall only one exception,—a gift of £250 from the late Hon. G. F. Angus, South Australia, whose heart the Lord had touched. Yet gently and steadily the required money began to come pouring in; and my personal outlays were reduced to a minimum by the hospitality of Christian friends and their kindly conveying of me from place to place. For all this I felt deeply grateful; it saved money for the Lord's work.

The work was unceasingly prosecuted. Meetings were urged upon me now from every quarter. Money flowed in so freely that, at the close of my tour, the fund had risen to £5000, including special Donations of £300 for the support of Native Teachers. Many Sabbath Schools, and many ladies and gentlemen, had individually promised the sum of £5 yearly to keep a Native

Teacher on one or other of the New Hebrides Islands. This happy custom prevails still, and is largely developed; the sum required being now £6 per annum at least—for which you may have your own personal representative toiling among the Heathen and telling them of Jesus.

Returning to Melbourne, the whole matter was laid before my Committee. I reported how God had blessed the undertaking, and what sums were now in the hands of the several Treasurers, indicating also larger hopes and plans which had been put into my soul. Dear Dr. Cairns rose and said, "Sir, it is of the Lord. This whole enterprise is of God, and not of us. Go home, and He will give you more Missionaries for the Islands."

Of the money which I had raised, £3000 were sent to Nova Scotia, to pay for the building of our new Mission Ship, the *Dayspring*. The Church which began the Mission on the New Hebrides was granted the honor of building our new Mission Ship. The remainder was set apart to pay for the outfit and passage of additional Missionaries for the field, and I was commissioned to return home to Scotland in quest of them. Dr. Inglis wrote, in vindication of this enterprise, to the friends whom he had just left, "From first to last, Mr. Paton's mission here has been a great success; and it has been followed up with such energy and promptitude in Nova Scotia, both in regard to the Ship and the Missionaries, that Mr. Paton's pledge to the Australian Churches has been fully redeemed. The hand of the Lord has been very visible in the whole movement from beginning to end, and we trust He has yet great blessing in store for the long and deeply-degraded Islanders."

CHAPTER XLVI.
AUSTRALIAN INCIDENTS.

HERE let me turn aside from the current of Missionary toils, and record a few wayside incidents that marked some of my wanderings to and fro in connection with the Floating of the *Dayspring*. Traveling in the Colonies in 1862-68 was vastly less developed than it is to-day; and a few of my experiences then will, for many reasons, be not unwelcome to most readers of this book. Besides, these incidents, one and all, will be felt to have a vital connection with the main purpose of writing this Autobiography, namely, to show that the Finger of God is as visible still, to those who have eyes to see, as when the fire-cloud Pillar led His People through the wilderness.

Twenty-six years ago, the roads of Australia, except those in and around the principal towns, were mere tracks over unfenced plains and hills, and on many of them packhorses only could be used in slushy weather. During long journeys through the bush the traveler could find his road only by following the deep notches, gashed by friendly precursors into the larger trees, and all pointing in one direction. If he lost his way, he had to struggle back to the last indented tree, and try to interpret more correctly its pilgrim notch. Experienced bush-travelers seldom miss the path; yet many others, losing the track, have wandered round and round till they sank and died. For then it was easy to walk thirty to forty miles, and see neither a person nor a house. The more intelligent do sometimes guide their steps by sun, moon, and stars, or by glimpses of mountain peaks or natural features on the far and high horizon, or by the needle of the compass; but the perils are not illusory, and occasionally the most experienced have miscalculated and perished.

An intelligent gentleman, a sheep farmer, who knew the country well, once kindly volunteered to lift me in an out-of-the-way place, and drive me to a meeting at his Station. Having a long spell before us, we started at midday in a buggy drawn by a pair of splendid horses, in the hope of reaching our destination before dusk. He turned into the usual bush-track through the forests, saying, "I know this road well; and we must drive steadily, as we have not a moment to lose."

Our conversation became absorbingly interesting. After we had driven about three hours, he remarked, "We must soon emerge into the open plain."

I doubtfully replied, "Surely we cannot have turned back! These trees and bushes are wonderfully like those we passed at starting."

He laughed, and made me feel rather vexed that I had spoken, when he said, "I am too old a hand in the bush for that. I have gone this road many a time before."

But my courage immediately revived, for I got what appeared to me a glint of the roof of the Inn beyond the bush, from which we had started at noon, and I repeated, "I am certain we have wheeled, and are back at the beginning of our journey; but there comes a Chinaman—let us wait and inquire."

My dear friend learned, to his utter amazement, that he had erred. The bush-track was entered upon once more, and followed with painful care, as he murmured, half to himself, "Well, this beats all reckoning! I could have staked my life that this was impossible."

Turning to me, he said, with manifest grief, "Our meeting is done for! It will be midnight before we can arrive."

The sun was beginning to set as we reached the thinly-timbered ground. Ere dusk fell, he took his bearing with the greatest possible care. Beyond the wood, a vast plain stretched before us, where neither fence nor house was visible, far as the eye could reach. He drove steadily towards a far-distant point, which was in the direction of his home. At last we struck upon the wire fence that bounded his property. The horses were now getting badly fagged; and, in order to save them a long round-about drive, he lifted and laid low a portion of the fence, led his horses cautiously over it, and, leaving it to be re-erected by a servant next day, he started direct for the Station. That seemed a long journey too; but it was for him familiar ground; and though amongst great patriarchal trees here and there, and safely past dangerous water-holes, we swung steadily on, reached his home in safety, and had a joyous welcome. The household had by this time got into great excitement over our non-appearance. The expected meeting had, of course, been abandoned hours ago: and the people were all gone, wondering in their hearts "whereto this would grow!"

At that time, in the depth of winter, the roads were often wrought into rivers of mire, and at many points almost impassable even for well-appointed conveyances. In connection therewith, I had one very perilous experience. I had to go from Clunes to a farm in the Learmouth district. The dear old Minister there, Mr. Downes, went with me to every place where a horse could be hired; but the owners positively refused—they would sell, but they would not hire, for the conveyance would be broken, and the horse would never return alive! Now, I was advertised to preach at Learmouth, and must somehow get over the nine miles that lay between. This would have been comparatively practicable, were it not that I carried with me an indispensable bag of "curios," and a heavy bundle of clubs, arrows, dresses, etc., from the Islands, wherewith to illustrate my lectures and enforce my appeals. No one could be hired to carry my luggage, nor could I get it sent after me by coach on that particular way. Therefore, seeing no alternative opening up my path, I committed myself once more to the Lord, as in harder trials before, shouldered my bundle of clubs, lifted my heavy bag, and started off on foot. They urged me fervently to desist; but I heard a voice repeating, "As thy days, so shall thy strength be." There came back to me also the old adage that had in youthful difficulties, spurred me on, "Where there's a will, there's a way." And I thought that with these two in his heart, a Scotchman and a Christian would not be easily beaten.

When I found the road wrought into mire, and dangerous, or impassable, I climbed the fence, and waded along in the plowed fields—though they were nearly as bad. My bundle was changed from shoulder to shoulder, and my bag from hand to hand, till I became thoroughly tired of both. Pressing on, however, I arrived at a wayside Public-house, where several roads met, and there I inquired the way to Learmouth, and how far it was. The innkeeper, pointing, answered—

"This is the road. If you are on horseback, it might be three to four miles just now, as your horse is able to take it. If you are in a conveyance, with a good horse, it might be six miles. And if you are walking, it might be eight or ten miles, or even more."

I said, "I am walking. How many English miles is it to Mr. Baird's farm?"

He laughingly replied, "You will find it a long way indeed this dark night, considering the state of the road, fenced in on both sides so that you cannot get off."

I passed on, leaving my Job's comforter; but a surly watchdog got upon my track, and I had much difficulty in keeping it from biting me. Its attacks, renewed upon me again and again, had one good effect,—they stirred up my spirits and made me hasten on.

Having persevered along the Learmouth road, I next met a company of men hastening on with a bundle of ropes. They were on their way to relieve a poor bullock, which by this time had almost disappeared, sinking in the mire on the public highway! They kindly pointed me to a light, visible through the dusk. That was the farm at which I was to stay, and they advised me to clear the fence, and make straight for that light, as the way was good.

With thankful heart, I did so. The light was soon lost to me, but I walked steadily on in the direction thereof, to the best of my judgment. Immediately I began to feel the ground all floating under me. Then at every step I took, or tried to take, I sank deeper and deeper, till at last I durst not move either backward or forward. I was floundering in a deadly swamp. I called out again and again, and "coo-ee-d" with all my strength, but there came no reply. It grew extremely dark, while I kept praying to God for deliverance. About midnight, I heard two men conversing, apparently at no very great distance. I began "coo-ee-ing" again, but my strength was failing. Fortunately, the night was perfectly calm. The conversation ceased for a while, but I kept on crying for help. At length I heard one voice remark to the other, "Some one is in the swamp." And then the question came, "Who's there?"

I answered, "A stranger. Oh, do help me!" Again a voice came through the darkness, "How did you get in there?"

And I feebly replied, "I have lost my way." I heard the one say to the other, "I will go and get him out, whoever he may be. We must not leave him there; he'll be dead before the morning. As you pass by our door, tell my wife that I'm helping some poor creature out of the swamp, and will be home immediately."

He kept calling to me, and I answering his call through the darkness, till, not without peril, he managed to reach and aid me. Once I was safely dragged out, he got my bag in his hand and slung my clubs on his shoulder, and in a very short time landed me at the farm, dripping and dirty and cold. Had God not sent that man to save me, I must have perished there, as many others have similarly perished before. The farmer's wife heartily welcomed me and kindly ministered to all my needs. Though not yet gone to rest, they had given up all hope of seeing me. I heard the kind servant say to his mistress, "I don't know where he came from, or how far he has carried his bundles; but I got him stuck fast in the swamp, and my shoulder is already sore from carrying his clubs!"

A cup of warm tea restored me. The Lord gave me a sound and blessed sleep. I rose next morning wonderfully refreshed, though arms and shoulders were rather sore with the burdens of yesterday. I conducted three Services, and told the story of my Mission, not without comfort and blessing; and with gratifying results in money. The people gave liberally to the work.

Thereafter, a Schoolmaster drove me a long distance across the country to Violet Town, where for the night we had to stay at an Inn. We had a taste of what Australian life really was, when the land was being broken in. A company of wild and reckless men were carousing there at the time, and our arrival was the signal for an outbreak of malicious mischief. A powerful fellow, who turned out to be a young Medical, rushed upon me as I left the conveyance, seized me by the throat, and shook me roughly, shouting, "A parson! a parson! I will do for the parson!"

Others with great difficulty relieved me from his grip, and dragged him away, cursing as if at his mortal enemy.

After tea, we got into the only bedroom in the house, available for two. The Teacher and I locked ourselves in and barricaded the door, hearing in the next room a large party of drunken men gambling and roaring over their cards. By and by they quarreled and fought; they smashed in and out of their room, and seemed to be murdering each other; every moment we expected our door to come crashing in, as they were thrown or lurched against it. Their very language made us tremble. One man in particular seemed to be badly abused; he shouted that they were robbing him of his money; and he groaned and cried for protection, all in vain. We spent a sleepless and most miserable night. At four in the morning I arose, and was glad to get away by the early coach. My friend also left in his own conveyance, and reached his home in safety. At that period, it was not only painful but dangerous for any decent traveler to stay at many of these wayside Inns in the new and rough country. Every man lived and acted just as he pleased, doing that which was right to his own eyes; and Might was Right.

CHAPTER XLVII.
AMONGST SQUATTERS AND DIGGERS.

AFTER this, I made a Mission tour, in a somewhat mixed and original fashion, right across the Colony of Victoria, from Albury in New South Wales to Mount Gambier in South Australia. I conducted Mission Services almost every day, and three or more every Sabbath, besides visiting all Sunday Schools that could be touched on the way. When I reached a gold-digging or township, where I had been unable to get any one to announce a meeting, the first thing I did on arriving was to secure some Church or Hall, and, failing that, to fix on some suitable spot in the open air. Then, I was always able to hire some one to go round with the bell, and announce the meeting. Few will believe how large were the audiences in this way gathered together, and how very substantial was the help that thereby came to the Mission fund.

Wheresover railway, steamboat, and coach were available, I always used them; but failing these, I hired, or was obliged to friends of Missions for driving me from place to place. On this tour, having reached a certain place, from which my way lay for many miles across the country, where there was no public conveyance, I walked to the nearest squatter's Station and frankly informed the owner how I was situated; that I could not hire, and that I would like to stay at his house all night, if he would kindly send me on in the morning by any sort of trap to the next Station on my list. He happened to be a good Christian and a Presbyterian, and gave me a right cordial welcome. A meeting of his servants was called, which I had the pleasure of addressing. Next morning, he gave me £20, and sent me forward with his own conveyance, telling me to retain it all day, if necessary.

On reaching the next squatter's Station, I found the master also at home, and said, "I am a Missionary from the South Sea Islands. I am crossing Victoria to plead the cause of the Mission. I would like to rest here for an hour or two. Could you kindly send me on to the next Station by your conveyance? If not, I am to keep the last squatter's buggy, until I reach it."

Looking with a queer smile at me, he replied, "You propose a rather novel condition on which to rest at my house! My horses are so employed to-day, I fear that I may have difficulty in sending you on. But come in; both you and your horses need rest; and my wife will be glad to see you."

I immediately discovered that the good lady came from Glasgow, from a street in which I had lodged when a student at the Free Normal College. I even knew some of her friends. All the places of her youthful associations were equally familiar to me. We launched out into deeply-interesting conversation, which finally led up, of course, to the story of our Mission.

The gentleman, by this time, had so far been won that he slipped out and sent my conveyance and horses back to their owner, and ordered his own to be ready to take me to the next Station, or, if need be, to the next again. At parting, the lady said to her husband, "The Missionary has asked no money, though he sees we have been deeply interested; yet clearly that is the object of his tour. He is the first Missionary from the Heathen that ever visited us here; and you must contribute something to his Mission fund."

I thanked her, explaining, "I never ask money directly from any person for the Lord's work. My part is done when I have told my story and shown the needs of the Heathen and the claims of Christ; but I gratefully receive all that the Lord moves His people to give for the Mission."

Her husband replied, rather sharply, "You know I don't keep money here." To which she retorted with ready tact and with a resistless smile, "But you keep a check-book; and your check is as good as gold! This is the first donation we ever gave to such a cause, and let it be a good one." He made it indeed handsome, and I went on my way, thanking them very sincerely, and thanking God.

At the next Station, the owner turned out to be a gruff Irishman, forbidding and insolent. Stating my case to him as to the others, he shouted at me, "Go on! I don't want to be troubled with the loikes o' you here."

I answered, "I am sorry if my coming troubles you; but I wish you every blessing in Christ Jesus. Good-by!"

As we drove off, he kept growling after us. On leaving his door, I heard a lady calling to him from the window, "Don't let that Missionary go away! Make haste and call him back. I want the children to see the idols and the South Sea curios."

At first he drowned her appeal in his own shoutings. But she must have persisted effectually; for shortly we heard him "coo-ee-ing," and stopped. When he came up to us, he explained, "That lady in my house heard you speaking in Melbourne. The ladies and children are very anxious to see your idols, dresses, and weapons. Will you please come back?"

We did so. I spent fifteen minutes or so, giving them information about the Natives and our Mission. As I left, our boisterous friend handed me a check for £5, and wished me great success.

The next Station at which we arrived was one of the largest of all. It happened to be a sort of payday, and men were assembled from all parts of the "run," and were to remain there over night. The squatter and his family were from home; but Mr. Todd, the overseer, being a good Christian and a Scotchman, was glad to receive us, arranged to hold a meeting that evening in the men's hut, and promised to set me forward on my journey next day. The meeting was very enthusiastic; and they subscribed £20 to the Mission—every man being determined to have so many shares in the new Mission Ship. With earnest personal dealing, I urged the claims of the Lord Jesus upon all who were present, seeking the salvation of every hearer. I ever found even the rough digger, and the lowest of the hands about far-away Stations, most attentive and perfectly respectful.

A lively and memorable extemporized meeting on this tour is associated in memory with one of my dearest friends. The district was very remote. He, the squatter, and his beloved wife were sterling Christians, and have been ever since warmly devoted to me. On my arrival, he invited the people from all the surrounding Stations, as well as his own numerous servants, to hear the story of our Mission. Next day he volunteered to drive me a long distance over the plains of St. Arnaud, his dear wife accompanying us. At that time there were few fences in such districts in Australia. The drive was long, but the day had been lovely, and the fellowship was so sweet that it still shines a sunny spot in the fields of memory.

Having reached our destination about seven o'clock, he ordered tea at the Inn for the whole party; and we sallied out meantime and took the only Hall in the place, for an extemporized meeting to be held that evening at eight o'clock. I then hired a man to go through the township with a bell, announcing the same; while I myself went up one side of the main street, and my friend up the other, inviting all who would listen to us to attend the Mission meeting where South Sea Islands idols, weapons, and dresses would be exhibited, and stories of the Natives told.

Running back for a hurried cup of tea, I then hasted to the Hall, and found it crowded to excess with rough and boisterous diggers. The hour struck as I was getting my articles arranged and spread out upon the table, and they began shouting, "Where's the Missionary?"—"Another hoax!"—indicating that they were not unwilling for a row. I learned that, only a few nights ago, a so-called Professor had advertised a lecture, lifted entrance money till the Hall was crowded, and then quietly slipped off the scene. In our case, though there was no charge, they seemed disposed to gratify themselves by some sort of promiscuous revenge.

Amidst the noisy chaff and rising uproar, I stepped up on the table, and said, "Gentlemen, I am the Missionary. If you will now be silent, the lecture will proceed. According to my usual custom, let us open the meeting with prayer."

The hush that fell was such a contrast to the preceding hubbub, that I heard my heart throbbing aloud! Then they listened to me for an hour, in perfect silence and with ever-increasing interest. At the close I intimated that I asked no collection; but if, after what they had heard, they would take a Collecting Card for the new Mission Ship, and send any contributions to the Treasurer at Melbourne, I would praise God for sending me amongst them. Many were heartily taken, and doubtless some souls felt the "constraining love," who had till then been living without God.

CHAPTER XLVIII.
JOHN GILPIN IN THE BUSH.

THE crowning adventure of my tour in Australia came about in the following manner. I was advertised to conduct Services at Narracoort on Sabbath, and at a Station on the way on Saturday evening. But how to get from Penola was a terrible perplexity. On Saturday morning, however, a young lady offered me, out of gratitude for blessings received, the use of her riding horse for the journey. "Garibaldi" was his name; and, though bred for a race-horse, I was assured that if I kept him firmly in hand, he would easily carry me over the two-and-twenty miles. He was to be left at the journey's end, and the lady herself would fetch him back. I shrank from the undertaking, knowing little of horses, and having vague recollections of being dreadfully punished for more than a week after my last and almost only ride. But every one in that country is quite at ease on the back of a horse. They saw no risk; and, as there appeared no other way of getting there to fulfil my engagements, I, for my part, began to think that God had unexpectedly provided the means, and that He would carry me safely through.

I accepted the lady's kind offer, and started on my pilgrimage. A friend showed me the road, and gave me ample directions. In the bush, I was to keep my eye on the notches in the trees, and follow them. He agreed kindly to bring my luggage to the Station, and leave it there for me by and by. After I had walked very quietly for some distance, three gentlemen on horseback overtook me. We entered into conversation. They inquired how far I was going, and advised me to sit a little "freer" in the saddle, as it would be so much easier for me. They seemed greatly amused at my awkward riding! Dark clouds were now gathering ahead, and the atmosphere prophesied a severe storm; therefore they urged that I should ride a little faster, as they, for a considerable distance, could guide me on the right way. I explained to them my plight through inexperience, said that I could only creep on slowly with safety, and bade them Good-by. As the sky was getting darker every minute, they consented, wishing me a safe journey, and started off at a smart pace.

I struggled to hold in my horse; but seizing the bit with his teeth, laying back his ears, and stretching out his eager neck, he manifestly felt that his honor was at stake; and in less time than I take to write it, the three friends cleared a way for us, and he tore past them all at an appalling speed. They tried for a time to keep within reach of us, but that sound only put fire into his blood; and in an incredibly short time I heard them not; nor, from the moment that he bore me swinging past them, durst I turn my head by one inch to look for them again. In vain I tried to hold him in; he tore on, with what appeared to me the speed of the wind. Then the thunderstorm broke around us, with flash of lightning and flood of rain, and at every fresh peal my "Garibaldi" dashed more wildly onward.

To me, it was a vast surprise to discover that I could sit more easily on this wild flying thing than when at a canter or a trot. At every turn I expected that he would dash himself and me against the great forest trees; but instinct rather than my hand guided him miraculously. Sometimes I had a glimpse of the road, but as for the "notches," I never saw one of them; we passed them with lightning speed. Indeed, I durst not lift my eyes for one moment from watching the horse's head and the trees on our track. My high-crowned hat was now drenched, and battered out of shape; for whenever we came to a rather clear space, I seized the chance and gave it another knock down over my head. I was spattered and covered with mud and mire.

Crash, crash, went the thunder, and on, on, went "Garibaldi" through the gloom of the forest, emerging at length upon a clearer ground with a more visible pathway. Reaching the top of the slope, a large house stood out far in front of us to the left; and the horse had apparently determined to make straight for that, as if it were his home. He skirted along the hill, and took the track as his own familiar ground, all my effort to hold him in or guide him having no more effect than that of a child. By this time, I suspect, I really had lost all power. "Garibaldi" had been at that house, probably frequently before; he knew those stables; and my fate seemed to be instant death against door or wall.

Some members of the family, on the outlook for the Missionary, saw us come tearing along as if mad or drunk; and now all rushed to the veranda, expecting some dread catastrophe. A tall and stout young groom, amazed at our wild career, throwing wide open the gate, seized the bridle at great risk to himself, and ran full speed, yet holding back with all his might, and shouting to me to do the same. We succeeded—"Garibaldi" having probably attained his purpose—in bringing him to a halt within a few paces of the door. Staring at me with open mouth, the man exclaimed, "I have saved your life. What madness to ride like that!" Thanking him, though I could scarcely by this time articulate a word, I told him that the horse had run away, and that I had lost all control.

Truly I was in a sorry plight, drenched, covered with mud, and my hat battered down over my eyes; little wonder they thought me drunk or mad! Finally, as if to confirm every suspicion, and amuse them all,—for master, mistress, governess, and children now looked on from the veranda,—when

I was helped off the horse, I could not stand on my feet! My head still went rushing on in the race; I staggered, and down I tumbled into the mud, feeling chagrin and mortification; yet there I had to sit for some time, before I recovered myself, so as either to rise or to speak a word. When I did get to my feet, I had to stand holding by the veranda for some time, my head still rushing on in the race. At length the master said, "Will you not come in?"

I knew that he was treating me for a drunken man; and the giddiness was so dreadful still, that my attempts at speech seemed more drunken than even my gait.

As soon as I could stand, I went into the house, and drew near to an excellent fire in my dripping clothes. The squatter sat opposite me in silence, reading the newspapers, and taking a look at me now and again over his spectacles. By and by he remarked, "Wouldn't it be worth while to change your clothes?"

Speech was now returning to me. I replied, "Yes, but my bag is coming on in the cart, and may not be here to-night."

He began to relent. He took me into a room, and laid out for me a suit of his own. I being then very slender, and he a big-framed farmer, my new dress, though greatly adding to my comfort, enhanced the singularity of my appearance!

Returning to him, washed and dressed, I inquired if he had arranged for a meeting? My tongue, I fear, was still unsteady, for the squatter looked at me rather reproachfully, and said, "Do you really consider yourself fit to appear before a meeting to-night?"

I assured him he was quite wrong in his suspicions, that I was a life-long Abstainer, and that my nerves had been so unhinged by the terrible ride and runaway horse. He smiled rather suggestively, and said we would see how I felt after tea.

We went to the table. All that had occurred was now consummated by my appearing in the lusty farmer's clothes; and the lady and other friends had infinite difficulty in keeping their amusement within decent bounds. I again took speech in hand, but I suspect my words had still the thickness of the tippler's utterance, for they seemed not to carry much conviction, "Dear friends, I quite understand your feelings; appearances are so strangely against me. But I am not drunken, as ye suppose. I have tasted no intoxicating drink, I am a life-long Total Abstainer!"

This fairly broke down their reserve. They laughed aloud, looking at each other and at me, as if to say, "Man, you're drunk at this very moment."

Before tea was over they appeared, however, to begin to entertain the idea that I *might* address the meeting; and so I was informed of the arrangements that had been made. At the meeting, my incredulous friends became very deeply interested. Manifestly their better thoughts were gaining the ascendency. And they heaped thereafter every kindness upon me, as if to make amends for harder suspicions.

Next morning the master drove me about ten miles farther on to the Church. A groom rode the racehorse, who took no scathe from his thundering gallop of the day before. It left deeper traces upon me. I got through the Services, however, and with good returns for the Mission. Twice since, on my Mission tours, I have found myself at that same memorable house; and on each occasion, a large company of friends were regaled by the good lady there with very comical descriptions of my first arrival at her door.

CHAPTER XLIX.
THE ABORIGINES OF AUSTRALIA.

DETAINED for nearly a week at Balmoral by the breakdown of the coach on these dreadful roads, I telegraphed to Hamilton for a conveyance; and the Superintendent of the Sunday School, dear Mr. Laidlaw, volunteered, in order to reduce expenses, to spend one day of his precious time coming for me, and another driving me down. While awaiting him, I came into painful and memorable contact with the Aborigines of Australia. The Publicans had organized a day of sports, horse-racing, and circus exhibitions. Immense crowds assembled, and, amongst the rest, tribe after tribe of the Aborigines from all the surrounding country. Despite the law prohibiting the giving of strong drinks to these poor creatures, foolish and unprincipled dealers supplied them with the same, and the very blankets which the Government had given them were freely exchanged for the fire-water which kindled them to madness.

Next day was the Sabbath. The morning was hideous with the yells of the fighting savages. They tore about on the Common in front of the Church, leading gentlemen having tried in vain to quiet them, and their wild voices without jarred upon the Morning Service. About two o'clock, I tried to get into conversation with them. I appealed to them whether they were not all tired and hungry? They replied that they had had no food all that day; they had fought since the morning! I said, "I love you, black fellows. I go Missionary black fellows far away. I love you, want you rest, get food. Come all of you, rest, sit round me, and we will talk, till the *Jins* (=women) get ready tea. They boil water, and I take tea with you, and then you will be strong!"

By broken English and by many symbols, I won their ear. They produced tea and *damper, i. e.* a rather forbidding-looking bread, without yeast, baked on the coals. Their wives hasted to boil water. I kept incessantly talking, to interest them, and told them how Jesus, God's dear Son, came and died to make them happy, and how He grieved to see them beating and fighting and killing each other.

When the tea was ready we squatted on the green grass, their tins were filled, the *damper* was broken into lumps, and I asked the blessing of God on the meal. To me it was unpleasant eating! Many of them looked strong and healthy; but not a few were weak and dying creatures. The strong, devouring all they could get, urged me to be done, and let them finish their fighting, eager for the fray. But having gained their confidence, I prayed with them, and thereafter said, "Now, before I leave, I will ask of you to do one thing for my sake, which you can all easily do." With one voice they replied, "Yes, we all do whatever you say."

I got their leaders to promise to me one by one. I then said, "Now you have got your tea; and I ask every man and boy among you to lie down in the bush and take a sleep, and your wives will sit by and watch over your safety!"

In glum silence, their war weapons still grasped in their hands, they stood looking intently at me, doubting whether I could be in earnest. I urged then, "You all promised to do what I asked. If you break your promise, these white men will laugh at me, and say that black fellows only lie and deceive. Let them see that you can be trusted. I wait here till I see you all asleep."

One said that his head was cut, and he must have revenge before he could lie down. Others filed past showing their wounds, and declaring that it was too bad to request them to go to sleep. I praised them as far as I could, but urged them for once to be men and to keep their word. Finally, they all agreed to lie down, I waiting till the last man had disappeared; and being doubly exhausted with the debauch and the fighting, they were soon all fast asleep. I prayed that the blessed Sleep might lull their savage passions.

Before daylight next morning, the Minister and I were hastening to the scene to prevent further fighting; but as the sun was rising we saw the last tribe of the distant Natives disappearing over the brow of a hill. A small party belonging to the district alone remained. They shouted to us, "Black fellows all gone! No more fight. You too much like black fellow!"

For three days afterwards I had still to linger there; and if their dogs ran or barked at me, the women chased them with sticks and stones, and protected me. One little touch of kindness and sympathy had unlocked their darkened hearts.

Who wonders that the *dark* races melt away before the *whites?* The pioneers of Civilization *will* carry with them this demon of strong drink, the fruitful parent of every other vice. The black people drink, and become unmanageable; and through the white man's own poison-gift, an excuse is found for sweeping the poor creatures off the face of the earth. Marsden's writings show how our Australian blacks are destroyed. But I have myself been on the track of such butcheries again and again. A Victorian lady told me the following incident. She heard a child's pitiful cry in the bush. On tracing it, she found a little girl weeping over her younger brother.

She said, "The white men poisoned our father and mother. They threaten to shoot me, so that I dare not go near them, I am here, weeping over my brother till we die!"

The compassionate lady promised to be a mother to the little sufferers, and to protect them. They instantly clung to her, and have proved themselves to be loving and dutiful ever since.

CHAPTER L.
NORA.

WHILE I was pondering over Kingsley's words,—about the blacks of Australia being "poor brutes in human shape," and too low to take in the Gospel,—the story of Nora, an Aboriginal Christian woman, whom I myself actually visited and corresponded with, was brought under my notice, as if to shatter to pieces everything that the famous preacher had proclaimed. A dear friend told me how he had seen Nora encamped with the blacks near Hexham in Victoria. Her husband had lost, through drink, their once comfortable home at a Station where he was employed. The change back to life in camp had broken her health, and she lay sick on the ground within a miserable hut. The visitors found her reading a Bible, and explaining to a number of her own poor people the wonders of redeeming love. My friend, Roderick Urquhart, Esq., overcome by the sight, said, "Nora, I am grieved to see you here, and deprived of every comfort in your sickness."

She answered, not without tears, "The change has indeed made me unwell; but I am beginning to think that this too is far the best; it has at last brought my poor husband to his senses, and I will grudge nothing if God thereby brings him to the Saviour's feet!"

She further explained that she had found wonderful joy in telling her own people about the true God and His Son Jesus, and was quite assured that the Lord in His own way would send her relief. The visitors who accompanied Mr. Urquhart showed themselves to be greatly affected by the true and pure Christian spirit of this poor Aboriginal, and on parting she said, "Do not think that I like this miserable hut, or the food, or the company: but I am and have been happy in trying to do good amongst my people."

For my part, let that dear Christlike soul look out on me from her Aboriginal hut, and I will trample under foot all teachings or theorizings that dare to say that she or her kind are but poor brutes, as mere blasphemies against Human Nature! "I thank thee, O Father, Lord of Heaven and Earth, that Thou hast hid these things from the wise and prudent, and hast revealed them unto babes."

It is easy to understand how even experienced travelers may be deluded to believe that the Aborigines have no idols and no religion. One must have lived amongst them or their kindred ere he can authoritatively decide these questions. Before I left Melbourne, for instance, I had met Nathaniel

Pepper, a converted Aboriginal from Wimmera. I asked him if his people had any "Doctors," *i. e.* Sacred Men or priests. He said they had. I inquired if they had any objects of Worship, or any belief in God? He said, "No! None whatever."

But on taking from my pocket some four small stone idols, his expression showed at once that he recognized them as objects of Worship. He had seen the Sacred Men use them; but he refused to answer any more questions. I resolved now, if possible, to secure some of their idols, and set this whole problem once for all at rest.

At Newstead, on another occasion, I persuaded a whole camp of the Aborigines to come to my meeting. After the address, they waited to examine the idols and stone gods which I had shown. Some of the young men admitted that their "doctors" had things like these, which they and the old people prayed to; but they added jauntily, "We young fellows don't worship; we know too much for that!" No "doctors" were, however, in that camp; so I could not meet with them; but I already felt that the testimony of nearly all white people that the "blacks" had "no idols and no worship" was quickly crumbling away.

On returning to Horsham, from a visit to a great camp of the blacks at Wonwondah, and having purchased, in the presence of witnesses, specimens of their idols from the Doctor or Sacred Man of these tribes, I informed my dear friends, Rev. P. Simpson and his excellent lady, of my exploits and possessions. He replied, "There is a black 'doctor' gone round our house just now to see one of his people who is washing here to-day. Let us go and test them, whether they know these objects."

Carrying them in his hand, we went to them. The woman instantly on perceiving them dropped what she was washing, and turned away in instinctive terror. Mr. Simpson asked, "Have you ever before seen stones like these?"

The wily "doctor" replied, "Plenty on the plains, where I kick them out of my way."

Taking others out of my pocket, I said, "These make people sick and well, don't they?"

His rage overcame his duplicity, and he exclaimed, "What black fellow give you these? If I know him I do for him!"

The woman, looking the picture of terror, and pointing to one of the objects, cried, "That fellow no good! he kill men. No good, no good! Me too much afraid."

Then, looking at me, she said, pointing with her finger, "That fellow savvy (knows) too much! No white man see them. He no good."

There was more in this scene and in all its surroundings, than in many arguments; and Mr. Simpson thoroughly believed that these were objects of idolatrous worship.

And now let me relate the story of my visit to Nora, the converted Aboriginal referred to above. Accompanied by Robert Hood, Esq., J. P., Victoria, I found my way to the encampment near Hexham. She did not know of our coming, nor see us till we stood at the door of her hut. She was clean and tidily dressed, as were also her dear little children, and appeared glad to see us. She had just been reading the *Presbyterian Messenger*, and the Bible was lying at her elbow. I said, "Do you read the *Messenger*?"

She replied, "Yes; I like to know what is going on in the Church."

We found her to be a sensible and humble Christian woman, conversing intelligently about religion and serving God devotedly. Next Sabbath she brought her husband, her children, and six blacks to church, all decently dressed, and they all listened most attentively.

At our first meeting I said, "Nora, they tell me you are a Christian. I want to ask you a few questions about the blacks; and I hope that as a Christian you will speak the truth." Rather hurt at my language, she raised her right hand, and replied, "I am a Christian. I fear and serve the true God. I always speak the truth."

Taking from my pocket the stone idols from the Islands, I inquired if her people had or worshipped things like these. She replied, "The 'doctors' have them."

"Have you a 'doctor' in your camp?" I asked. She said, "Yes, my uncle is the Sacred Man; but he is now far away from this."

"Has he the idols with him now?" I inquired. She answered, "No; they are left in my care."

I then said, "Could you let us see them?"

She consulted certain representatives of the tribe who were at hand. They rose, and removed to a distance. They had consented. Mr. Hood assured me that no fault would be found with her, as she was the real, or at least virtual head of the tribe. Out of a larger bag she then drew two smaller bags, and opened them. They were filled with the very objects which I had brought from the Islands. I asked her to consult the men of her tribe whether they would agree to sell four or five of them to me, that I might by them convince the white people that they had gods of their own, and are, therefore, above the brutes of the field; the money to be given to their Sacred Man on his return. This, also, after a time was agreed to. I selected three of the objects, and paid the stipulated price. And I have the recorded testimony of "Robert Hood, J. P., Hexham, Victoria, 28th February, 1863," certifying on his honor all that I am here affirming.

Mr. Hood asked Nora how he had never heard of or seen these things before, living so long amongst them, and blacks constantly coming and going about his house. She replied, "Long ago white men laughed at black fellows praying to their idols. Black fellows said, white men never see them again! Suppose this white man not know all about them, he would not now see them. No white men live now have seen what you have seen."

Thus it has been demonstrated on the spot, and in presence of the most reliable witnesses, that the Aborigines, before they saw the white invaders, were not "brutes" incapable of knowing God, but human beings, yearning after a God of some kind. Nor do I believe that any tribe of men will ever be found, who, when their language and customs are rightly interpreted, will not display their consciousness of the need of a God, and that Divine capacity of holding fellowship with the Unseen Powers, of which the brutes are without one faintest trace.

Poor, dear, Christian-hearted Nora! The Christ-spirit shines forth unmistakably through thee,—praying for and seeking to save husband and children, enduring trials and miseries by the aid of communion with thy Lord, weeping over the degradation of thy people, and seeking to lift them up by telling them of the true God and of His love to Mankind through Jesus Christ.

CHAPTER LI.
BACK TO SCOTLAND.

EACH of my Australian Committees strongly urged my return to Scotland, chiefly to secure, if possible, more Missionaries for the New Hebrides. Dr. Inglis, just arrived from Britain, where he had the Aneityumese New Testament carried through the press, also zealously enforced this appeal.

Constrained by what appeared to me the Voice of God, I sailed for London in the *Kosciusko*, an Aberdeen clipper, on the 17th May, 1863. Captain Stuart made the voyage most enjoyable to all. The Rev. Mr. Stafford, friend of the good Bishop Selwyn and tutor to his son, conducted along with myself, alternately, an Anglican and a Presbyterian Service. We passed through a memorable thunder-burst in rounding the Cape. Our good ship was perilously struck by lightning. The men on deck were thrown violently down. The copper in the bulwarks was twisted and melted—a specimen of which the Captain gave me and I still retain. When the ball of fire struck the ship, those of us sitting on chairs, screwed to the floor around the cabin table, felt as if she were plunging to the bottom. When she sprang aloft again, a military man and a medical officer were thrown heavily into the back passage between the cabins, the screws that held their seats having snapped asunder. I, in grasping the table, got my leg severely bruised, being jammed betwixt the seat and the table, and had to be carried to my berth. All the men were attended to, and quickly recovered consciousness; and immediately the good Captain, an elder of the Church, came to me, and said, "Lead us in prayer, and let us thank the Lord for this most merciful deliverance; the ship is not on fire, and no one is seriously injured!"

Poor fellow! whether hastened on by this event I know not, but he struggled for three weeks thereafter in a fever, and it took our united care and love to pull him through. The Lord, however, restored him; and we cast anchor safely in the East India Docks, at London, on 26th August, 1863, having been three months and ten days at sea from port to port.

It was 5.30 P. M. when we cast anchor, and the gates closed at 6 o'clock. My little box was ready on deck. The Custom House officers kindly passed me, and I was immediately on my way to Euston Square. Never before had I been within the Great City, and doubtless I could have enjoyed its palaces and memorials. But the King's business entrusted to me, "required haste," and I felt constrained to press forward, looking neither to the right hand nor to the left.

At nine o'clock that evening, I left for Scotland by train. Next morning, about the same hour, I reported myself at the manse of the Rev. John Kay, Castle Douglas, the Convener of the Foreign Mission Committee of the Reformed Presbyterian Church, to which I then belonged. We arranged for a meeting of said Committee, at earliest practicable date, that my scheme and plans might at once be laid before them.By the next train I was on my way to Dumfries, and thence by conveyance to my dear old home at Torthorwald. There I had a Heavenly Welcome from my saintly parents, yet not unmixed with many fast-falling tears. Five brief years only had elapsed, since I went forth from their Sanctuary, with my young bride; and now, alas! alas! that grave on Tanna held mother and son locked in each other's embrace till the Resurrection Day.Not less glowing, but more terribly agonizing, was my reception, a few days thereafter, at Coldstream, when I first gazed on the bereaved father and mother of my beloved; who, though godly people, were conscious of a heart-break under that stroke, from which through their remaining years they never fully rallied. They murmured not against the Lord; but all the same, heart and flesh began to faint and fail, even as our Divine Exemplar Himself fainted under the Cross, which yet He so uncomplainingly bore.The Foreign Mission Committee of the Reformed Presbyterian Church met in Edinburgh, and welcomed me kindly, nay, warmly. A full report of all my doings for the past, and of all my plans and hopes, was laid before them. They at once agreed to my visiting and addressing every Congregation and Sabbath School in the Church. They opened to me their Divinity Hall, that I might appeal to the Students. My Address there was published and largely circulated, under the motto—"Come over and help us." It was used of God to deepen vastly the interest in our Mission.The Committee generously and enthusiastically did everything in their power to help me. By their influence, the Church in 1864 conferred on me the undesired and undeserved honor, the highest which they could confer—the honor of being the Moderator of their Supreme Court. No one can understand how much I shrank from all this; but, in hope of the Lord's using it and me to promote His work amongst the Heathen, I accepted the Chair, though, I fear, only to occupy it most unworthily, for Tanna gave me little training for work like that!

I have ever regarded it as a privilege and honor that I was born and trained within the old covenanting Reformed Presbyterian Church of Scotland. As a separate Communion, that Church was small amongst the thousands of Israel; but the principles of Civil and Religious Liberty for which her founders suffered and died are, at this moment, the heart and soul of all that is best and divinest in the Constitution of our British Empire. I am more proud that the blood of Martyrs is in my veins, and their truths in my heart, than other men can be of noble pedigree or royal names.

CHAPTER LII.
TOUR THROUGH THE OLD COUNTRY.

My tour through Scotland brought me into contact with every Minister, Congregation, and Sabbath School in the Church of my fathers. They were never at any time a rich people, but they were always liberal. At this time they contributed beyond all previous experience, both in money and in boxes of useful articles for the Islanders.

Unfortunately, my visit to the far North, to our Congregations at Wick and Stromness, had been arranged for the month of January; and thereby a sore trial befell me in my pilgrimages. The roads were covered with snow and ice. I reached Aberdeen and Wick by steamer from Edinburgh, and had to find my way thence to Thurso. The inside seats on the mail coach being all occupied, I had to take my place outside. The cold was intense, and one of my feet got bitten by the frost. The storm detained me nearly a week at Thurso, but feeling did not return to the foot.

We started, in a lull, by steamer for Stromness; but the storm burst again, all were ordered below, and hatches and doors made fast. The passengers were mostly very rough, the place was foul with whisky and tobacco. I appealed to the Captain to let me crouch somewhere on deck and hold on as best I could. He shouted, "I dare not! You'll be washed overboard."

On seeing my appealing look, he relented, directed his men to fasten a tarpaulin over me, and lash it and me to the mast, and there I lay till we reached Stromness. The sea broke heavily and dangerously over the vessel. But the Captain, finding shelter for several hours under the lee of a headland, saved both the ship and the passengers. When at last we landed, my foot was so benumbed and painful that I could move a step only with greatest agony. Two meetings, however, were in some kind of way conducted; but the projected visit to Dingwall and other places had to be renounced, the snow lying too deep for any conveyance to carry me, and my foot crying aloud for treatment and skill.

On returning Southwards I was confined for about two months, and placed under the best medical advice. All feeling seemed gradually to have departed from my foot; and amputation was seriously proposed both in Edinburgh and in Glasgow. Having somehow managed to reach Liverpool, my dear friend, the Rev. Dr. Graham, took me there to a Doctor who had wrought many wonderful recoveries by galvanism. Time after time he applied the battery, but I felt nothing. He declared that the power used would "have killed six ordinary men," and that he had never seen any part of the human body so dead to feeling on a live and healthy person. Finally, he covered it all over with a dark plaster, and told me to return in three days. But next day, the throbbing feeling of insufferable coldness in the foot compelled me to return at once. After my persistent appeals, he removed the plaster; and, to his great astonishment, the whole of the frosted part adhered to it! Again, dressing the remaining parts, he covered it with plaster as before, and assured me that with care and rest it would now completely recover. By the blessing of the Lord it did, though it was a bitter trial to me amidst all these growing plans to be thus crippled by the way; and to this day I am sometimes warned in over-walking that the part is capable of many a painful twinge. And humbly I feel myself crooning over the graphic words of the Greatest Missionary, "I bear about in my body the marks of the Lord Jesus."

On that tour, the Sabbath Schools joyfully adopted my scheme, and became "Shareholders" in the Mission Ship. It was thereafter ably developed by an elder of the Church. A *Dayspring* collecting box found its way into almost every family; and the returns from Scotland have yielded ever since about £250 per annum, as their proportion for the expenses of the Children's Mission Ship to the New Hebrides. The Church in Nova Scotia heartily accepted the same idea, and their Sabbath School children have regularly contributed their £250 per annum too. The Colonial children have contributed the rest, throughout all these years, with unfailing interest. And whensoever the true and full history of the South Sea Islands Mission is written for the edification of the Universal Church, let it not be forgotten that the children of Australasia, and Nova Scotia, and Scotland, did by their united pennies keep the *Dayspring* floating in the New Hebrides; that the Missionaries and their families were thereby supplied with the necessaries of life, and that the Islanders were thus taught to clothe themselves and to sit at the feet of Jesus. This was the Children's Holy League, erewhile referred to; and one knows that on such a Union the Divine Master smiles well pleased.

The Lord also crowned this tour with another precious fruit of blessing, though not all by any means due to my influence. Four new Missionaries volunteered from Scotland, and three from Nova Scotia. By their aid we not only re-claimed for Jesus the posts that had been abandoned, but we took possession of other Islands in His most blessed Name. But I did not wait and take them out with me. They had matters to look into and to learn about, that would be infinitely helpful to them in the Mission field. Especially, and far above everything else in addition to their regular Clerical course, some Medical instruction was an absolute prerequisite. Every Missionary was urged to obtain all insight that was practicable at the Medical Mission Dispensary, and otherwise, especially on lines known to be most requisite for these Islands. For this, and similar objects, all that I raised over and above what was required for the *Dayspring* was entrusted to the Foreign Mission Committee, that the new Missionaries might be fully equipped, and their outfit and traveling expenses be provided for without burdening the Church at home. Her responsibilities were already large enough for her resources. But she could give men, God's own greatest gift, and His people elsewhere gave the money,—the Colonies and the Home Country thus binding themselves to each other in this Holy Mission of the Cross.

CHAPTER LIII.
MARRIAGE AND FAREWELL.

BUT I did not return alone. The dear Lord had brought to me one prepared, all unknown to either of us, by special culture, by godly training, by many gifts and accomplishments, and even by family associations, to share my lot on the New Hebrides. Her brother had been an honored Missionary in the Foreign field, and had fallen asleep while the dew of youth was yet upon him; her sister was the wife of a devoted Minister of our Church in Adelaide, both she and her husband being zealous promoters of our work; and her father had left behind him a fragrant memory through his many Christian works at Edinburgh, Kenneth, and Alloa, besides being not unknown to fame as the author of those still popular books, *Whitecross's Anecdotes*, illustrative of the Shorter Catechism and of the Holy Scriptures. Ere I left Scotland in 1864, I was married to Margaret Whitecross, and God spares us to each other still (1892); and the family which He has been pleased in His love to grant unto us we have dedicated to His service, with the prayer and hope that He may use every one of them in spreading the Gospel throughout the Heathen World.

Our marriage was celebrated at her sister's house in Edinburgh; and I may be pardoned for recalling a little event which characterized the occasion. My youngest brother, then tutor to a gentleman studying at the University, stepped forth at the close of the ceremony and recited an Epithalamium composed for the day. For many a month and year the refrain, a play upon the Bride's name, kept singing itself through my memory:—

"Long may the *Whitecross* banner wave,
By the battle blasts unriven;
Long may our Brother and Sister brave
Rejoice in the light of Heaven."

He describes the Bride as hearing a "Voice from the far Pacific Seas"; and turning to us both, he sang of an Angel "beckoning us to the Tanna-land," to gather a harvest of souls:—

"The warfare is brief, the crown is bright,
The pledge is the souls of men;
Go, may the Lord defend the Right,
And restore you safe again!"

But the verse which my dear wife thought most beautiful for a bridal day, and which her memory cherishes still, was this:—

"May the ruddy Joys, and the Graces fair,
Wait fondly around you now;
Sweet angel Hopes and young Loves repair
To your home and bless your vow!"

My last scene in Scotland was kneeling at the family altar in the old Sanctuary Cottage at Torthorwald, while my venerable father, with his high-priestly locks of snow-white hair streaming over his shoulders, commenced us once again to "the care and keeping of the Lord God of the families of Israel." It was the last time that ever on this Earth those accents of intercession, loaded with a pathos of deathless love, would fall upon my ears. I knew to a certainty that when we rose from our knees and said farewell, our eyes would never meet again till they were flooded with the lights of the Resurrection Day. But he and my darling mother gave us away once again with a free heart, not unpierced with the sword of human anguish, to the service of our common Lord and to the Salvation of the Heathen. And we went forth, praying that a double portion of their spirit, along with their precious blessing, might rest upon us in all the way that we had to go.

Our beloved mother, always more self-restrained, and less demonstrative in the presence of others, held back her heart till we were fairly gone from the door; and then, as my dear brother afterward informed me, she fell back into his arms with a great cry, as if all the heart-strings had broken, and lay for long in a deathlike swoon. Oh, all ye that read this page, think most tenderly of the cries of Nature, even where Grace and Faith are in perfect triumph. Read, through scenes like these, a fuller meaning into the words addressed to that blessed Mother, whose Son was given for us all, "Yea, a sword shall pierce through thine own soul also."

CHAPTER LIV.
FIRST PEEP AT THE "DAYSPRING."

WE embarked at Liverpool for Australia in *The Crest o' the Wave*, Captain Ellis; and, after what was then considered a fast passage of ninety-five days, we landed at Sydney on 17th January, 1865. Within an hour we had to grapple with a new and amazing perplexity. The Captain of our *Dayspring* came to inform me that his ship had arrived three days ago and now lay in the stream,—that she had been to the Islands, and had settled the Gordons, M'Cullaghs, and Morrisons on their several stations,—that she had left Halifax in Nova Scotia fourteen months ago, and that now, on arriving at Sydney, he could not get one penny of money, and that the crew were clamoring for their pay, etc. etc. He continued, "Where shall I get money for current expenses? No one will lend unless we mortgage the *Dayspring*. I fear there is nothing before us but to sell her!" I gave him £50 of my own to meet clamant demands, and besought him to secure me a day or two of delay that something might be done.

Having landed, and been heartily welcomed by dear Dr. and Mrs. Moon and other friends, I went with a kind of trembling joy to have my first look at the *Dayspring*, like a sailor getting a first peep at the child born to him whilst far away on the sea. Some of the irritated ship's company stopped us by the way, and threatened prosecution and all sorts of annoyance. I could only urge again for a few days' patience. I found her to be a beautiful two-masted Brigantine, with a deck-house (added when she first arrived at Melbourne), and every way suitable for our necessities,—a thing of beauty, a white-winged Angel set a-floating by the pennies of the children to bear the Gospel to these sin-darkened but sun-lit Southern Isles. To me she became a sort of living thing, the impersonation of a living and throbbing love in the heart of thousands of "shareholders"; and I said, with a deep, indestructible faith,—"The Lord has provided—the Lord will provide."

Since she sailed, £1400 had been expended; for present liabilities at least £700 more were instantly required: and, at any rate, as large a sum to pay her way and meet expenses of next trip to the Islands. Having laid our perplexing circumstances before our dear Lord Jesus, having "spread out" all the details in His sympathetic presence, pleading that the Ship itself and the new Missionaries were all His own, not mine, I told Him that this money was needed to do His own blessed work.

On Friday morning, I consulted friends of the Mission, but no help was visible. I tried to borrow, but found that the lender demanded 20 per cent for interest, besides the title-deeds of the ship for security. I applied for a loan from the agent of the London Missionary Society (then agent for us too) on the credit of the Reformed Presbyterian Church's Foreign Committee, but he could not give it without a written order from Scotland. There were some who seemed rather to enjoy our perplexity!

Driven thus to the wall, I advertised for a meeting of Ministers and other friends, next morning at eleven o'clock, to receive my report and to consult *re* the *Dayspring*. I related my journeyings since leaving them and the results, and then asked for advice about the ship.

"Sell her," said some, "and have done with it."—"What," said others, "have the Sabbath Schools given you the *Dayspring* and can you not support her yourselves?"

I pointed out to them that the salary of each Missionary was then only £120 per annum, that they gave their lives for the Heathen, and that surely the Colonial Christians would undertake the up-keep of the ship, which was necessary to the very existence of the Mission. I appealed to them that, as my own Church in Scotland had now one Missionary abroad for every six Ministers at home, and the small Presbyterian Church of Nova Scotia had actually three Missionaries now on our Islands, it would be a blessed privilege for the Australian Churches and Sabbath Schools to keep the *Dayspring* afloat, without whose services the Missionaries could not live nor the Islanders be evangelized.

Being Saturday, the morning Services for Sabbath were all arranged for, or advertised; but Dr. M'Gibbon offered me a meeting for the evening, and Dr. Steel an afternoon Service at three o'clock, combined with his Sabbath School. Rev. Mr. Patterson of Piermont, offered me a Morning Service; but, as his was only a Mission Church, he could not give me a collection. These openings I accepted, as from the Lord, however much they fell short of what I desired.

At the Morning Service I informed the congregation how we were situated, and expressed the hope that under God and their devoted pastor they would greatly prosper, and would yet be able to help in supporting our Mission to their South Sea neighbors. Returning to the vestry, a lady and gentleman waited to be introduced to me. They were from Launceston, Tasmania.

"I am," said he, "Captain and owner of that vessel lying at anchor opposite the *Dayspring*. My wife and I, being too late to get on shore to attend any Church in the city, heard this little Chapel bell ringing, and followed, when we saw you going up the hill. We have so enjoyed the Service. We do heartily sympathize with you. This check for £50 will be a beginning to help you out of your difficulties."

The reader knows how warmly I would thank them; and how in my own heart I knew *Who* it was that made them arrive too late for *their* plans, but not for *His*, and led them up that hill, and opened their hearts. Jehovah-Jireh?

At three o'clock, Dr. Steel's Church was filled with children and others. I told them in my appeal what had happened in the Mission Chapel, and how God had led Captain Frith and his wife, entire strangers, to sound the first note of our deliverance. One man stood up and said, "I will give £10." Another, "I will give £5." A third, "I shall send you £20 to-morrow morning." Several others followed their example, and the general collection was greatly encouraging.

In the evening I had a very large as well as sympathetic congregation. I fully explained the difficulty about the *Dayspring*, and told them what God had already done for us, announcing an address to which contributions might be sent. Almost every mail brought me the free-will offerings of God's people; and on Wednesday, when the adjourned meeting was held, the sum had reached in all £456. Believing that the Lord thus intervened at a vital crisis in our Mission, I dwell on it to the praise of His blessed Name. Trust in Him, obey Him, and He will not suffer you to be put to shame.

Clearing out from her sister ships, then in harbor, the *John Williams* and the *John Wesley*, our little *Dayspring* sailed for Tasmania. At Hobart we were visited by thousands of children and parents, and afterwards at Launceston, who were proud to see their own Ship, in which they were "shareholders" for Jesus. Daily, all over the Colony, I preached in churches, and addressed public meetings, and got collections, and gave out Collection Cards to be returned within two weeks.

We received many tokens of interest and sympathy. The steam tug was granted to us free, and the harbor dues were remitted. Many presents were also sent on board the *Dayspring*. Still, after meeting all necessary outlays, the trip to Tasmania gave us only £227: 8: 11 clear for the Mission fund.

Sailing now for South Australia, we arrived at Adelaide. Many friends there showed the deepest interest in our plans. Thousands of children and parents came to visit their own Mission Ship by several special trips. Daily and nightly I addressed meetings, and God's people were moved greatly in the cause. After meeting all expenses while in port, there remained a sum of £634: 9: 2 for the up-keep of the vessel. The Honorable George Fife Angus gave me £241—a dear friend belonging to the Baptist Church. But there was still a deficit of £400 before the *Dayspring* could sail free of debt, and my heart was sore as I cried for it to the Lord.

Leaving the ship to sail direct for Sydney, I took steamer to Melbourne; but, on arriving there, sickness and anxiety laid me aside for three days. Under great weakness, I crept along to my dear friends at the Scotch College, Dr. and Mrs. Morrison, and Miss Fraser, and threw myself on their advice.

"Come along," said the Doctor cheerily, "and I'll introduce you to Mr. Butchart and one or two friends in East Melbourne, and we'll see what what can be done!"

I gave all information, being led on in conversation by the Doctor, and tried to interest them in our work, but no subscriptions were asked or received. Ere I sailed for Sydney however, the whole deficiency was sent to me. I received in all, on this tour, the sum of £1726: 9: 10. Our *Dayspring* once more sailed free, and our hearts overflowed with gratitude to the Lord and to His stewards!

CHAPTER LV.
THE FRENCH IN THE PACIFIC.

We went down to the Islands with the *Dayspring* in 1865. The full story of the years that had passed was laid before my Missionary brethren at their Annual Synod. They resolved that permanent arrangements must now be made for the vessel's support, and that I must return to the Colonies and see these matured, to prevent any such crisis as that through which we had recently passed. This, meantime, appeared to all of them, the most clamant of all Missionary duties,—their very lives, and the existence of the Mission itself, depending thereon. The Lord seemed to leave me no alternative: and, with great reluctance, my back was again turned away from the Islands.

The *Dayspring*, doing duty among the Loyalty Islands, left me, along with my dear wife, on Mare, there to await an opportunity of getting to New Caledonia, and thence to Sydney. Detained there for some time, we saw the noble work done by Messrs. Jones and Creagh, of the London Missionary Society, all being cruelly undone by the tyranny and Popery of the French. One day, in an inland walk, Mrs. Paton and I came on a large Conventicle in the bush. They were teaching each other, and reading the Scriptures which the Missionaries had translated into their own language, and which the French had forbidden them to use. They cried to God for deliverance from their oppressors! Missionaries were prohibited from teaching the Gospel to the Natives without the permission of France; their books were suppressed, and they themselves placed under military guard on the Island of Lifu. Even when, by Britain's protest, the Missionaries were allowed to resume their work, the French language was alone to be used by them; and some, like Rev. J. Jones (as far down as 1888), were marched on board a Man-of-war, at half an hour's notice, and, without crime laid to their charge, forbidden ever to return to the Islands. While, on the other hand, the French Popish Missionaries were everywhere fostered and protected, presenting to the Natives as many objects of idolatry as their own, and following, as is the custom of the Romish Church in those Seas, in the wake of every Protestant Mission, to pollute and to destroy.

Being delayed also for two weeks on Noumea, we saw the state of affairs under military rule. English Protestant residents, few in number, appealed to me to conduct worship, but liberty could not be obtained from the authorities, who hated everything English. Again a number of Protestant parents, some French, others English and German, applied to me to baptize their children at their own houses. To have asked permission would have been to court refusal, and to falsify my position. I laid the matter before the Lord, and baptized them all. Within two days the Private Secretary of the Governor arrived with an interpreter, and began to inquire of me, "Is it true that you have been baptizing here?"

I replied quite frankly, "It is."

"We are sent to demand on whose authority?"

"On the authority of my Great Master."

"When did you get that authority?"

"When I was licensed and ordained to preach the Gospel, I got that authority from my Great Master."

Here a spirited conversation followed betwixt the two in French, and they politely bowed, and left me.

Very shortly they returned, saying, "The Governor sends his compliments, and he wishes the honor of a visit from you at Government House at three o'clock, if convenient for you."

I returned my greeting, and said that I would have pleasure in waiting upon his Excellency at the appointed hour. I thought to myself that I was in for it now, and I earnestly cried for Divine guidance.

He saluted me graciously as "de great Missionary of de New Hebrides." He conversed in a very friendly manner about the work there, and seemed anxious to find any indication as to the English designs. I had to deal very cautiously. He spoke chiefly through the interpreter; but, sometimes dismissing him, he talked to me as good, if not better English himself. He was eager to get my opinions as to how Britain got and retained her power over the Natives. After a very prolonged interview, we parted without a single reference to the baptisms or to religious services!

That evening the Secretary and interpreter waited upon us at our Inn, saying, "The Governor will have pleasure in placing his yacht and crew at your disposal to-morrow. Mrs. Paton and you can sail all around, and visit the Convict Island, and the Government Gardens, where lunch will be prepared for you."

It was a great treat to us indeed. The crew were in prison garments, but all so kind to us. By Convict labor all the public works seemed to be carried on, and the Gardens were most beautiful. The carved work in bone, ivory, cocoanuts, shells, etc., was indeed very wonderful. We bought a few specimens, but the prices were beyond our purse. It was a strange spectacle—these things of beauty and joy, and beside them the chained gangs of fierce and savage Convicts, kept down only by bullet and sword!

Thanking the Governor for his exceeding kindness, I referred to their Man-of-war about to go to Sydney, and offered to pay full passage money if they would take me, instead of leaving me to wait for a "trader." He at once granted my request, and arranged that we should be charged only at the daily cost for the sailors. At his suggestion, however, I took a number of things on board with me, and presented them to be used at the cabin table. We were most generously treated—the Captain giving up his own room to my wife and myself, as they had no special accommodation for passengers.

Noumea appeared to me at that time to be wholly given over to drunkenness and vice, supported as a great Convict Settlement by the Government of France, and showing every extreme of reckless, worldly pleasure, and of cruel, slavish toil. When I saw it again, three-and-twenty years thereafter, it showed no signs of progress for the better. It there be a God of justice and of love, His blight cannot but rest on a nation whose pathway is stained with corruption and steeped in blood, as is undeniably the case with France in the Pacific Isles.

CHAPTER LVI.
THE GOSPEL AND GUNPOWDER.

Arriving at Sydney, I was at once plunged into a whirlpool of horrors. H. M. S. *Curaçoa* had just returned from her official trip to the Islands, in which the Commodore, Sir William Wisenian, had thought it his duty to inflict punishment on the Natives for murder and robbery of Traders and others. On these Islands, as in all similar cases, the Missionaries had acted as interpreters, and of course always used their influence on the side of mercy, and in the interests of peace. But Sydney, and indeed Australia and the Christian World, were thrown into a ferment just a few days before our arrival, by certain articles in a leading publication there, and by the pictorial illustrations of the same. They were professedly from an officer on board Her Majesty's ship, and the sensation was increased by their apparent truthfulness and reality. Tanna was the scene of the first event, and a series was to follow in succeeding numbers. The *Curaçoa* was pictured lying at anchor off the shore having the *Dayspring* astern. The Tannese warriors were being blown to pieces by shot and shell, and lay in heaps on the bloody coast. And the Missionaries were represented as safe in the lee of the Man-of-war, directing the onslaught, and gloating over the carnage.

Without a question being asked or a doubt suggested, without a voice being raised in fierce denial that such men as these Missionaries were known to be could be guilty of such conduct,—men who had jeoparded their lives for years on end rather than hurt one hair on a Native's head,—a cry of execration, loud and deep, and even savage, arose from the Press, and was apparently joined in by the Church itself. The common witticism about the "Gospel and Gunpowder" headed hundreds of bitter and scoffing articles in the journals; and, as we afterwards learned, the shocking news had been telegraphed to Britain and America, losing nothing in force by the way, and, while filling friends of Missions with dismay, was dished up day after day with every imaginable enhancement of horror for the readers of the secular and infidel Press. As I stepped ashore at Sydney I found myself probably the best-abused man in all Australia, and the very name of the New Hebrides Mission stinking in the nostrils of the people.

The gage of battle had been thrown and fell at my feet. Without one moment's delay I lifted it in the name of my Lord and of my maligned brethren. That evening my reply was in the hands of the editor, denying that such battles ever took place, retailing the actual facts of which I had been myself an eyewitness, and intimating legal prosecution unless the most ample and unequivocal withdrawal and apology were at once published.

The Newspaper printed my rejoinder, and made satisfactory amends for having been imposed upon and deceived. I waited upon the Commodore and appealed for his help in redressing this terrible injury to our Mission. He informed me that he had already called his officers to account, but that all denied any connection with the articles or the picture. He had little doubt, all the same, that some one on board was the prompter, who gloried in the evil that was being done to the cause of Christ. He offered every possible assistance, by testimony or otherwise, to place all the facts before the Christian public and to vindicate our Missionaries.

The outstanding facts are best presented in the following extract from the official report of the Mission Synod:—

"When the New Hebrides Missionaries were assembled at their annual meeting on Aneityum, H. M. S. *Curaçoa*, Sir Wm. Wiseman, Bart., C. B., arrived in the harbor to investigate many grievances of white men and trading vessels among the Islands. A petition having been previously presented to the Governor in Sydney, as drawn out by the Revs. Messrs. Geddie and Copeland, after the murder of Mr. and Mrs. Gordon on Erromanga, requesting an investigation into the sad event, and the removal of a Sandal-wood Trader, a British subject, who had incited the Natives to it,—the Missionaries gave the Commodore a memorandum on the loss of life and property that had been sustained by the Mission on Tanna, Erromanga, and Efate. He requested the Missionaries to supply him with interpreters, and requested the *Dayspring* to accompany him with them. The request was at once acceded to. Mr. Paton was appointed to act as interpreter for Tanna, Mr. Gordon (brother of the martyr) for Erromanga, and Mr. Morrison for Efate.

"At each of these Islands, the Commodore summoned the principal Chiefs near the harbors to appear before him, and explained to them that his visit was to inquire into the complaints British subjects had made against them, and to see if they had any against British subjects; and when he had found out the truth he would punish those who had done the wrong and protect those who had suffered wrong. The Queen did not send him to compel them to become Christians, or to punish them for not becoming Christians. She left them to do as they liked in this matter; but she was very angry at them because they had encouraged her subjects to live amongst them, sold them land, and promised to protect them, and afterwards murdered some of them and attempted to murder others, and stolen and destroyed their property; that the inhabitants of these islands were talked of over the whole world for their treachery, cruelty, and murders; and that the Queen would no longer allow them to murder or injure her subjects, who were living peaceably among them either as Missionaries or Traders. She would send a Ship of War every year to inquire into their conduct, and if any white man injured any Native they were to tell the Captain of the Man-of-war, and the white man would be punished as fast as the black man."

After spending much time, and using peaceably every means in his power in trying to get the guilty parties on Tanna, and not succeeding, he shelled two villages,—having the day before informed the Natives that he would do so, and advising to have all women, children, and sick removed, which in fact they did. Indeed nearly the whole of the inhabitants, young and old, went to Nowar's land, where they were instructed they would be safe, while they witnessed what a Man-of-war could do in punishing murderers. But before the hour approached, a foolish host of Tannese warriors had assembled on the beach, painted and armed and determined to fight the Man-of-war! And the Chief of a village on the other side of the bay was at that moment assembled with his men on the high ground within our view, and dancing to a war song in defiance.

The Commodore caused a shell to strike the hill and explode with terrific fury just underneath the dancers. The earth and the bush were torn and thrown into the air above and around them; and next moment the whole host were seen disappearing over the brow of the hill. Two shots were sent over the heads of the warriors on the shore, with terrific noise and uproar: in an instant, every man was making haste for Nowar's land, the place of refuge. The Commodore then shelled the villages, and destroyed their property. Beyond what I have here recorded, absolutely nothing was done.

We returned then for a moment to Sydney. The public excitement made it impossible for me to open my lips in the promotion of our Mission. The Rev. Drs. Dunmore, Lang and Steel, along with Professor Smith of the University, waited on the Commodore, and got an independent version of the facts. They then called a meeting on the affair by public advertisement. Without being made acquainted with the results of their investigations, I was called upon to give my own account of the *Curaçoa's* visit and of the connection of the Missionaries therewith. They then submitted the Commodore's statement, given by him in writing. He exonerated the Missionaries from every shadow of blame and from all responsibility. In the interests of mercy as well as justice, and to save life, they had acted as his interpreters; and there all that they had to do with the *Curaçoa* began and ended. All this was published in the newspapers next day, along with the speeches of the three deputies. The excitement began to subside. But the poison had been lodged in many hearts, and the ejectment of it was a slow and difficult process.

Feeling absolutely conscious that I had only done my Christian duty, I left all results in the hands of my Lord Jesus, and pressed forward in His blessed work. But more than one dear personal friend had to be sacrificed over this painful affair. A presbyterian Minister, and a godly elder and his wife, all most excellent and well-beloved, at whose houses I had been received as a brother, intimated to me that owing to this case of the *Curaçoa* their friendship and mine must entirely cease in this world. And it did cease; but my esteem never changed. I had learned not to think unkindly of friends, even when they manifestly misunderstood my actions. Nor would these things merit being recorded here, were it not that they may be at once a beacon and a guide. God's people are still belied. And the mob is still as ready as ever to cry, "Crucify! Crucify!"

CHAPTER LVII.
A PLEA FOR TANNA.

EVERYTHING having been at length arranged for in the Colonies, in connection with the Mission and *Dayspring*, as far as could possibly be,—and I having been adopted by the Victorian Assembly of 1866, as the first Missionary from the Presbyterian Church of Australia to the New Hebrides,—we sailed for the Islands on the 8th August of that year. Besides my wife and child, the following accompanied us to the field: Revs. Copeland, Cosh, and M'Nair, along with their respective wives. On 20th August we reached Aneityum; and, having landed some of our friends, we sailed Northwards, as far as Efate, to let the new Missionaries see all the Islands open for occupation, and to bring all our Missionaries back to the annual meeting, where the permanent settlements would be finally agreed upon.

While staying at Aneityum, I learned with as deep emotion as man ever felt for man, that noble old Abraham, the sharer of my Tannese trials, had during the interval peacefully fallen asleep in Jesus. He left for me his silver watch—one which I had myself sent to the dear soul from Sydney, and which he greatly prized. In his dying hour he said, "Give it to Missi, my own Missi Paton; and tell him that I go to Jesus, where Time is dead."

I learned also, and truly human-hearted readers will need no apology for introducing this news in so grave a story—that my faithful dog *Clutha*, entrusted to the care of a kindly Native to be kept for my return, had, despite all coaxing, grown weary of heart amongst all these dark faces, and fallen asleep too, truly not unworthy of a grateful tear!

At our annual Synod, after much prayerful deliberation and the careful weighing of every vital circumstance, I was constrained by the united voice of my brethren not to return to Tanna, but to settle on the adjoining island of Aniwa (=A-neé-wa). It was even hoped that thereby Tanna might eventually be the more surely reached and evangelized.

By the new Missionaries all the other old Stations were reoccupied and some fresh Islands were entered upon in the name of Jesus. As we moved about with our *Dayspring*, and planted the Missionaries here and there, nothing could repress the wonder of Natives.

"How is this?" they cried. "We slew or drove them all away! We plundered their houses and robbed them. Had we been so treated, nothing would have made us return. But they come back with a beautiful new ship, and with more and more Missionaries. And is it to trade and to get money, like the other white men? No! no! But to tell us of their Jehovah God and of His Son Jesus. If their God makes them do all that, we may well worship Him too."

In this way, island after island was opened up to receive the Missionary, and their Chiefs bound themselves to protect and cherish him, before they knew anything whatever of the Gospel, beyond what they saw in the disposition and character of its Preachers or heard rumored regarding its fruits on other Islands. Imagine *Cannibals* found thus prepared to welcome the Missionary, and to make not only his property but his life comparatively safe. The Isles "wait" for Christ.

On our way to Aniwa, the *Dayspring* had to call at Tanna. By stress of weather we lay several days in Port Resolution. And there many memories were again revived—wounds that after five-and-twenty years, when I now write, still bleed afresh! Nowar, the old Chief, unstable but friendly, was determined to keep us there by force or by fraud. The Captain told him that the council of the Missionaries had forbidden him to land our boxes at Tanna.

"Don't land them," said the wily Chief, "just throw them over; my men and I will catch everything before it reaches the water, and carry them all safely ashore!"

The Captain said he durst not. "Then," persisted Nowar, "just point them out to us; you will have no further trouble; we will manage everything for Missi."

They were in distress when he refused; and poor old Nowar tried another tack. Suspecting that my clear wife was afraid of them, he got us on shore to see his extensive plantations. Turning eagerly to her, he said, leaving me to interpret, "Plenty of food! While I have a yam or a banana, you shall not want."

She answered, "I fear not any lack of food."

Pointing to his warriors, he cried, "We are many! We are strong! We can always protect you."

"I am not afraid," she calmly replied.

He then led us to that chestnut tree, in the branches of which I had sat during a lonely and memorable night, when all hope had perished of any earthly deliverance, and said to her with a manifest touch of genuine emotion, "The God who protected Missi there will always protect you."

She told him that she had no fear of that kind, but explained to him that we must for the present go to Aniwa, but would return to Tanna, if the Lord opened up our way. Nowar, Arkurat, and the rest, seemed to be genuinely grieved, and it touched my soul to the quick.

A beautiful incident was the outcome, as we learned only in long after years. There was at that time an Aniwan Chief on Tanna, visiting friends. He was one of their great Sacred Men. He and his people had been promised a passage home in the *Dayspring*, with their canoes in tow. When old Nowar saw that he could not keep us with himself, he went to this Aniwan Chief, and took the white shells, the insignia of Chieftainship, from his own arm, and bound them on the Sacred Man, saying, "By these you promise to protect my Missi and his wife and child on Aniwa. Let no evil befall them; or, by this pledge, I and my people will revenge it."

In a future crisis, this probably saved our lives, as shall be afterwards related. After all, a bit of the Christ-Spirit had found its way into that old cannibal's soul! And the same Christ-Spirit in me yearned more strongly still, and made it a positive pain to pass on to another Island, and leave him in that dim-groping twilight of the soul.

CHAPTER LVIII.
OUR NEW HOME ON ANIWA.

ANIWA became my Mission Home in November, 1866; and for the next fifteen years it was the heart and center of my personal labors in the Heathen World. Since 1881, alas! my too frequent deputation pilgrimages among Churches in Great Britain and in the Colonies have rendered my visits to Aniwa but few and far between. God never guided me back to Tanna; but others, my dear friends, have seen His Kingdom planted and beginning to grow amongst that slowly relenting race. Aniwa was to be the land wherein my past years of toil and patience and faith were to see their fruits ripening at length. I claimed Aniwa for Jesus, and by the grace of God Aniwa now worships at the Saviour's feet.

The Island of Aniwa is one of the smaller isles of the New Hebrides. It measures scarcely seven miles by two, and is everywhere girt round with a belt of coral reef. The sea breaks thereon heavily, with thundering roar, and the white surf rolls in furious and far. But there are days of calm, when all the sea is glass, and the spray on the reef is only a fringe of silver.

Aniwa, having no hills to attract and condense the clouds, suffers badly for lack of genial rains; and the heavy rains of hurricane and tempest seem to disappear as if by magic through the light soil and porous rock. The moist atmosphere and the heavy dews, however keep the Island covered with green, while large and fruitful trees draw wondrous nourishment from their rocky beds.

Aniwa has no harbor, or safe anchorage of any kind for ships; though, in certain winds, they have been seen at anchor on the outer edge of the reef, always a perilous haven! There is one rock in the coral belt, through which a boat can safely run to shore; but the little wharf, built there of the largest coral blocks that could be rolled together, has been once and again swept clean off by the hurricane, leaving "not a wrack behind."

When we landed, the Natives received us kindly. They and the Aneityumese Teachers led us to a temporary home, prepared for our abode. It was a large Native Hut. Walls and roof consisted of sugar-cane leaf and reeds, intertwisted on a strong wooden frame. It had neither doors nor windows, but open spaces instead of these. The earthen floor alone looked beautiful, covered thick with white coral broken small. It had only one apartment; and that, meantime, had to serve also for Church and School and Public Hall. We screened off a little portion, and behind that screen planted our bed, and stored our valuables. All the natives within reach assembled to watch us taking our food! A box at first served for a chair, the lid of another box was our table, our cooking was all done in the open air under a large tree, and we got along with amazing comfort. But the house was under the shelter of a coral rock, and we saw at a glance that at certain seasons it would prove a very hotbed of fever and ague. We were, however, only too thankful to enter it, till a better could be built, and on a breezier site.

The Aniwans were not so violently dishonorable as the Tannese. But they had the knack of asking in a rather menacing manner whatever they coveted; and the tomahawk was sometimes swung to enforce an appeal. We strove to get along quietly and kindly, in the hope that when we knew their language, and could teach them the principles of Jesus, they would be saved, and life and property would be secure. But the rumor of the *Curaçoa's* visit and her punishment of murder and robbery did more, by God's blessing, to protect us during those Heathen days than all other influences combined. The savage cannibal was heard to whisper to his bloodthirsty mates, "not to murder or to steal, for the Man-of-war that punished Tanna would blow up their little island!"

Sorrowful experience on Tanna had taught us to seek the site of our Aniwan house on the highest ground, and away from the malarial influences near the shore. There was one charming mound, covered with trees, whose roots ran down into the crevices of coral, and from which Tanna and Erromanga are clearly seen. But there the Natives for some superstitious reason forbade us to build, and we were constrained to take another rising ground somewhat nearer the shore. In the end, this turned out to be the very best site on the island for us, central and suitable every way. But we afterwards learned that perhaps superstition also led them to sell us this site, in the malicious hope that it would prove our ruin. The mounds on the top, which had to be cleared away, contained the bones and refuse of their Cannibal feasts for ages. None but their Sacred Men durst touch them; and the Natives watched us hewing and digging, certain that their gods would strike us dead! That failing, their thoughts may probably have been turned to reflect that after all the Jehovah God was stronger than they.

In leveling the site, and gently sloping the sides of the ground for good drainage purposes, I had gathered together two large baskets of human bones. I said to a Chief in Tannese, "How do these bones come to be here?"

And he replied, with a shrug worthy of a cynical Frenchman, "Ah, we are not Tanna-men! We don't eat the bones!"

CHAPTER LIX.
HOUSE-BUILDING FOR GOD.

THE site being now cleared, we questioned whether to build only a temporary home, hoping to return to dear old Tanna as soon as possible, or, though the labor would be vastly greater, a substantial house—for the comfort of our successors, if not of ourselves. We decided that, as this was work for God, we would make it the very best we could. We planned two central rooms, sixteen feet by sixteen, with a five feet wide lobby between, so that other rooms could be added when required. About a quarter of a mile from the sea, and thirty-five feet above its level, I laid the foundations of the house. Coral blocks raised the wall about three feet high all round. Air passages carried sweeping currents underneath each room, and greatly lessened the risk of fever and ague. A wide trench was dug all round, and filled up as a drain with broken coral. At back and front, the verandah stretched five feet wide; and pantry, bath-room, and tool-house were partitioned off under the verandah behind. The windows sent to me had hinges; I added two feet to each, with wood from Mission-boxes, and made them French door-windows, opening from each room to the verandah. And so we had, by God's blessing, a healthy spot to live in, if not exactly a thing of beauty!

The Mission House, as ultimately finished, had six rooms, three on each side of the lobby, and measured ninety feet in length, surrounded by a verandah, one hundred feet by five, which kept everything shaded and cool. Underneath two rooms a cellar was dug eight feet deep, and shelved all round for a store. In more than one terrific hurricane that cellar saved our lives,—all crushing into it when trees and houses were being tossed like feathers on the wings of the wind. Altogether, the house at Aniwa has proved one of the healthiest and most commodious of any that have been planted by Christian hands on the New Hebrides. In selecting site and in building "the good hand of our God was upon us for good."

I built also two small Orphanages, almost as inevitably necessary as the Missionary's own house. They stood on a line with the front of my own dwelling, one for girls, the other for boys, and we had them constantly under our own eyes. The orphans were practically boarded at the Mission premises, and adopted by the Missionaries. Their clothing was a heavy drain upon our resources; and every odd and curious article that came in any of the boxes or parcels was utilized. We trained these young people for Jesus. And at this day many of the best of our Native Teachers, and most devoted Christian helpers, are amongst those who would probably have perished but for these Orphanages.

Every day after dinner we set the bell a-ringing—intimating, from, our first arrival on Aniwa, readiness to give advice or medicine to all who were sick. We spoke to them, so soon as we had learned, a few words about Jesus. The weak received a cup of tea and a piece of bread. The demand was sometimes great, especially when epidemics befell them. But some rather fled from us as the cause of their sickness, and sought refuge from our presence in remotest corners, or rushed off at our approach and concealed themselves in the bush. They were but children, and full of superstition; and we had to win them by kindly patience, never losing faith in them and hope for them, any more than the Lord did with us!

Our learning the language on Aniwa was marked by similar incidents to those of Tanna related in a preceding chapter; though a few of them could understand my Tannese, and that greatly helped me. One day a man, after carefully examining some article, turned to his neighbor and said, "Taha tinei?"

I inferred that he was asking, "What is this?" Pointing to another article, I repeated their words; they smiled at each other, and gave me its name.

On another occasion, a man said to his companion, looking toward me, "Taha neigo?" Concluding that he was asking my name, I pointed towards him, and repeated the words, and they at once gave me their names.

Readers would be surprised to discover how much you can readily learn of any language, with these two short questions constantly on your lips, and with people ready at every turn to answer—"What's this?" "What's your name?" Every word was at once written down, spelled phonetically and arranged in alphabetic order, and a note appended as to the circumstances in which it was used. By frequent comparison of these notes, and by careful daily and even hourly imitation of all their sounds, we were able in a measure to understand each other before we had gone far in the house-building operations, during which some of them were constantly beside me.

One incident of that time was very memorable, and God turned it to good account for higher ends. I often tell it as "the miracle of the speaking bit of wood"; and it has happened to other Missionaries exactly as to myself. While working at the house, I required some nails and tools. Lifting a piece of planed wood, I penciled a few words on it, and requested our old Chief to carry it to Mrs. Paton, and she would send what I wanted. In blank wonder, he innocently stared at me, and said, "But what do you want?"

I replied, "The wood will tell her." He looked rather angry, thinking that I befooled him, and retorted, "Who ever heard of wood speaking?"

By hard pleading I succeeded in persuading him to go. He was amazed to see her looking at the wood and then fetching the needed articles. He brought back the bit of wood, and eagerly made signs for an explanation. Chiefly in broken Tannese I read to him the words, and informed him that in the same way God spoke to us through His Book. The will of God was written there, and by and by, when he learned to read, he would hear God speaking to him from its page, as Mrs. Paton heard me from the bit of wood. A great desire was thus awakened in the poor man's soul to see the very Word of God printed in his own language. He helped me to learn words and master ideas with growing enthusiasm. And when my work of translating portions of Holy Scripture began, his delight was unbounded and his help invaluable. The miracle of a speaking page was not less wonderful than that of speaking wood! One day, while building the house, an old Inland Chief and his three sons came to see us. Everything was to them full of wonder. After returning home one of the sons fell sick, and the father at once blamed us and the Worship, declaring that if the lad died we all should be murdered in revenge. By God's blessing, and by our careful nursing and suitable medicine, he recovered and was spared. The old Chief superstitiously wheeled round almost to another extreme. He became not only friendly, but devoted to us. He attended the Sabbath Services, and listened to the Aneityumese Teachers, and to my first attempts, partly in Tannese, translated by the orator Taia or the Chief Namakei, and explained in our hearing to the people in their mother tongue.

But on the heels of this, another calamity overtook us. So soon as two rooms of the Mission House were roofed in, I hired the stoutest of the young men to carry our boxes thither. Two of them started off with a heavy box suspended on a pole from shoulder to shoulder, their usual custom. They were shortly after attacked with vomiting of blood; and one of them, an Erromangan, actually died. The father of the other swore that, if his son did not get better, every soul at the Mission House should be slain in revenge. But God mercifully restored him.

As the boat-landing was nearly three-quarters of a mile distant, and such a calamity recurring would be not only sorrowful in itself but perilous in the extreme for us all, I steeped my wits, and with such crude materials as were at hand, I manufactured not only a hand-barrow, but a wheel-barrow, for the pressing emergencies of the time. In due course, I procured a more orthodox hand-cart from the Colonies, and coaxed and bribed the Natives to assist me in making a road for it. Perhaps the ghost of *Macadam* would shudder at the appearance of that road, but it has proved immensely useful ever since.

CHAPTER LX.
A CITY OF GOD.

When, in the course of years, everything had been completed to our taste, we lived practically in the midst of a beautiful village,—the Church, the School, the Orphanage, the Smithy and Joiner's Shop, the Printing Office, the Banana and Yam House, the Cook House, etc.; all very humble indeed, but all standing sturdily up there among the orange-trees, and preaching the Gospel of a higher civilization and of a better life for Aniwa. The little road leading to each door was laid with the white coral broken small. The fence around all shone fresh and clean with new paint. Order and taste were seen to be laws in the white man's New Life; and several of the Natives began diligently to follow our example.

Many and strange were the arts which I had to try to practise, such as handling the adze, the mysteries of tenon and mortise, and other feats of skill. If a Native wanted a fish-hook, or a piece of red calico to bind his long whip-cord hair, he would carry me a block of coral or fetch me a beam; but continuous daily toil seemed to him a mean existence. The women were tempted, by calico and beads for pay, to assist in preparing the sugar-cane leaf for thatch, gathering it in the plantations, and tying it over reeds four or six feet long with strips of bark of pandanus leaf, leaving a long fringe hanging over on one side. How differently they acted when the Gospel began to touch their hearts! They built their Church and their Schools then, by their own free toil, rejoicing to labor without money or price; and they have ever since kept them in good repair, for the service of the Lord, by their voluntary offerings of wood and sugar-cane leaf and coral-lime.

The roof was firmly tied on and nailed; thereon were laid the reeds, fringed with sugar-cane leaf, row after row tied firmly to the wood; the ridge was bound down by cocoanut leaves, dexterously plaited from side to side and skewered to the ridge-pole with hard wooden pins; and over all, a fresh storm-roof was laid on yearly for the hurricane months, composed of folded cocoanut leaves, held down with planks of wood, and bound to the frame-work below—which, however, had to be removed again in April to save the sugar-cane leaf from rotting beneath it. There you were snugly covered in, and your thatching good to last from eight years to ten; that is, provided you were not caught in the sweep of the hurricane, before which trees went flying like straws, huts disappeared like autumn leaves, and your Mission House, if left standing at all, was probably swept bare alike of roof and thatch at a single stroke! Well for you at such times if you have a good barometer indicating the approach of the storm; and better still, a large cellar like ours, four-and-twenty feet by sixteen, built round with solid coral blocks,—where goods may be stored, and whereinto also all your household may creep for safety, while the tornado tosses your dwelling about, and sets huge trees dancing around you! We had also to invent a lime-kiln, and this proved one of the hardest nuts of all that had to be cracked. The kind of coral required could be obtained only at one spot, about three miles distant. Lying at anchor in my boat, the Natives dived into the sea, broke off with hammer and crowbar piece after piece, and brought it up to me, till I had my load. We then carried it ashore, and spread it out in the sun to be blistered there for two weeks or so. Having thus secured twenty or thirty boat-loads, and had it duly conveyed round to the Mission Station, a huge pit was dug in the ground, dry wood piled in below, and green wood above to the height of several feet, and on the top of all the coral blocks were orderly laid. When this pile had burned for seven or ten days, the coral had been reduced to excellent lime, and the plasterwork made therefrom shone like marble.

On one of these trips the Natives performed an extraordinary feat. The boat with full load was struck heavily by a wave, and the reef drove a hole in her side. Quick as thought the crew were all in the sea, and, to my amazement, bearing up the boat with their shoulder and one hand, while swimming and guiding us ashore with the other! There on the land we were hauled up, and four weary days were spent fetching and carrying from the Mission Station every plank, tool, and nail, necessary for her repair. Every boat for these seas ought to be built of cedar wood and copper-fastened, which is by far the most economical in the end. And all houses should be built of wood which is as full as possible of gum or resin, since the large white ants devour not only other soft woods, but even Colonial blue gum-trees, the hard cocoanut, and window sashes, chairs, and tables!

Glancing back on all these toils, I rejoice that such exhausting demands are no longer made on our newly-arrived Missionaries. Houses, all ready for being set up, are now brought down from the Colonies. Zinc roofs and other improvements have been introduced. The Synod appoints a deputation to accompany the young Missionary, and plant the house along with himself at the Station committed to his care. Precious strength is thus saved for higher uses; and not only property but life itself is oftentimes preserved.

I will close this chapter with an incident which, though it came to our knowledge only years afterwards, closely bears upon our Settlement on Aniwa. At first we had no idea why they so determinedly refused us one site, and fixed us to another of their own choice. But after the old Chief

Namakei became a Christian, he one day addressed the Aniwan people in our hearing to this effect:—

"When Missi came we saw his boxes. We knew he had blankets and calico, axes and knives, fish-hooks and all such things. We said, 'Don't drive him off, else we will lose all these things. We will let him land. But we will force him to live on the Sacred Plot. Our gods will kill him, and we will divide all that he has amongst the men of Aniwa.' But Missi built his house on our most sacred spot. He and his people lived there, and the gods did not strike. He planted bananas there, and we said, 'Now when they eat of these they will all drop down dead, as our fathers assured us, if any one ate fruit from that ground, except only our Sacred Men themselves.' These bananas ripened. They did eat them. We kept watching for days and days, but no one died! Therefore what we say, and what our fathers have said, is not true. Our gods cannot kill them. Their Jehovah God is stronger than the gods of Aniwa."

I enforced old Namakei's appeal, telling them that, though they knew it not, it was the living and true and only God who had sent them every blessing which they possessed, and had at last sent us to teach them how to serve and love and please Him. In wonder and silence they listened, while I tried to explain to them that Jesus, the Son of this God, had lived and died and gone to the Father to save them, and that He was now willing to take them by the hand and lead them through this life to glory and immortality together with Himself.

The old Chief led them in prayer—a strange, dark, groping prayer, with streaks of Heathenism coloring every thought and sentence; but still a heart-breaking prayer, as the cry of a soul once Cannibal, but now being thrilled through and through with the first conscious pulsations of the Christ-Spirit, throbbing into the words—"Father, Father; our Father."

When these poor creatures began to wear a bit of calico or a kilt, it was an outward sign of a change, though yet far from civilization. And when they began to look up and pray to One whom they called "Father, our Father," though they might be far, very far, from the type of Christian that dubs itself "respectable," my heart broke over them in tears of joy; and nothing will ever persuade me that there was not a Divine Heart in the Heavens rejoicing too.

CHAPTER LXI.
THE RELIGION OF REVENGE.

ON landing in November, 1866, we found the Natives of Aniwa, some very shy and distrustful, and others forward and imperious. No clothing was worn; but the wives and elder women had grass aprons or girdles like our first parents in Eden. The old Chief interested himself in us and our work; but the greater number showed a far deeper interest in the axes, knives, fishhooks, strips of red calico, and blankets, received in payment for work or for bananas. Even for payment they would scarcely work at first, and they were most unreasonable, easily offended, and started off in a moment at any imaginable slight.

For instance, a Chief once came for medicine. I was so engaged that I could not attend to him for a few minutes. So off he went, in a great rage, threatening revenge, and muttering, "I must be attended to! I won't wait on *him*." Such were the exactions of a naked savage!

Shortly before our arrival, an Aneityumese Teacher was sacrificed on Aniwa. The circumstances are illustrative of what may be almost called their worship of revenge. Many long years ago, a party of Aniwans had gone to Aneityum on a friendly visit; but the Aneityumese, then all savages, murdered and ate every man of them save one, who escaped into the bush. Living on cocoanuts, he awaited a favorable wind, and, launching his canoe by night, he arrived in safety. The bereaved Aniwans, hearing his terrible story, were furious for revenge; but the forty-five miles of sea between proving too hard an obstacle, they made a deep cut in the earth and vowed to renew that cut from year to year till the day of revenge came round. Thus the memory of the event was kept alive for nearly eighty years.

At length the people of Aneityum came to the knowledge of Jesus Christ. They strongly yearned to spread their saving Gospel to the Heathen Islands all around. Amid prayers and strong cryings to God they, like the Church at Antioch, designated two of their leading men to go as Native Teachers and evangelize Aniwa, viz. Navalak and Nemeyan; whilst others went forth to Fotuna, Tanna, and Erromanga, as opportunity arose. Namakei, the principal Chief of Aniwa, had promised to protect and be kind to them. But as time went on, it was discovered that the Teachers belonged to the Tribe on Aneityum, and one of them to the very land, where long ago the Aniwans had been murdered. The Teachers had from the first known their danger, but were eager to make known the Gospel to Aniwa. It was resolved that they should die. But the Aniwans, having promised to protect them, shrank from doing it themselves; so they hired two Tanna-men and an Aniwan Chief, one of whose parents had belonged to Tanna, to waylay and shoot the Teachers as they returned from their tour of Evangelism among the villages on Sabbath afternoon. Their muskets did not go off, but the murderers rushed upon them with clubs and left them for dead.

Nemeyan was dead, and entered that day amongst the noble army of the Martyrs. Poor Navalak was still breathing, and the Chief Namakei carried him to his village and kindly nursed him. He pleaded with the people that the claims of revenge had been satisfied, and that Navalak should be cherished and sent home,—the Christ-Spirit beginning to work in that darkened soul! Navalak was restored to his people and is yet living (1888)— a high class Chief on Aneityum, and an honor to the Church of God, bearing on his body "the marks of the Lord Jesus." And often since has he visited Aniwa, in later years, and praised the Lord amongst the very people who once thirsted for his blood and left him by the wayside as good as dead!

For a time, Aniwa was left without any witness for Jesus,—the London Missionary Society Teachers, having suffered dreadfully for lack of food and from fever and ague, being also removed. But on a visit of a Mission vessel, Namakei sent his orator Taia to Aneityum, to tell them that now revenge was satisfied, the cut in the earth filled up, and a cocoanut tree planted and flourishing where the blood of the Teachers had been shed, and that no person from Aneityum would ever be injured by Aniwans. Further, he was to plead for more Teachers, and to pledge his Chiefs word that they would be kindly received and protected. They knew not the Gospel, and had no desire for it; but they wanted friendly intercourse with Aneityum, where trading vessels called, and whence they might obtain mats, baskets, blankets, and iron tools. At length two Aneityumese again volunteered to go, Kangaru and Nelmai, one from each side of the Island, and were located by the Missionaries, along with their families, on Aniwa, one with Namakei, and the other at the south end, to lift up the Standard of a Christlike life among their Heathen neighbors.

Taia, who went on the Mission to Aneityum, was a great speaker and also a very cunning man. He was the old Chief's appointed "Orator" on all state occasions, being tall and stately in appearance, of great bodily strength, and possessed of a winning manner. On the voyage to Aneityum he was constantly smoking and making things disagreeable to all around him. Being advised not to smoke while on board, he pleaded with the Missionary just to let him take a whiff now and again till he finished the tobacco he had in his pipe, and then he would lay it aside. But, like the widow's meal, it lasted all the way to Aneityum, and never appeared to get less—at which the innocent Taia expressed much astonishment!

CHAPTER LXII.
FIRST FRUITS ON ANIWA.

THE two Teachers and their wives on Aniwa were little better than slaves when we landed there, toiling in the service of their masters and living in constant fear of being murdered. Doubtless, however, the mighty contrast presented by the life, character, and disposition of these godly Teachers was the sowing of the seed that bore fruit in other days,—though as yet no single Aniwan had begun to wear clothing out of respect to Civilization, much less been brought to know and love the Saviour.

So soon as I could speak a little to them in their own language, we began to visit regularly at their villages and to talk to them about Jesus and His love. We tried also to get them to come to our Church under the shade of the banyan tree. Nasi and some of the worst characters would sit scowling not far off, or follow us with loaded muskets. Using every precaution, we still held on doing our work; sometimes giving fish-hooks or beads to the boys and girls, showing them that our objects were kind and not selfish. And however our hearts sometimes trembled in the presence of imminent death and sank within us, we stood fearless in their presence, and left all results in the hands of Jesus. Often have I had to run into the arms of some savage, when his club was swung or his musket leveled at my head, and, praying to Jesus, so clung round him that he could neither strike nor shoot me till his wrath cooled down, and I managed to slip away. Often have I seized the pointed barrel and directed it upwards, or, pleading with my assailant, uncapped his musket in the struggle. At other times, nothing could be said, nothing done, but stand still in silent prayer, asking God to protect us or to prepare us for going home to His Glory. He fulfilled His own promise—"I will not fail thee nor forsake thee."

The first Aniwan that ever came to the knowledge and love of Jesus was the old Chief Namakei. We came to live on his land, as it was near our diminutive harbor; and, upon the whole, he and his people were the most friendly, though his only brother, the Sacred Man of the tribe, on two occasions tried to shoot me. Namakei came a good deal about us at the Mission House, and helped us to acquire the language. He discovered that we took tea evening and morning. When we gave him a cup and a piece of bread, he liked it well, and gave a sip to all around him. At first he came for the tea, perhaps, and disappeared suspiciously soon thereafter; but his interest manifestly grew, till he showed great delight in helping us in every possible way. Along with him and as his associates came also the Chief Naswai and his wife Katua. These three grew into the knowledge of the

Saviour together. From being savage Cannibals they rose before our eyes, under the influence of the Gospel, into noble and beloved characters, and they and we loved each other exceedingly.

Namakei brought his little daughter, his only child, the Queen of her race, called Litsi Soré (=Litsi the Great), and said, "I want to leave my Litsi with you, I want you to train her for Jesus."

She was a very intelligent child, learned things like any white girl, and soon became quite a help to Mrs. Paton. On seeing his niece dressed, and so smart-looking, the old Chief's only brother, the Sacred Man that had attempted to shoot me, also brought his child, Litsi Sisi (=the Little) to be trained like her cousin. The mothers of both were dead. The children reported all they saw, and all we taught them, and so their fathers became more deeply interested in our work, and the news of the Gospel spread far and wide. Soon we had all the Orphans committed to us, whose guardians were willing to part with them, and our Home become literally the School of Christ—the boys growing up to help all my plans, and the girls to help my wife and to be civilized and trained by her, and many of them developing into devoted Teachers and Evangelists.

Our earlier Sabbath Services were sad affairs. Every man came armed—indeed, every man slept with his weapons of war at his side—and bow and arrow, spear and tomahawk, club and musket, were always ready for action. On fair days we assembled under the banyan tree, on rainy days in a Native hut partly built for the purpose. One or two seemed to listen, but the most lay about on their backs or sides, smoking, talking, sleeping! When we stopped the feast at the close, which the Aneityumese Teacher had been forced to prepare before our coming, and for which they were always ready, the audiences at first went down to two or three; but these actually came to learn, and a better tone began immediately to pervade the Service. We informed them that it was for their good that we taught them, and that they would get no "pay" for attending Church or School, and the greater number departed in high dudgeon as very ill-used persons! Others of a more commercial turn came offering to sell their "idols," and when we would not purchase them, but urged them to give up and cast them away for love to Jesus, they carried them off, saying they would have nothing to do with this new Worship.

Amidst our frequent trials and dangers in those earlier times on Aniwa, our little Orphans often warned us privately and and saved our lives from cruel plots. When, in baffled rage, our enemies demanded who had revealed things to us, I always said, "It was a little bird from the bush." So the dear children grew to have perfect confidence in us. They knew we would not betray them; and they considered themselves the guardians of our lives.

CHAPTER LXIII.
TRADITIONS AND CUSTOMS.

WHAT a suggestive tradition of the Fall came to me in one of those early days on Aniwa! Upon our leaving the hut and removing to our new house, it was seized upon by Tupa for his sleeping-place, though still continuing to be used by the Natives as club-house, court of law, etc. One morning at daylight this Tupa came running to us in great excitement, wielding his club furiously, and crying, "Missi, I have killed the Tebil. I have killed Teapolo. He came to catch me last night. I raised all the people, and we fought him round the house with our clubs. At daybreak he came out and I killed him dead. We will have no more bad conduct or trouble now. Teapolo is dead!"

I said, "What nonsense; Teapolo is a spirit, and cannot be seen."

But in mad excitement he persisted that he had killed him. And at Mrs. Paton's advice, I went with the man, and he led me to a great Sacred Rock of coral near our old hut, over which hung the dead body of a huge and beautiful sea-serpent, and exclaimed, "There he lies! Truly I killed him."

I protested, "That is not the Devil; it is only the body of a serpent."

The man quickly answered, "Well? but it is all the game! He is Teapolo. He makes us bad, and causes all our troubles."

Following up this hint by many inquiries, then and afterwards, I found that they clearly associated man's troubles and sufferings somehow with the serpent. They worshiped the Serpent, as a spirit of evil, under the name of Matshiktshiki; that is to say, they lived in abject terror of his influence, and all their worship was directed towards propitiating his rage against man.

Their story of Creation, at least of the origin of their own Aniwa and the adjacent Islands, is much more an outcome of the unaided Native mind. They say that Matshiktshiki fished up these lands out of the sea. And they show the deep print of his foot on the coral rocks, opposite each island, whereon he stood as he strained and lifted them up above the waters. He then threw his great fishing-line round Fotuna, thirty-six miles distant, to draw it close to Aniwa and make them one land; but, as he pulled, the line broke and he fell, where his mark may still be seen upon the rock—so the Islands remain separated unto this day.

Matshiktshiki placed men and women on Aniwa. On the southern end of the Island there was a beautiful spring and a freshwater river, with rich land all around, for plantations. But the people would not do what Matshiktshiki wanted them; so he got angry, and split off the richer part of Aniwa, with the spring and river, and sailed with them across to Aneityum, leaving them where Dr. Inglis has since built his beautiful Mission Station. To this day, the river there is called "the water of Aniwa" by the inhabitants of both islands; and it is the ambition of all Aniwans to visit Aneityum and drink of that spring and river, as they sigh to each other, "Alas, for the waters of Aniwa!"

Their picture of the Flood is equally grotesque. Far back, when the volcano now on Tanna was part of Aniwa, the rain fell and fell from day to day, and the sea rose till it threatened to cover everything. All were drowned except the few who climbed up on the volcano mountain. The sea had already put out the volcano at the southern end of Aniwa; and Matshiktshiki, who dwelt in the greater volcano, becoming afraid of the extinction of his big fire too, split it off from Aniwa with all the land on the southeastern side, and sailed it across to Tanna on the top of the flood. There, by his mighty strength, he heaved the volcano to the top of a high mountain in Tanna, where it remains to this day. For, on the subsiding of the sea, he was unable to transfer his big fire to Aniwa; and so it was reduced to a very small island, without a volcano, and without a river, for the sins of the people long ago.

Even where there are no snakes they apply the superstitions about the serpent to a large, black, poisonous lizard called *Kekvau*. They call it Teapolo, and women or children scream wildly at the sight of one.

One of the darkest and most hideous blots on Heathenism is the practice of Infanticide. Only three cases came to our knowledge on Aniwa; but we publicly denounced them at all hazards, and awoke not only natural feeling, but the selfish interests of the community for the protection of the children. These three were the last that died there by parents' hands. A young husband, who had been jealous of his wife, buried their male child alive as soon as born. An old Tanna woman, who had no children living, having at last a fine healthy boy born to her, threw him into the sea before any one could interfere to save. And a savage, in anger with his wife, snatched her baby from her arms, hid himself in the bush till night, and returned without the child, refusing to give any explanation, except that he was dead and buried. Praise be to God, these three murderers of their own children were by and by touched with the story of Jesus, became members of the Church, and each adopted little orphan children, towards whom they continued to show the most tender affection and care.

Wife-murder was also considered quite legitimate. In one of our inland villages dwelt a young couple, happy in every respect except that they had no children. The man, being a Heathen, resolved to take home another wife, a widow with two children. This was naturally opposed by his young wife. And, without the slightest warning, while she sat plaiting a basket, he discharged a ball into her from his loaded musket. It crashed through her arm and lodged in her side. Everything was done that was in my power to save her life; but on the tenth day tetanus came on, and she soon after passed away. The man appeared very attentive to her all the time; but, being a Heathen, he insisted that she had no right to oppose his wishes! He was not in any way punished or disrespected by the people of his village, but went out and in amongst them as usual, and took home the other woman as his wife a few weeks thereafter. His second wife began to attend Church and School regularly with her children; and at last he also came along with them, changing very manifestly from his sullen and savage former self. They have a large family; they are avowedly trying to train them all for the Lord Jesus, and they take their places meekly at the Lord's Table.

It would give a wonderful shock, I suppose, to many namby-pamby Christians to whom the title "Mighty to Save" conveys no ideas of reality, to be told that nine or ten converted murderers were partaking with them the Holy Communion of Jesus! But the Lord who reads the heart, and weighs every motive and circumstance, has perhaps much more reason to be shocked by the presence of some of themselves. Penitence opens all the heart of God—"To-day shalt thou be with Me in Paradise."

CHAPTER LXIV.
NELWANG'S ELOPEMENT.

SOME most absurd and preposterous experiences were forced upon us by the habits and notions of the people. Amongst these I recall very vividly the story of Nelwang's elopement with his bride. I had begun, in spare hours, to lay the foundation of two additional rooms for our house, and felt rather uneasy to see a well-known savage hanging around every day with his tomahawk, and eagerly watching me at work. He had killed a man, before our arrival on Aniwa; and had also startled my wife by suddenly appearing from amongst the boxes, and causing her to run for life. On seeing him hovering so alarmingly near, tomahawk in hand, I saluted him, "Nelwang, do you want to speak to me?"

"Yes, Missi," he replied; "if you will help me now, I will be your friend forever."

I answered, "I am your friend. That brought me here and keeps me here."

"Yes," said he very earnestly, "but I want you to be strong as my friend, and I will be strong for you!"

I replied, "Well, how can I help you?"

He quickly answered, "I want to get married, and I need your help."

I protested,—"Nelwang, you know that marriages here are all made in infancy, by children being bought and betrothed to their future husbands. How can I interfere? You don't want to bring evil on me and my wife and child? It might cost us our lives."

"No! no! Missi," earnestly retorted Nelwang. "No one hears of this, or can hear. Only help me now. You tell me, if you were my circumstances, how would you act?"

"That's surely very simple," I answered. "Every man knows how to go about that business, if he wants to be honest! Look out for your intended, find out if she loves you and the rest will follow naturally,—you will marry her."

"Yes," argued Nelwang, "but just there my trouble comes in!"

"Do you know the woman you would like to get?" I asked, wishing to bring him to some closer issue.

"Yes," replied he very frankly, "I want to marry Yakin, the Chiefs' widow up at the inland village, and that will break no infant betrothals."

"But," I persevered, "do you know if she loves you or would take you?"

"Yes," replied Nelwang; "one day I met her on the path and told her I would like to have her for my wife. She took out her ear-rings and gave them to me, and I know thereby that she loves me. I was one of her late husband's men; and if she had loved any of them more than she loved me, she would have given them to another. With the ear-rings she gave me her heart."

"Then why," I insisted, "don't you go and marry her?"

"There," said Nelwang gravely, "begins my difficulty. In her village there are thirty young men for whom there are no wives. Each of them wants her, but no one has the courage to take her, for the other nine-and-twenty will shoot him!"

"And if you take her," I suggested, "the disappointed thirty will shoot you!"

"That's exactly what I see, Missi," continued Nelwang; "but I want you just to think you are in my place, and tell me how you would carry her off. You white men can always succeed. Missi, hear my plans, and advise me."

With as serious a face as I could command, I had to listen to Nelwang, to enter into his love affair, and to make suggestions, with a view to avoiding bloodshed and other miseries. The result of the deliberations was that Nelwang was to secure the confidence of two friends, his brother and the orator Taia, to place one at each end of the coral rocks above the village as watchmen, to cut down with his American tomahawk a passage through the fence at the back, and to carry off his bride at dead of night into the seclusion and safety of the bush! Nelwang's eyes flashed as he flourished his tomahawk about and cried, "I see it now, Missi! I shall win her from them all. Yakin and I will be strong for you all our days."

Next morning Yakin's house was found deserted. They sent to all the villages around, but no one had seen her. The hole in the fence behind was then discovered, and the thirty whispered to each other that Yakin had been wooed and won by some daring lover. Messengers were despatched to all the villages, and Nelwang was found to have disappeared on the same night as the widow, and neither could anywhere be found.

The usual revenge was taken. The houses of the offenders burned, their fences broken down, and all their property either destroyed or distributed. Work was suspended, and the disappointed thirty solaced themselves by feasting at Yakin's expense.

Three weeks passed. The runaways were nowhere to be found. It was generally believed that they had gone in a canoe to Tanna or Erromanga. But one morning, as I began my work at my house alone, the brave Nelwang appeared at my side!

"Hillo!" I said, "where have you come from? and where is Yakin?"

"I must not," he replied, "tell you yet. We are hid. We have lived on cocoanuts gathered at night. Yakin is well and happy. I come now to fulfil my promise: I will help you, and Yakin will help Missi Paton the woman, and we shall be your friends. I have ground to be built upon and fenced, whenever we dare; but we will come and live with you, till peace is secured. Will you let us come to-morrow morning?"

"All right!" I said. "Come to-morrow!" And, trembling with delight, he disappeared into the bush.

Thus strangely God provided us with wonderful assistance. Yakin soon learnt to wash and dress and clean everything, and Nelwang served me like a faithful disciple. They clung by us like our very shadow, partly through fear of attack, partly from affection; but as each of them could handle freely both musket and tomahawk, which, though laid aside, were never far away, it was not every enemy that cared to try issues with Nelwang and his bride. After a few weeks had thus passed by, and as both of them were really showing an interest in things pertaining to Jesus and His Gospel, I urged them strongly to appear publicly at the Church on Sabbath, to show that they were determined to stand their ground together as true husband and wife, and that the others must accept the position and become reconciled. Delay now could gain no purpose, and I wished the strife and uncertainty to be put to an end.

Nelwang knew our customs. Every worshiper has to be seated, when our Church bell ceases ringing. Aniwans would be ashamed to enter after the Service had actually begun. As the bell ceased, Nelwang, knowing that he would have a clear course, marched in, dressed in shirt and kilt, but grasping very determinedly his tomahawk! He sat down as near to me as he could conveniently get, trying hard to conceal his manifest agitation. Silently smiling towards me, he then turned and looked eagerly at the other door through which the women entered and left the Church, as if to say, "Yakin is coming!" But his tomahawk was poised ominously on his shoulder, and his courage gave him a defiant and almost impudent air. He was evidently quite ready to sell his life at a high price, if any one was prepared to risk the consequences.

In a few seconds Yakin entered; and if Nelwang's bearing and appearance were rather inconsistent with the feeling of worship,—what on earth was I to do when the figure and costume of Yakin began to reveal itself marching in? The first visible difference betwixt a Heathen and a Christian is,—that the Christian wears some clothing, the Heathen wears none. Yakin had determined to show the extent of her Christianity by the amount of clothing she could carry upon her person. Being a Chief's widow before she became Nelwang's bride, she had some idea of state occasions, and appeared dressed in every article of European apparel, mostly portions of male attire, that she could beg or borrow from about the premises! Her bridal gown was a man's drab-colored great-coat, put on above her Native grass skirts, and sweeping down to her heels, buttoned tight. Over this she had hung on a vest, and above that again, most amazing of all, she had superinduced a pair of men's trousers, planting the body of them on her neck and shoulders, and leaving her head and face looking out from between the legs—a leg from either side streaming over her bosom arid dangling down absurdly in front! Fastened to the one shoulder also there was a red shirt, and to the other a striped shirt, waving about her like wings as she sailed along. Around her head a red shirt had been twisted like a turban, and her notions of art demanded that a sleeve thereof should hang aloft over each of her ears! She seemed to be a moving monster loaded with a mass of rags. The day was excessively hot, and the perspiration poured over her face in streams. She, too, sat as near to me as she could get on the women's side of the Church. Nelwang looked at me and then at her, smiling quietly, as if to say, "You never saw, in all your white world, a bride so grandly dressed!"

I little thought what I was bringing on myself when I urged them to come to Church. The sight of that poor creature sweltering before me constrained me for once to make the service very short—perhaps the shortest I ever conducted in all my life! The day ended in peace. The two souls were extremely happy; and I praised God that what might have been a scene of bloodshed had closed thus, even though it were in a kind of wild grotesquerie!

CHAPTER LXV.
THE CHRIST-SPIRIT AT WORK.

THE progress of God's work was most conspicuous in, relation to wars and revenges among the Natives. The two high Chiefs, Namakei and Naswai, frequently declared, "We are the men of Christ now. We must not fight. We must put down murders and crimes among our people."

Two young fools, returning from Tanna with muskets, attempted twice to shoot a man in sheer wantonness and display of malice. The Islanders met, and informed them that if man or woman was injured by them, the other men would load their muskets and shoot them dead in general council. This was a mighty step towards public order, and I greatly rejoiced before the Lord. His Spirit, like leaven, was at work!

My constant custom was, in order to prevent war, to run right in between the contending parties. My faith enabled me to grasp and realize the promise, "Lo, I am with you always." In Jesus I felt invulnerable and immortal, so long as I was doing His work. And I can truly say that these were the moments when I felt my Saviour to be most truly and sensibly present, inspiring and empowering me.

Another scheme had an excellent educative and religious influence. I tried to interest all the villages, and to treat all the Chiefs equally. In our early days, after getting into my two-roomed house, I engaged the Chief, or representative man of each district, to put up one or other at the many outhouses required at the Station. One, along with his people, built the cookhouse; another, the store; another, the banana and yam-house; another, the washing-house; another, the boys and girls' house; the houses for servants and teachers, the Schoolhouse, and the large shed, a kind of shelter where Natives sat and talked when not at work about the premises. Of course these all were at first only Native huts, of larger or smaller dimensions. But they were all built by contract for articles which they highly valued, such as axes, knives, yards of prints and calico, strings of beads, blankets, etc. They served our purpose for the time, and when another party, by contract also, had fenced around our premises, the Mission Station was really a beautiful, little, lively, and orderly village, and in itself no bad emblem of Christian and civilized life. The payments, made to all irrespectively, but only for work duly done and according to reasonable bargain, distributed property and gifts amongst them on wholesome principles, and encouraged a well-conditioned rivalry which had many happy effects.

Heathenism made many desperate and some strange efforts to stamp out our Cause on Aniwa, but the Lord held the helm. One old Chief, formerly friendly, turned against us. He ostentatiously set himself to make a canoe, working at it very openly and defiantly on Sabbaths. He, becoming sick and dying, his brother started, on a Sabbath morning and in contempt of the Worship, with an armed company to provoke our people to war. They refused to fight; and one man, whom he struck with his club, said, "I will leave my revenge to Jehovah."

A few days thereafter, this brother also fell sick and suddenly died. The Heathen party made much of these incidents, and some clamored for our death in revenge, but most feared to murder us; so they withdrew and lived apart from our friends, as far away as they could get. By and by, however, they set fire to a large district belonging to our supporters burning cocoanut and breadfruit trees and plantations. Still our people refused to fight, and kept near to protect us. Then all the leading men assembled to talk it over. Most were for peace, but some insisted upon burning our house and driving us away or killing us, that they might be left to live as they had hitherto done. At last a Sacred Man, a Chief who had been on Tanna when the Curaçoa punished the murderers and robbers, but protected the villages of the friendly Natives there, stood up and spoke in our defense, and warned them what might happen; and other three, who had been under my instruction on Tanna, declared themselves to be the friends of Jehovah and of His Missionary. Finally, the Sacred Man rose again, and showed them rows of beautiful white shells strung round his left arm, saying—

"Nowar, the great Chief at Port Resolution on Tanna, when he saw that Missi and his wife could not be kept there, took me to his heart, and pledged me by these, the shells of his office as Chief, taken from his own arm and bound on mine, to protect them from all harm. He told me to declare to the men of Aniwa that if the Missi be injured or slain, he and his warriors will come from Tanna and take the full revenge in blood." This turned the scale. The meeting closed in our favor.

Close on the heels of this, another and a rather perplexing incident befell us. A party of Heathens assembled and made a great display of fishing on the Lord's Day, in contempt of the practice of the men on Jehovah's side, threatening also to waylay the Teachers and myself in our village circuits. A meeting was held by the Christian party, at the close of the Sabbath Services. All who wished to serve Jehovah were to come to my house next morning, unarmed, and accompany me on a visit to our enemies, that we might talk and reason together with them. By daybreak, the Chiefs and nearly eighty men assembled at the Mission House, declaring that they were on Jehovah's side, and wished to go with me. But, alas! they refused to lay down their arms, or leave them behind; nor would they either refrain from going or suffer me to go alone. Pledging them to peace, I was reluctantly placed at their head, and we marched off to the village of the unfriendly party.

The villagers were greatly alarmed. The Chief's two sons came forth with every available man to meet us. That whole day was consumed in talking and speechifying, sometimes chanting their replies—the Natives are all inveterate talkers! To me the day was utterly wearisome; but it had one redeeming feature,—their rage found vent in hours of palaver, instead of blows and blood. It ended in peace. The Heathen were amazed at the number of Jehovah's friends; and they pledged themselves henceforth to leave the Worship alone, and that every one who pleased might come to it unmolested. For this, worn out and weary, we returned, praising the Lord.

CHAPTER LXVI.
THE SINKING OF THE WELL.

BUT I must here record the story of the Sinking of the Well, which broke the back of Heathenism on Aniwa. Being a flat coral island, with no hills to attract the clouds, rain is scarce there as compared with the adjoining mountainous islands; and even when it does fall heavily, with tropical profusion, it disappears, as said before, through the light soil and porous rock, and drains itself directly into the sea. The rainy season is from December to April, and then the disease most characteristic of all these regions is apt to prevail, viz., fever and ague.

At certain seasons, the Natives drink very unwholesome water; and, indeed, the best water they had at any time for drinking purposes was from the precious cocoanut, a kind of Apple of Paradise for all these Southern Isles! They also cultivate the sugar-cane very extensively, and in great variety; and they chew it, when we would fly to water for thirst; so it is to them both food and drink. The black fellow carries with him to the field, when he goes off for a day's work, four or five sticks of sugar-cane, and puts in his time comfortably enough on these. Besides, the sea being their universal bathing-place, in which they swattle like fish, and little water, almost none, being required for cooking purposes, and none whatever for washing clothes, the lack of fresh-springing water was not the dreadful trial to them that it would be to us. Yet they appreciate and rejoice in it immensely too; though the water of the green cocoanut is refreshing, and in appearance, taste, and color not unlike lemonade—one nut filling a tumbler; and though when mothers die they feed the babies on it and on the soft white pith, and they flourish on the same, yet the Natives themselves show their delight in preferring, when they can get it, the water from the well.

Aniwa, having therefore no permanent supply of fresh water, in spring or stream or lake, and my own household also suffering sadly for lack of the same, I resolved by the help of God to sink a well near the Mission Premises, hoping that a wisdom higher than my own would guide me to the source of some blessed spring. Of the scientific conditions of such an experiment I was comparatively ignorant; but I counted on having to dig through earth and coral above thirty feet, and my constant fear was, that owing to our environment, the water, if water I found, could only be salt water after all my toils! Still I resolved to sink that shaft in hope, and in faith that the Son of God would be glorified thereby.

One morning I said to the old Chief and his fellow-Chief, both now earnestly inquiring about the religion of Jehovah and of Jesus, "I am going to sink a deep well down into the earth, to see if our God will send us fresh water up from below."

They looked at me with astonishment, and said in a tone of sympathy approaching to pity, "O Missi! Wait till the rain comes down, and we will save all we possibly can for you."

I replied, "We may all die for lack of water. If no fresh water can be got, we may be forced to leave you."

The old Chief looked imploringly, and said "O Missi! you must not leave us for that. Rain comes only from above. How could you expect our Island to send up showers of rain from below?"

I told him, "Fresh water does come up springing from the earth in my Land at home, and I hope to see it here also."

The old Chief grew more tender in his tones, and cried, "O Missi, your head is going wrong; you are losing something, or you would not talk wild like that! Don't let our people hear you talking about going down into the earth for rain, or they will never listen to your word or believe you again."

But I started upon my hazardous job, selecting a spot near the Mission Station and close to the public path, that my prospective well might be useful to all. I began to dig, with pick and spade and bucket at hand, an American axe for a hammer and crowbar, and a ladder for service by and bye. The good old Chief now told off his men in relays to watch me, lest I should attempt to take my own life, or do anything outrageous, saying, "Poor Missi! That's the way with all who go mad. There's no driving of a notion out of their heads. We must just watch him now. He will find it harder to work with pick and spade than with his pen, and when he's tired we'll persuade him to give it up."

I did get exhausted sooner than I expected, toiling under that tropical sun; but we never own before the Natives that we are beaten; so I went into the house and filled my vest pocket with large, beautiful English-made fish-hooks. These are very tempting to the young men as compared with their own,—skilfully made though they be out of shell, and serving their purposes wonderfully. Holding up a large hook, I cried, "One of these to every man who fills and turns over three buckets out of this hole!"

A rush was made to get the first turn, and back again for another and another. I kept those on one side who had got a turn, till all the rest in order had a chance, and bucket after bucket was filled and emptied rapidly. Still the shaft seemed to lower very slowly, while my fish-hooks were disappearing very quickly. I was constantly there, and took the heavy share of everything, and was thankful one evening to find that we had cleared more than twelve feet deep,—when lo! next morning, one side had rushed in, and our work was all undone. The old Chief and his best men now came around me more earnestly than ever. He remonstrated with me very gravely. He assured me for the fiftieth time that rain would never be seen coming up through the earth on Aniwa!

"Now," said he, "had you been in that hole last night, you would have been buried, and a Man-of-war would have come from Queen 'Toria to ask for the Missi that lived here. We would have to say, 'He is down in that hole.' The Captain would ask, 'Who killed him and put him down there?' We would have to say, 'He went down there himself!' The Captain would answer, 'Nonsense! Who ever heard of a white man going down into the earth to bury himself? You killed him, you put him there; don't hide your bad conduct with lies!' Then he would bring out his big guns and shoot us, and destroy our Island in revenge. You are making your own grave, Missi, and you will make ours too. Give up this mad freak, for no rain will be found by going downwards on Aniwa. Besides, all your fish-hooks cannot tempt my men again to enter that hole; they don't want to be buried with you. Will you not give it up now?" I said all that I could to quiet his fears, explained to them that this falling in had happened by my neglect of precautions, and finally made known that by the help of my God, even without all other help, I meant to persevere. Steeping my poor brains over the problem, I became an extemporized engineer. Two trees were searched for, with branches on opposite sides, capable of sustaining a cross tree betwixt them. I sank them on each side firmly into the ground, passed the beam across them over the center of the shaft, fastened thereon a rude home-made pulley and block, passed a rope over the wheel, and swung my largest bucket to the end of it. Thus equipped, I began once more sinking away at the well, but at so great an angle that the sides might not again fall in. Not a Native, however, would enter that hole, and I had to pick and dig away till I was utterly exhausted. But a Native Teacher, in whom I had confidence, took charge above, managing to hire them with axes, knives, etc., to seize the end of the rope and walk along the ground, pulling it till the bucket rose to the surface, and then he himself swung it aside, emptied it, and lowered it down again. I rang a little bell which I had with me, when the bucket was loaded, and that was the signal for my brave helpers to pull their rope. And thus I toiled on from day to day, my heart almost sinking sometimes with the sinking of the well, till we reached a depth of about thirty feet. And the phrase, "living water," "living water," kept chiming through my soul like music from God, as I dug and hammered away!

CHAPTER LXVII.
RAIN FROM BELOW.

AT this depth the earth and coral began to be soaked with damp. I felt that we were nearing water. My soul had a faith that God would open a spring for us; but side by side with this faith was a strange terror that the water would be salt. So perplexing and mixed are even the highest experiences of the soul; the rose-flower of a perfect faith, set round and round with prickly thorns. One evening I said to the old Chief, "I think that Jehovah God will give us water to-morrow from that hole!"

The Chief said, "No, Missi; you will never see rain coming up from the earth on this Island. We wonder what is to be the end of this mad work of yours. We expect daily, if you reach water, to see you drop through into the sea and the sharks will eat you! That will be the end of it; death to you, and danger to us all."

I still answered, "Come to-morrow. I hope and believe that Jehovah God will send you the rain water up through the earth."

At the moment I knew I was risking much, and probably incurring sorrowful consequences, had no water been given; but I had faith that the Lord was leading me on, and I knew that I sought His glory, not my own.

Next morning, I went down again at daybreak and sank a narrow hole in the center about two feet deep. The perspiration broke over me with uncontrollable excitement, and I trembled through every limb, when the water rushed up and began to fill the hole. Muddy though it was, I eagerly tasted it, lapping it with my trembling hand, and then I almost fell upon my knees in that muddy bottom as my heart burst up in praise to the Lord. It was water! It was fresh water. It was living water from Jehovah's well! True, it was a little brackish, but nothing to speak of; and no spring in the desert, cooling the parched lips of a fevered pilgrim, ever appeared more worthy of being called a Well of God than did that water to me!

The Chiefs had assembled with their men near by. They waited on in eager expectancy. It was a rehearsal, in a small way, of the Israelites coming round, while Moses struck the rock and called for water. By and by, when I had praised the Lord, and my excitement was a little calmed, the mud being also greatly settled, I filled a jug, which I had taken down empty in the sight of them all, and ascending to the top called for them to come and see the rain which Jehovah God had given us through the well. They closed around me in haste, and gazed on it in superstitious fear. The old Chief shook it to see if it would spill, and then touched it to see if it felt like water. At last he tasted it, and rolling it in his mouth with joy for a moment, he swallowed it, and shouted, "Rain! Rain! Yes, it is Rain! But how did you get it?"

I repeated, "Jehovah my God gave it out of His own Earth in answer to our labors and prayers. Go and see it springing up for yourselves!"

Now, though every man there could climb the highest tree as swiftly and as fearlessly as a squirrel or an opossum, not one of them had courage to walk to the side and gaze down into that well. To them this was miraculous! But they were not without a resource that met the emergency. They agreed to take firm hold of each other by the hand, to place themselves in a long line, the foremost man to lean cautiously forward, gaze into the well, and then pass to the rear, and so on till all had seen "Jehovah's rain" far below. It was somewhat comical, yet far more pathetic, to stand by and watch their faces, as man after man peered down into the mystery, and then looked up at me in blank bewilderment! When all had seen it with their own very eyes, and were "weak with wonder," the old Chief exclaimed—

"Missi, wonderful, wonderful is the work of your Jehovah God! No god of Aniwa ever helped us in this way. The world is turned upside down since Jehovah came to Aniwa! But, Missi," continued he, after a pause that looked liked silent worship, "will it always rain up through the earth? or will it come and go like the rain from the clouds?"

I told them that I believed it would always continue there for our use, as a good gift from Jehovah.

"Well, but, Missi," replied the Chief some glimmering of self-interest beginning to strike his brain, "will you or your family drink it all, or shall we also have some?"

"You and all your people," I answered, "and all the people of the Island, may come and drink and carry away as much of it as you wish. I believe there will always be plenty for us all, and the more of it we can use the fresher it will be. That is the way with many of our Jehovah's best gifts to men, and for it and for all we praise His Name!"

"Then, Missi," said the Chief, "it will be our water, and we may all use it as our very own."

"Yes," I answered, "whenever you wish it, and as much as you need, both here and at your own houses, as far as it can possibly be made to go."

The Chief looked at me eagerly, fully convinced at length that the well contained a treasure, and exclaimed, "Missi, what can we do to help you now?"

I was thankful, indeed, to accept of the Chief's assistance, now sorely needed, and I said, "You have seen it fall in once already. If it falls again, it will conceal the rain from below which our God has given us. In order to preserve it for us and for our children in all time, we must build it round and round with great coral blocks from the bottom to the very top. I will now clear it out, and prepare the foundation for this wall of coral. Let every man and woman carry from the shore the largest block they can bring. It is well worth all the toil thus to preserve our great Jehovah's gift!"

Scarcely were my words uttered, when they rushed to the shore, with shoutings and songs of gladness; and soon every one was seen struggling under the biggest block of coral with which he dared to tackle. They lay like limestone rocks, broken up by the hurricanes, and rolled ashore in the arms of mighty billows; and in an incredibly short time scores of them were tumbled down for my use at the mouth of the well. Having prepared a foundation, I made ready a sort of bag-basket, into which every block was firmly tied and then let down to me by the pulley—a Native Teacher, a faithful fellow, cautiously guiding it. I received and placed each stone in its position, doing my poor best to wedge them one against the other, building circularly, and cutting them to the needed shape with my American ax. The wall is about three feet thick, and the masonry may be guaranteed to stand till the coral itself decays. I wrought incessantly, for fear of any further collapse, till I had it raised about twenty feet; and now, feeling secure, and my hands being dreadfully cut up, I intimated that I would rest a week or two, and finish the building then. But the Chief advanced and said—

"Missi, you have been strong to work. Your strength has fled. But rest here beside us; and just point out where each block is to be laid. We will lay them there, we will build them solidly behind like you. And no man will sleep till it is done."

With all their will and heart they started on the job; some carrying, some cutting and squaring the blocks, till the wall rose like magic, and a row of the hugest rocks laid round the top, bound all together, and formed the mouth of the well. Women, boys, and all wished to have a hand in building it, and it remains to this day, a solid wall of masonry, the circle being thirty-four feet deep, eight feet wide at the top, and six at the bottom. I floored it over with wood above all, and fixed the windlass and bucket, and there it stands as one of the greatest material blessings which the Lord has given to Aniwa. It rises and falls with the tide, though a third of a mile distant from the sea; and when, after using it, we tasted the pure fresh water on board the *Dayspring*, the latter seemed so insipid that I had to slip a little salt into my tea along with the sugar before I could enjoy it! All visitors are taken to see the well, as one of the wonders of Aniwa; and an Elder of the Native

Church said to me, on a recent visit, "But for that water, during the last two years of drought, we would have all been dead!"

Very strangely, though the Natives themselves have since tried to sink six or seven wells in the most likely places near their different villages, they have either come to coral rock which they could not pierce, or found only water that was salt. And they say amongst themselves, "Missi not only used pick and spade, but he prayed and cried to his God. We have learned to dig, but not how to pray, and therefore Jehovah will not give us the rain, from below!"

CHAPTER LXVIII.
THE OLD CHIEF'S SERMON.

THE well was now finished. The place was neatly fenced in. And the old Chief said, "Missi, I think I could help you next Sabbath. Will you let me preach a sermon on the well?"

"Yes," I at once replied, "if you will try to bring all the people to hear you."

"Missi, I will try," he eagerly promised. The news spread like wildfire that the Chief Namakei was to be Missionary on the next day for the Worship, and the people, under great expectancy, urged each other to come and hear what he had to say.

Sabbath came round. Aniwa assembled in what was for that island a great crowd. Namakei appeared dressed in shirt and kilt. He was so excited, and flourished his tomahawk about at such a rate, that it was rather lively work to be near him. I conducted short opening devotions, and then called upon Namakei. He rose at once, with eye flashing wildly, and his limbs twitching with emotion. He spoke to the following effect, swinging his tomahawk to enforce every eloquent gesticulation:—

"Friends of Namakei, men and women and children of Aniwa, listen to my words! Since Missi came here he has talked many strange things we could not understand—things things all too wonderful; and we said regarding many of them that they must be lies. White people might believe such nonsense, but we said that the black fellow knew better than to receive it. But of all his wonderful stories, we thought the strangest was about sinking down through the earth to get rain! Then we said to each other, The man's head is turned; he's gone mad. But the Missi prayed on and wrought on, telling us that Jehovah God heard and saw, and that his God would give him rain. Was he mad? Has he not got the rain deep down in the earth? We mocked at him; but the water was there all the same. We have laughed at other things which the Missi told us, because we could not see them. But from this day I believe that all he tells us about his Jehovah God is true. Some day our eyes will see it. For to-day we have seen the rain from the earth."

Then rising to a climax, first the one foot and then the other making the broken coral on the floor fly behind like a war-horse pawing the ground, he cried with great eloquence:—

"My people, the people of Aniwa, the world is turned upside down since the word of Jehovah came to this land! Who ever expected to see rain coming up through the earth? It has always come from the clouds! Wonderful is the work of this Jehovah God. No god of Aniwa ever answered prayers as the Missi's God has done. Friends of Namakei, all the powers of the world could not have forced us to believe that rain could be given from the depths of the earth, if we had not seen it with our eyes, felt it and tasted it as we here do. Now, by the help of Jehovah God the Missi brought that invisible rain to view, which we never before heard of or saw, and"—(beating his hand on his breast, he exclaimed):—

"Something here in my heart tells me that the Jehovah God does exist, the Invisible One, whom we never heard of nor saw till the Missi brought Him to our knowledge. The coral has been removed, the land has been cleared away, and lo! the water rises. Invisible till this day, yet all the same it was there, though our eyes were too weak. So I, your Chief, do now firmly believe that when I die, when the bits of coral and the heaps of dust are removed which now blind my old eyes, I shall then see the Invisible Jehovah God with my soul, as Missi tells me, not less surely than I have seen the rain from the earth below. From this day, my people, I must worship the God who has opened for us the well, and who fills us with rain from below. The gods of Aniwa cannot hear, cannot help us, like the God of Missi. Henceforth I am a follower of Jehovah God. Let every man that thinks with me go now and fetch the idols of Aniwa, the gods which our fathers feared, and cast them down at Missi's feet. Let us burn and bury and destroy these things of wood and stone, and let us be taught by the Missi how to serve God who can hear, the Jehovah who gave us the well, and who will give us every other blessing, for He sent His Son Jesus to die for us and bring us to Heaven. This is what the Missi has been telling us every day since he landed on Aniwa. We laughed at him, but now we believe him. The Jehovah God has sent us rain from the earth. Why should He not also send us His Son from Heaven? Namakei stands up for Jehovah!"

This address, and the Sinking of the Well, broke the back of Heathenism on Aniwa. That very afternoon, the old Chief and several of his people brought their idols and cast them down at my feet beside the door of our house. Oh, the intense excitement of the weeks that followed! Company after company came to the spot, loaded with their gods of wood and stone, and piled them up in heaps, amid the tears and sobs of some, and the shoutings of others, in which was heard the oft-repeated word, "Jehovah! Jehovah!" What could be burned, we cast into the flames; others we buried in pits twelve or fifteen feet deep; and some few, more likely than the rest to feed or awaken superstition, we sank far out into the deep sea. Let no Heathen eyes ever gaze on them again!

One of the very first steps in Christian discipline to which they readily and almost unanimously took was the asking of God's blessing on every meal and praising the great Jehovah for their daily bread. Whosoever did not do so was regarded as a Heathen. (Query: how many white Heathens are there?) The next step, and it was taken in a manner as if by some common consent that was not less surprising than joyful, was a form of Family Worship every morning and evening. Doubtless the prayers were often very queer, and mixed up with many remaining superstitions; but they were prayers to the great Jehovah, the compassionate Father, the Invisible One—no longer to gods of stone!

Necessarily these were the conspicuous features of our life as Christians in their midst—morning and evening Family Prayer, and Grace at Meat; and hence, most naturally, their instinctive adoption and imitation of the same as the first outward tokens of Christian discipline. Every house in which there was not Prayer to God in the family was known thereby to be Heathen. This was a direct and practical evidence of the New Religion; and, so far as it goes (and that is very far indeed, where there is any sincerity beneath it), the test was one about which there could be no mistake on either side.

A third conspicuous feature stood out distinctly and at once,—the change as to the Lord's Day. Village after village followed in this also the example of the Mission House. All ordinary occupation ceased. Sabbath was spoken of as the Day for Jehovah. Saturday came to be called "Cooking Day," referring to the extra preparations for the coming day of rest and worship. They believed that it was Jehovah's will to keep the first day holy. The reverse was a distinctive mark of Heathenism.

The first traces of a new Social Order began to rise visibly on the delighted eye. The whole inhabitants, young and old, now attended School,—three generations sometimes at the one copy or A B C book! Thefts, quarrels, crimes, etc., were settled now, not by club law, but by fine or bonds or lash, as agreed upon by the Chiefs and their people. Everything was rapidly and surely becoming "New" under the influence of the leaven of Jesus. Industry increased. Huts and plantations were safe. Formerly every man, in traveling, carried with him all his valuables; now they were secure, left at home.

Even a brood of fowls or a litter of pigs would be carried in bags on their person in Heathen days. Hence at Church we had sometimes lively episodes, the chirruping of chicks, the squealing of piggies, and the barking of puppies, one gaily responding to the other, as we sang, or prayed, or preached the Gospel! Being glad to see the Natives there, even with all their belongings, we carefully refrained from finding fault; but the thread of devotion was sometimes apt to slip through one's fingers, especially when the conflict of the owner to silence a baby pig inspired the little wretch to drown everything in a long-sustained and high-pitched scream.

The natives, finding this state of matters troublesome to themselves and disagreeable all round, called a General Assembly, unanimously condemned dishonesty, agreed upon severe fines and punishments for every act of theft, and covenanted to stand by each other in putting it down. The chiefs, however found this a long and difficult task, but they held at it under the inspiration of the gospel and prevailed. Even the trials and difficulties with which they met were overruled by God, in assisting them to form by the light of their own experience a simple code of Social Laws, fitted to repress the crimes there prevailing, and to encourage the virtues specially needing to be cultivated there. Heathen Worship was gradually extinguished; and, though no one was compelled to come to Church, every person on Aniwa, without exception, became ere many years an avowed worshipper of Jehovah God. Again, "O Galilean, Thou hast conquered!"

CHAPTER LXIX.
THE FIRST BOOK AND THE NEW EYES.

THE printing of my first Aniwan book was a great event, not so much for the toil and worry which it cost me, though that was enough to have broken the heart of many a compositor, as rather for the joy it gave to the old Chief Namakei.

The break-up at Tanna had robbed me of my own neat little printing-press. I had since obtained at Aneityum the remains of one from Erromanga, that had belonged to the murdered Gordon. But the supply of letters, in some cases, was so deficient that I could print only four pages at a time; and, besides, bits of the press were wanting, and I had first to manufacture substitutes from scraps of iron and wood. I managed, however, to make it go, and by and by it did good service. By it I printed our Aniwan Hymn-Book, a portion of Genesis in Aniwan, a small book in Erromangan for the second Gordon, and some other little things.

The old Chief had eagerly helped me in translating and preparing this first book. He had a great desire "to hear it speak," as he graphically expressed it. It was made up chiefly of short passages from the Scriptures that might help me to introduce them to the treasures of Divine truth and love. Namakei came to me, morning after morning, saying, "Missi, is it done? Can it speak?"

At last I was able to answer, "Yes!"

The old Chief eagerly responded, "Does it speak my words?"

I said, "It does."

With rising interest, Namakei exclaimed, "Make it speak to me, Missi! Let me hear it speak."

I read to him a part of the book, and the old man fairly shouted in an ecstasy of joy, "It does speak! It speaks my own language, too! Oh, give it to me!"

He grasped it hurriedly, turned it all round every way, pressed it to his bosom, and then, closing it with a look of great disappointment, handed it back to me, saying, "Missi, I cannot make it speak! It will never speak to me."

"No," said I; "you don't know how to read it yet, how to make it speak to you; but I will teach you to read, and then it will speak to you as it does to me."

"O Missi, dear Missi, show me how to make it speak!" persisted the bewildered Chief. He was straining his eyes so, that I suspected they were dim with age, and could not see the letters. I looked out for him a pair of spectacles, and managed to fit him well. He was much afraid of putting them on at first, manifestly in dread of some sort of sorcery. At last, when they were properly placed, he saw the letters and everything so clearly that he exclaimed in great excitement and joy—

"I see it all now! This is what you told us about Jesus. He opened the eyes of a blind man. The word of Jesus has just come to Aniwa. He has sent me these glass eyes. I have gotten back again the sight that I had when a boy. O Missi, make the book speak to me now!"

I walked out with him to the public Village Ground. There I drew A B C in large characters upon the dust, showed him the same letters in the book, and left him to compare them, and find out how many occurred on the first page. Fixing these in his mind, he came running to me, and said, "I have lifted up A B C. They are here in my head and I will hold them fast. Give me other three."

This was repeated time after time. He mastered the whole Alphabet, and soon began to spell out the smaller words. Indeed, he came so often, getting me to read it over and over, that before he himself could read it freely, he had it word for word committed to memory. When strangers passed him, or young people came around, he would get out the little book, and say, "Come, and I will let you hear how the book speaks our own Aniwan words. You say, it is hard to learn to read and make it speak. But be strong to try! If an old man like me has done it, it ought to be much easier for you."

One day I heard him read to a company with wonderful fluency. Taking the book, I asked him to show me how he had learned to read so quickly. Immediately I perceived that he could recite the whole from memory! He became our right-hand helper in the Conversion of Aniwa.

Next after God's own Word, perhaps the power of Music was most amazingly blessed in opening up our way. Amongst many other illustrations, I may mention how Namakei's wife was won. The old lady positively shuddered at coming near the Mission House, and dreaded being taught anything. One day she was induced to draw near the door, and fixing a hand on either post, and gazing inwards, she exclaimed, "Awái, Missi! Kái, Missi!"—the Native cry for unspeakable wonder. Mrs. Paton began to play on the harmonium, and sang a simple hymn in the old woman's language. Manifestly charmed, she drew nearer and nearer, and drank in the music, as it were, at every pore of her being. At last she ran off, and we thought it was with fright, but it was to call together all the women and girls from her village "to hear the *bokis* sing!" (Having no *x*, the word *box* is pronounced thus.) She returned with them all at her heels. They listened with dancing eyes. And ever after the sound of a hymn, and the song of the *bokis*, made them flock freely to class or meeting.

Being myself as nearly as possible destitute of the power of singing, all my work would have been impaired and sadly hindered, and the joyous side of the Worship and Service of Jehovah could not have been presented to the Natives, but for the gift bestowed by the Lord on my dear wife. She led our songs of praise, both in the Family and in the Church, and that was the first avenue by which the New Religion winged its way into the heart of Cannibal and Savage.

The old Chief was particularly eager that this same aged lady, his wife Yauwaki, should be taught to read. But her sight was far gone. So, one day, he brought her to me, saying, "Missi, can you give my wife also a pair of new glass eyes like mine? She tries to learn, but she cannot see the letters. She tries to sew, but she pricks her finger, and throws away the needle, saying, 'The ways of the white people are not good!' If she could get a pair of glass eyes, she would be in a new world like Namakei." In my bundle I found a pair that suited her. She was in positive terror about putting them on her face, but at last she cried with delight, "Oh, my new eyes! my new eyes! I have the sight of a little girl. Oh, my new eyes!"

CHAPTER LXX.
A ROOF-TREE FOR JESUS.

AT first we moved about amongst the Natives from village to village, acquired their language, and taught them everywhere,—by the roadside, under the shade of a tree, or on the public Tillage Ground. Our old Native Hut, when we removed to the Mission House formerly referred to, was also used for all sorts of public meetings. Feeling by and by, however, that the time had come to interest them in building a new Church, and that it would be every way helpful, I laid the proposal before them, carefully explaining that for this work no one would be paid, that the Church was for all the Islanders and for the Worship alone, and that every one must build purely for the love of Jesus.

I told them that God would be pleased with such materials as they had to give, that they must not begin till they had divided the work and counted the cost, and that for my part I would do all that I could to direct and help, and would supply the sinnet (= cocoanut fiber rope) which I had brought from Aneityum, and the nails from Sydney.

They held meeting after meeting throughout the Island. Chiefs made long speeches; orators chanted their palavers; and warriors acted their part by waving of club and tomahawk. An unprecedented friendliness sprang up amongst them. They agreed to sink every quarrel, and unite in building the first Church on Aniwa,—one Chief only holding back. Women and children began to gather and prepare the sugar-cane leaf for thatch. Men searched for and cut down suitable trees.

The Church measured sixty-two feet by twenty-four. The wall was twelve feet high. The studs were of hard ironwood, and were each by tenon and mortise fastened into six ironwood trees forming the upper wall plates. All were not only nailed, but strongly tied together by sinnet-rope, so as to resist the hurricanes. The roof was supported by four huge ironwood trees, and a fifth of equally hard wood, sunk about eight feet into the ground, surrounded by building at the base, and forming massive pillars. There were two doorways and eight window spaces; the floor was laid with white coral, broken small, and covered with cocoanut tree leaf-mats, on which the people sat. I had a small platform, floored and surrounded with reeds; and Mrs. Paton had a seat enclosing the harmonium, also made of reeds and in keeping. Great harmony prevailed all the time, and no mishap marred the work. One hearty fellow fell from the roof-tree to the ground, and was badly stunned. But, jumping up, he shook himself, and saying—"I was working for Jehovah! He has saved me from being hurt!"—he mounted the roof again and went on cheerily with his work.

But our pride in this New Church soon met with a dreadful blow. That very season a terrific hurricane leveled it with the ground. After much wailing, the principal Chief, in a public Assembly, said, "Let us not weep, like boys over their broken bows and arrows! Let us be strong, and build a yet stronger Church for Jehovah."

By our counsel, ten days were spent first in repairing houses and fences, and saving food from the plantations, many of which had been swept into utter ruin. Then they assembled on the appointed day. A hymn was sung. God's blessing was invoked, and all the work was dedicated afresh to Him. Days were spent in taking the iron wood roof to pieces, and saving everything that could be saved. The work was allocated equally amongst the villages, and a wholesome emulation was created. One Chief still held back. After a while, I visited him and personally invited his help,—telling him that it was God's House, and for all the people of Aniwa; and that if he and his people did not do their part, the others would cast it in their teeth that they had no share in the House of God. He yielded to my appeal, and entered vigorously upon the work.

One large tree was still needed to complete the couples, and could nowhere be found. The work was at a standstill; for, though the size was now reduced to fifty feet by twenty-two, the roof lowered by four feet, and there was still plenty of smaller wood on Aniwa, the larger trees were apparently exhausted. One morning, however, we were awakened at early daybreak by the shouting and singing of a company of men, carrying a great black tree to the Church, with this same Chief dancing before them, leading the singing, and beating time with the flourish of his tomahawk. Determined not to be beaten, though late in the field, he had lifted the roof-tree out of his own house, as black as soot could make it, and was carrying it to complete the couplings. The rest of the builders shouted against this. All the other wood of the Church was white and clean, and they would not have this black tree, conspicuous in the very center of all. But I praised the old Chief for what he had done, and hoped he and his people would come and worship Jehovah under his own roof-tree. At this all were delighted! and the work went on apace, with many songs and shoutings.

Whenever the Church was roofed in, we met in it for Public Worship. Coral was being got and burned, and preparations made for plastering the walls. The Natives were sharp enough to notice that I was not putting up the bell; and suspicions arose that I kept it back in order to take it with me when I returned to Tanna. It was a beautiful Church bell, cast and sent out by our dear friend, James Taylor, Esq., Birkenhead. The Aniwans, therefore, gave me no rest till I agreed to have it hung on their new Church. They found a large ironwood tree near the shore, cut a road for half a mile through the bush, tied poles across it every few feet, and with shouts lifted it bodily on their shoulders—six men or so at each pole—and never set it down again till they reached the Church; for as one party got exhausted, others were ready to rush in and relieve them at every stage of the journey. The two old Chiefs, flourishing their tomahawks, went capering in front of all the rest, and led the song to which they marched, joyfully bearing their load. They dug a deep hole, into which to sink it; I squared the top and screwed on the bell; then we raised the tree by ropes, letting it sink into the hole, and built it round eight feet deep with coral blocks and lime; and there from its top swings and rings ever since the Church bell of Aniwa.

CHAPTER LXXI.
"KNOCK THE TEVIL OUT!"

ONE of the last attempts ever made on my life resulted, by God's blessing, in great good to us all and to the work of the Lord. It was when Nourai, one of Nasi's men, struck at me again and again with the barrel of his musket; but I evaded the blows, till rescued by the women—the men looking on stupefied. After he escaped into the bush I assembled our people, and said, "If you do not now try to stop this bad conduct, I shall leave Aniwa, and go to some island where my life will be protected."

Next morning at daybreak, about one hundred men arrived at my house, and in answer to my query why they came armed they replied, "We are now going to that village where the men of wicked conduct are gathered together. We will find out why they sought your life, and we will rebuke their Sacred Man for pretending to cause hurricanes and diseases. We cannot go unarmed. We will not suffer you to go alone. We are your friends and the friends of the Worship. And we are resolved to stand by you, and you must go at our head to-day!"

In great perplexity, yet believing that my presence might prevent bloodshed, I allowed myself to be placed at their head. The old Chief followed next, then a number of fiery young men; then all the rest, single file, along the narrow path. At a sudden turn, as we neared their village, Nourai, who had attacked me the Sabbath day before, and his brother were seen lurking with their muskets; but our young men made a rush in front, and they disappeared into the bush.

We took possession of the Village Public Ground; and the Chief, the Sacred Man, and others soon assembled. A most characteristic Native Palaver followed. Speeches, endless speeches, were fired by them at each other. My friends declared, in every conceivable form of language and of graphic illustration, that they were resolved at any cost to defend me and the Worship of Jehovah, and that they would as one man punish every attempt to injure me or take my life. The orator, Taia, exclaimed, "You think that Missi is here alone, and that you can do with him as you please! No! We are now all Missi's men. We will fight for him and his rather than see him injured. Every one that attacks him attacks us. That is finished to-day!"

In the general scolding, the Sacred Man had special attention for pretending to cause hurricanes. One pointed out that he had himself a stiff knee, and argued, "If he can make a hurricane, why can't he restore the joint of his own knee? It is surely easier to do the one than the other!"

The Natives laughed heartily, and taunted him. Meantime he sat looking down to the earth in sullen silence; and a ludicrous episode ensued. His wife, a big, strong woman, scolded him roundly for the trouble he had brought them all into; and then, getting indignant as well as angry, she seized a huge cocoanut leaf out of the bush, and with the butt end thereof began thrashing his shoulders vigorously as she poured out the vials of her wrath in torrents of words, always winding up with the cry, "I'll knock the Tevil out of him! He'll not try hurricanes again!"

The woman was a Malay, as all the Aniwans were. Had a Papuan woman on Tanna or Erromanga dared such a thing, she would have been killed on the spot. But even on Aniwa, the unwonted spectacle of a wife beating her husband created uproarious amusement. At length I remonstrated, saying, "You had better stop now! You don't want to kill him, do you? You seem to have knocked 'the Tevil' pretty well out of him now! You see how he receives it all in silence, and repents of all his bad talk and bad conduct."

They exacted from him a solemn promise as to the making of no more diseases or hurricanes, and that he would live at peace with his neighbors. The offending villagers at length presented a large quantity of sugar-cane and food to us as a peace-offering; and we returned, praising God that the whole day's scolding had ended in talk, not blood. The result was every way most helpful. Our friends knew their strength and took courage. Our enemies were disheartened and afraid. We saw the balance growing heavier every day on the side of Jesus; and our souls blessed the Lord.

CHAPTER LXXII.
THE CONVERSION OF YOUWILI.

THESE events suggest to me another incident of those days, full at once of trial and of joy. It pertains to the story of our young Chief Youwili. From the first, and for long, he was most audacious and troublesome. Observing that for several days no Natives had come near the Mission House, I asked the old Chief if he knew why, and he answered, "Youwili has *tabooed* the paths, and threatens death to any one who breaks through it."

I at once replied, "Then I conclude that you all agree with him, and wish me to leave. We are here only to teach you and your people. If he has power to prevent that we shall leave with the *Dayspring*."

The old Chief called the people together, and they came to me, saying, "Our anger is strong against Youwili. Go with us and break down the *taboo*. We will assist and protect you."

I went at their head and removed it. It consisted simply of reeds stuck into the ground, with twigs and leaves and fiber tied to each in a peculiar way, in a circle round the Mission House. The Natives had an extraordinary dread of violating the taboo, and believed that it meant death to the offender or to some one of his family. All present entered into a bond to punish on the spot any man who attempted to replace the *taboo* or to revenge its removal. Thus a mortal blow was publicly struck at this most miserable superstition, which had caused bloodshed and misery untold.

One day, thereafter, I was engaged in clearing away the bush around the Mission House, having purchased and paid for the land for the very purpose of opening it up, when suddenly Youwili appeared and menacingly forbade me to proceed. For the sake of peace I for the time desisted. But he went straight to my fence, and with his tomahawk cut down the portion in front of our house, also some bananas planted there—the usual declaration of war, intimating that he only awaited his opportunity similarly to cut down me and mine. We saw the old Chief and his men planting themselves here and there to guard us, and the Natives prowling about armed and excited. On calling them, they explained the meaning of what Youwili had done, and that they were determined to protect us. I said. "This must not continue. Are you to permit one young fool to defy us all, and break up the Lord's work on Aniwa? If you cannot righteously punish him, I will shut myself up in my house and withdraw from all attempts to teach or help you, till the vessel comes, and then I can leave the island."

Now that they had begun really to love us, and to be anxious to learn more, this was always my most powerful argument. We retired into the Mission House. The people surrounded our doors and windows and pleaded with us. After long silence, we replied, "You know our resolution. It is for you now to decide. Either you must control that foolish young man, or we must go!"

Much speech-making, as usual, followed. The people resolved to seize and punish Youwili; but he fled, and had hid himself in the bush. Coming to me, the Chief said, "It is left to you to say what shall be Youwili's punishment. Shall we kill him?"

I replied firmly, "Certainly not! Only for murder can life be lawfully taken away."

"What then?" they continued. "Shall we burn his houses and destroy his plantations?"

I answered, "No."

"Shall we bind him and beat him?"

"No."

"Shall we place him in a canoe, thrust him out to sea, and let him drown or escape as he may?"

"No! by no means."

"Then, Missi," said they, "these are our ways of punishing. What other punishment remains that Youwili cares for?"

I replied, "Make him with his own hands, and alone, put up a new fence, and restore all that he has destroyed; and make him promise publicly that he will cease all evil conduct towards us. That will satisfy me."

This idea of punishment seemed to tickle them greatly. The Chiefs reported our words to the Assembly; and the Natives laughed and cheered, as if it were a capital joke! They cried aloud, "It is good! Obey the word of the Missi."

After considerable hunting, the young Chief was found. They brought him to the Assembly and scolded him severely and told him their sentence. He was surprised by the nature of the punishment, and cowed by the determination of the people.

"To-morrow," said he, "I will fully repair the fence. Never again will I oppose the Missi. His word is good."

By daybreak next morning Youwili was diligently repairing what he had broken down, and before evening he had everything made right better than it was before. While he toiled away, some fellows of his own rank twitted him, saying, "Youwili, you found it easier to cut down Missi's fence than to repair it again. You will not repeat that in a hurry!"

But he heard all in silence. Others passed with averted heads, and he knew they were laughing at him. He made everything tight and then left without uttering a single word. My heart yearned after the poor fellow, but I thought it better to let his own mind work away, on its new ideas as to punishment and revenge, for a little longer by itself alone. I instinctively felt that Youwili was beginning to turn, that the Christ-Spirit had touched his darkly-groping soul. My doors were now thrown open, and every good work went on as before. We resolved to leave Youwili entirely to Jesus, setting apart a portion of our prayer every day for the enlightenment and conversion of the young Chief, on whom all other means had been exhausted apparently in vain.

A considerable time elapsed. No sign came, and our prayers seemed to fail. But one day, I was toiling between the shafts of a hand-cart, assisted by two boys, drawing it along from the shore loaded with coral blocks. Youwili came rushing from his house, three hundred yards or so off the path, and said, "Missi, that is too hard for you. Let me be your helper!"

Without waiting for a reply, he ordered the two boys to seize one rope, while he grasped the other, threw it over his shoulder and started off, pulling with the strength of a horse. My heart rose in gratitude, and I wept with joy as I followed him. I knew that that yoke was but a symbol of the yoke of Christ, which Youwili with his change of heart was beginning to carry! Truly there is only one way of regeneration, being born again by the power of the Spirit of God, the new heart; but there are many ways of conversation, of outwardly turning to the Lord, of taking the actual first step that shows on whose side we are.

Like those of old praying for the deliverance of Peter, and who could not believe their ears and eyes when Peter knocked and walked in amongst them, so we could scarcely believe our eyes and ears when Youwili became a disciple of Jesus, though we had been praying for his conversion every day. His once sullen countenance became literally bright with inner light. His wife came immediately for a book and a dress saying, "Youwili sent me. His opposition to the Worship is over now. I am to attend Church and School. He is coming too. He wants to learn how to be strong, like you, for Jehovah and for Jesus."

Oh, Jesus! to Thee alone be all the glory. Thou hast the key to unlock every heart that Thou hast created.

CHAPTER LXXIII.
FIRST COMMUNION ON ANIWA.

AND this leads me to relate the story of our First Communion on Aniwa. It was Sabbath, 24th October 1869; and surely the Angels of God and the Church of the Redeemed in Glory were amongst the "great cloud of witnesses" who eagerly "peered" down upon the scene,—when we sat around the Lord's Table and partook the memorials of His body and blood with those few souls rescued out of the Heathen World. My Communicants' Class had occupied me now a considerable time. The conditions of attendance at this early stage were explicit, and had to be made very severe, and only twenty were admitted to the roll. At the final examination only twelve gave evidence of understanding what they were doing, and of having given their hearts to the service of the Lord Jesus. At their own urgent desire, and after every care in examining and instructing, they were solemnly dedicated in prayer to be baptized and admitted to the Holy Table. On that Lord's Day, after the usual opening Service, I gave a short and careful exposition of the Ten Commandments and of the Way of Salvation according to the Gospel. The twelve Candidates then stood up before all the inhabitants there assembled; and, after a brief exhortation to them as Converts, I put to them the two questions that follow, and each gave an affirmative reply, "Do you, in accordance with your profession of the Christian Faith, and your promises before God and the people, wish me now to baptize you?"

And—"Will you live henceforth for Jesus only, hating all sin and trying to love and serve your Saviour?"

Then, beginning with the old Chief, the twelve came forward, and I baptized them one by one according to the Presbyterian usage. Two of them had also little children, and they were at the same time baptized, and received as the lambs of the flock. Solemn prayer was then offered, and in the name of the Holy Trinity the Church of Christ on Aniwa was formally constituted. I addressed them on the words of the Holy Institution—1 Corinthians xi. 23—and then, after the prayer of Thanksgiving and Consecration, administered the Lord's Supper, the first time since the Island of Aniwa was heaved out of its coral depths! Mrs. M'nair, my wife, and myself, along with six Aneityumese Teachers, communicated with the newly baptized twelve. And I think, if ever in all my Earthly experience, on that day I might truly add the blessed words—"Jesus in the midst."

The whole Service occupied nearly three hours. The Islanders looked on with a wonder whose unwonted silence was almost painful to bear. Many were led to inquire carefully about everything they saw, so new and strange. For the first time the Dorcas Street Sabbath School Teachers' gift from South Melbourne Presbyterian Church was put to use—a new Communion Service of silver. They gave it in faith that we would require it, and in such we received it. And now the day had come and gone! For three years we had toiled and prayed and taught for this. At the moment when I put the bread and wine into those dark hands, once stained with the blood of Cannibalism, but now stretched out to receive and partake the emblems and seals of the Redeemer's love, I had a foretaste of the joy of Glory that well-nigh broke my heart to pieces. I shall never taste a deeper bliss till I gaze on the glorified face of Jesus Himself.

On the afternoon of that Communion Day an open-air Prayer Meeting was held under the shade of the great banyan tree in front of our Church. Seven of the new Church members there led the people in prayer to Jesus, a hymn being sung after each. My heart was so full of joy that I could do little else but weep. Oh, I wonder, I wonder, when I see so many good Ministers at home, crowding each other and treading on each other's heels, whether they would not part with all their home privileges, and go out to the Heathen World and reap a joy like this—"the joy of the Lord."

CHAPTER LXXIV.
THE NEW SOCIAL ORDER.

THE new Social Order, referred to already in its dim beginnings, rose around us like a sweet-scented flower. I never interfered directly, unless expressly called upon or appealed to. The two principal Chiefs were impressed with the idea that there was but one law—the Will of God; and one rule for them and their people as Christians—to please the Lord Jesus. In every difficulty they consulted me. I explained to them and read in their hearing the very words of Holy Scripture, showing what appeared to me to be the will of God and what would please the Saviour; and then sent them away to talk it over with their people, and to apply these principles of the Word of God as wisely as they could according to their circumstances. Our own part of the work went on very joyfully, notwithstanding occasional trying and painful incidents. Individual cases of greed and selfishness and vice brought us many a bitter pang. But the Lord never lost patience with us, and we durst not therefore lose patience with them! We trained the Teachers, we translated and printed and expounded the Scriptures, we ministered to the sick and dying; we dispensed medicines every day, we taught them the use of tools, we advised them as to laws and penalties; and the New Society grew and developed, and bore amidst all its imperfections some traces of the fair Kingdom of God amongst men.

Our life and work will reveal itself to the reader if I briefly outline a Sabbath Day on Aniwa. Breakfast is partaken of immediately after daylight. The Church bell then rings, and ere it stops every worshiper is seated. The Natives are guided in starting by the sunrise, and are forward from farthest corners at this early hour. The first Service is over in about an hour; there is an interval of twenty minutes; the bell is again rung, and the second Service begins. We follow the ordinary Presbyterian ritual; but in every Service I call upon an Elder or a Church Member to lead in one of the prayers, which they do with great alacrity and with much benefit to all concerned.

As the last worshiper leaves, at close of second Service, the bell is sounded twice very deliberately, and that is the signal for the opening of my Communicants' Class. I carefully expound the Church's Shorter Catechism, and show how its teachings are built upon Holy Scripture, applying each truth to the conscience and the life. This class is conducted all the year round; and from it, step by step, our Church Members are drawn as the Lord opens up their way, the most of them attending two full years at least before being admitted to the Lord's Table. This discipline accounts for the fact that so very few of our baptized converts have ever fallen away—as few in proportion, I verily believe, as in Churches at home. Meantime, many of the Church members have been holding a prayer-meeting amongst themselves in the adjoining School,—a thing started of their own free accord,—in which they invoke God's blessing on all the work and worship of the day.

Having snatched a brief meal of tea, or a cold dinner cooked on Saturday, the bell rings within an hour, and our Sabbath School assembles,—in which the whole inhabitants, young and old, take part, myself superintending and giving the address, as well as questioning on the lesson, Mrs. Paton teaching a large class of adult women, and the Elders and best readers instructing the ordinary classes for about half-an-hour or so.

About one o'clock the School is closed, and we then start off on our village tours. An experienced Elder, with several Teachers, takes one side of the Island this Sabbath, I with another company taking the other side, and next Sabbath we reverse the order. A short Service is conducted in the open air, or in Schoolrooms, at every village that can be reached and on their return they report to me cases of sickness, or any signs of progress in the work of the Lord. The whole Island is thus steadily and methodically evangelized.

As the sun is setting I am creeping home from my village tour; and when darkness begins to approach, the canoe drum is beat at every village, and the people assemble under the banyan tree for evening village prayers. The Elder or Teacher presides. Five or six hymns are joyously sung, and five or six short prayers offered between, and thus the evening hour passes happily in the fellowship of God. On a calm evening, after Christianity had fairly taken hold of the people, and they loved to sing over and over again their favorite hymns, these village prayer-meetings formed a most blessed close to every day, and set the far-distant bush echoing with the praises of God.

Nor is our week-day life less crowded or busy, though in different ways. At gray dawn on Monday, and every morning, the *Tavaka* (= the canoe drum) is struck in every village on Aniwa. The whole inhabitants turn in to the early School, which lasts about an hour and a half, and then the Natives are off to their plantations. Having partaken of breakfast, I then spend my forenoon in translating or printing, or visiting the sick, or whatever else is most urgent. About two o'clock the Natives return from their work, bathe in the sea, and dine off cocoanut, breadfruit, or anything else that comes handily in the way. At three o'clock the bell rings, and the afternoon School for the Teachers and the more advanced learners then occupy my wife and myself for about an hour and a half. After this, the Natives spend their time in fishing or lounging or preparing supper,—which is amongst them always *the* meal of the day. Towards sundown the *Tavaka* sounds again, and the day closes amid the echoes of village prayers from under their several banyan trees.

Thus day after day and week after week passed over us on Aniwa; and much the same on all the Islands where the Missionary has found a home. In many respects it is a simple and happy and beautiful life; and the man whose heart is full of things that are dear to Jesus, feels no desire to exchange it for the poor frivolities of what calls itself "Society," which seems to find its life in pleasures that Christ cannot be asked to share, and in which, therefore, Christians should have neither lot nor part.

CHAPTER LXXV.
THE ORPHANS AND THEIR BISCUITS.

THE habits of morning and evening Family Prayer and of Grace at Meat took a very wonderful hold upon the people; and became, as I have shown elsewhere, a distinctive badge of Christian versus Heathen. This was strikingly manifested during a time of bitter scarcity that befell us. I heard a father, for instance, at his hut door, with his family around him, reverently blessing God for the food provided for them, and for all His mercies in Christ Jesus. Drawing near and conversing with them, I found that their meals consisted of fig leaves which they had gathered and cooked—a poor enough dish, but hunger makes a healthy appetite, and contentment is a grateful relish.

During the same period of privation, my Orphans suffered badly also. Once they came to me, saying, "Missi, we are very hungry."

I replied, "So am I, dear children, and we have no more white food till the *Dayspring* comes."

They continued, "Missi, you have two beautiful fig-trees. Will you let us take one feast of the young and tender leaves? We will not injure branch or fruit."

I answered, "Gladly, my children, take your fill!"

In a twinkling each child was perched upon a branch; and they feasted there happy as squirrels. Every night we prayed for the vessel, and in the morning our Orphan boys rushed to the coral rocks and eagerly scanned the sea for an answer. Day after day they returned with sad faces, saying, "Missi, *Tavaka jimra*!" (= No vessel yet).

But at gray dawn of a certain day we were awoke by the boys shouting from the shore and running for the Mission House with the cry,—"*Tavaka oa! Tavaka oa!*" (= The vessel, hurrah!)

We arose at once, and the boy exclaimed, "Missi, she is not our own vessel, but we think she carries her flag. She has three masts, and our *Dayspring* only two!"

I looked through my glass, and saw that they were discharging goods into the vessel's boats; and the children, when I told them that boxes and bags and casks were being sent on shore, shouted and danced with delight. As the first boat-load was discharged, the Orphans surrounded me, saying,

"Missi, here is a cask that rattles like biscuits? Will you let us take it to the Mission House?"

I told them to do so if they could; and in a moment it was turned into the path, and the boys had it flying before them, some tumbling and hurting their knees, but up and at it again, and never pausing till it rolled up at the door of our Storehouse. On returning I found them all around it, and they said, "Missi, have you forgotten what you promised us?"

I said, "What did I promise you?"

They looked very disappointed and whispered to each other, "Missi has forgot!"

"Forgot what?" inquired I.

"Missi," they answered, "you promised that when the vessel came you would give each of us a biscuit."

"Oh," I replied, "I did not forget; I only wanted to see if you remembered it?"

They laughed, saying, "No fear of that, Missi! Will you soon open the cask? We are dying for biscuits."

At once I got hammer and tools, knocked off the hoops, took out the end, and then gave girls and boys a biscuit each. To my surprise, they all stood round, biscuit in hand, but not one beginning to eat.

"What," I exclaimed, "you are dying for biscuits! Why don't you eat? Are you expecting another?"

One of the eldest said, "We will first thank God for sending us food, and ask Him to bless it to us all."

And this was done in their own simple and beautiful childlike way; and then they did eat, and enjoyed their food as a gift from the Heavenly Father's hand. (Is there any child reading this, or hearing it read, who never thanks God or asks Him to bless daily bread? Then is that child not a white Heathen?) We ourselves at the Mission House could very heartily rejoice with the dear Orphans. For some weeks past our European food had been all exhausted, except a little tea, and the cocoanut had been our chief support. It was beginning to tell against us. Our souls rose in gratitude to the Lord, who had sent us these fresh provisions that we might love Him better and serve Him more.

The children's sharp eyes had read correctly. It was not the *Dayspring*. Our brave little ship, as I afterwards learned, had gone to wreck on 6th January 1873; and this vessel was the *Paragon*, chartered to bring down our supplies.

Alas! the wreck had gone by auction sale to a French slaving company, who cut a passage through the coral reef, and had the vessel again floating in the Bay,—elated at the prospect of employing our Mission Ship in the blood-stained *Tanaka*-traffic (= a mere euphemism for South Sea slavery)! Our souls sank in horror and concern. Many Natives would unwittingly trust themselves to the *Dayspring* and revenge would be taken on us, as was done on noble Bishop Patteson, when the deception was found out. What could be done? Nothing but cry to God, which all the friends of our Mission did day and night, not without tears, as we thought of the possible degradation of our noble little ship. Listen! The French Slavers, anchoring their prize in the Bay, and greatly rejoicing, went ashore to celebrate the event. They drank and feasted and reveled. But that night a mighty storm arose, the old *Dayspring* dragged her anchor, and at daybreak she was seen again on the reef, but this time with her back broken in two and for ever unfit for service, either fair or foul. Oh, white winged Virgin, daughter of the waves, better for thee, as for thy human sisters, to die and pass away than to suffer pollution and live on in disgrace!

CHAPTER LXXVI.
THE FINGER-POSTS OF GOD.

I HAD often said that I would not again leave my beloved work on the Islands unless compelled to do so either by the breakdown of health, or by the loss of our Mission Ship and my services being required to assist in providing another. Very strange, that in this one season both of these events befell us! During the hurricanes, from January to April 1873, when the *Dayspring* was wrecked, we lost a darling child by death, my dear wife had a protracted illness, and I was brought very low with severe rheumatic fever. I was reduced so far that I could not speak, and was reported as dying. The Captain of a vessel, having seen me, called at Tanna, and spoke of me as in all probability dead by that time. Our unfailing and ever-beloved friends and fellow-Missionaries, Mr. and Mrs. Watt, at once started from Kwamera, in their open boat, and rowed and sailed thirty miles to visit us. But a few days before they arrived I had fallen into a long and sound sleep, out of which, when I awoke, consciousness had again returned to me. I had got the turn; there was no further relapse; but when I did regain a little strength, my weakness was so great that I had to travel about on crutches for many a day.

In the circumstances of our baby Lena's death, every form of heartrending tenderness seemed to meet. On Friday, 28th March, at 3 A.M. she came from God, and seemed to both of us the Angel-child of all our flock. Alas, on Saturday I was seized with sciatica, so dreadful and agonizing, that I had to be borne to my bed, and could not stir a limb any more than if my back had been broken. My dear wife struggled to attend to the baby, with such help as Native girls could give; and I directed the Teachers about the Services in Church next Sunday, the first time as yet that I had been unable to appear and lead them. From the beds where we lay, my wife and I could hear each other's voices, and tried to console one another in our sorrowful and helpless state. On Tuesday, 1st April, the child was bright and vigorous; but the mother's strength had been overtaxed, and she fell back, fainting in her bed, when helping to dress the baby. Next morning, to our dismay, there were symptoms of wheezing and feverishness in the little darling. All due measures were at once taken to check these; and Williag, an experienced Native, now having charge, kept everything warm and cozy. Before tea, when receiving a little food, Lena opened her dark blue eyes, and gazed up peacefully and gladly in her mother's face. But, immediately after tea, within less than an hour, when the nurse brought her and placed her in the mother's arms, the Angel-Soul fled away. Poor Williag, seeing the mother's pathetic look, and as if she herself had been guilty, fell on her knees and cried,—"I knew it, Missi, I knew it! She gave two big sighs, and went! Awai, Missi, Awai!" When the mother called to me something about the child having "fainted," I was talking with Koris, but my heart guessed the worst. Alas, all means were seen to be vain! I could not rise, could not move, nor could the mother, but we prayed, in each other's hearing, and in the hearing of our blessed Lord, and He did not leave us without consolation. In such cases, the Heathen usually fly away in terror, but our Teachers were faithful and obedient; and our little boys, Bob and Fred, six and four respectively, followed all our tearful directions. One of their small toy-boxes was readily given up to make the baby's coffin. Yawaci brought calico, and dressed the precious body at the mother's instructions. I then offered a prayer to the clear Lord, whilst the mother clasped the coffin in her arms. The little grave, dug by the Teachers in the Mission plot, was within earshot of where we lay, and there Bob and Fred, kneeling in their snow-white dresses, sang "There is a Happy Land," as their sister's dust was laid in the Earth and in the arms of Jesus who is the Resurrection and the Life. God only can ever know how our hearts were torn by the pathos of that event, as we lay helpless, almost dying, and listened to our children's trembling voices! Johna, the Teacher, then prayed; while the Heathen, in groups of wonder, but holding far aloof, had many strange ideas wakened in their puzzled brains. The mother and I gave ourselves once more away to God, and to the Service of our dear Lord Jesus, as we parted with our darling Lena; and when, by and by, we were raised up again, and able to move about, often, often, did we find ourselves meeting together at that precious grave.

Being ordered to seek health by change and by higher medical aid, and if possible in the cooler air of New Zealand, we took the first opportunity and arrived at Sydney, anxious to start the new movement to secure the *Paragon* there, and then to go on to the sister Colony. Being scarcely able to walk without the crutches, we called privately a preliminary meeting of friends for consultation and advice. The conditions were laid before them and discussed. The Insurance Company had paid £2000 on the first *Dayspring*. Of that sum £1000 had been spent on chartering and maintaining the *Paragon;* so that we required an additional £2000 to purchase her, according to Dr. Steel's bargain with the owners, besides a large sum for alterations and equipment for the Mission. The late Mr. Learmouth looked across to Mr. Goodlet, and said, "If you'll join me, we will at once secure this vessel for the Missionaries, that God's work may not suffer from the wreck of the *Dayspring*."

Those two servants of God, excellent Elders of the Presbyterian Church, consulted together, and the vessel was purchased next day. How I did praise God, and pray Him to bless them and theirs! The late Dr. Fullarton, our dear friend, said to them, "But what guarantee do you ask from the Missionaries for your money?"

Mr. Learmouth's noble reply was, and the other heartily re-echoed it— "God's work is our guarantee! From them we will ask none. What guarantee have they to give us, except their faith in God? That guarantee is ours already."

I answered, "You take God and His work for your guarantee. Rest assured that He will soon repay you, and you will lose nothing by this noble service."

Having secured St. Andrew's Church for a public meeting, I advertised it in all the papers. Ministers, Sabbath School Teachers, and other friends came in great numbers. The scheme was fairly launched, and Collecting Cards largely distributed. Committees carried everything out into detail, and all worked for the fund with great goodwill.

I then sailed from Sydney to Victoria, and addressed the General Assembly of the Presbyterian Church in session at Melbourne. The work was easily set agoing there, and willing workers fully and rapidly organized it through Congregations and Sabbath Schools. Under medical advice, I next sailed for New Zealand in the S. S. *Hero*, Captain Logan. Reaching Auckland, I was in time to address the General Assembly of the Church there also. They gave me cordial welcome, and every Congregation and Sabbath School might be visited as far as I possibly could. The Ministers promoted the movement with hearty zeal. The Sabbath Scholars took Collecting Cards for "shares" in the New Mission Ship. A meeting was held every day, and three every Sabbath. Auckland, Nelson, Wellington, Dunedin, and all towns and churches within reach of these were rapidly visited; and I never had greater joy or heartiness in any of my tours than in this happy intercourse with the Ministers and people of the Presbyterian Church in New Zealand.

I arrived in Sydney about the end of March. My health was wonderfully restored, and New Zealand had given me about £1700 for the new ship. With the £1000 of insurance money, and about £700 from New South Wales, and £400 from Victoria, besides the £500 for her support also from. Victoria, we were able to pay back the £3000 of purchase money, and about £800 for alterations and repairs, as well as equip and provision her to sail for her next year's work amongst the Islands free of debt. I said to our two good friends at Sydney:

"You took God and His work for your guarantee. He has soon relieved you from all responsibility. You have suffered no loss, and you have had the honor and privilege of serving your Lord. I envy you the joy you must feel in so using your wealth, and I pray God's double blessing on all your store."

Our agent. Dr. Steel, had applied to the Home authorities for power to change the vessel's name from *Paragon* to *Dayspring*, so that the old associations might not be broken. This was cordially granted. And so our second *Dayspring*, owing no man anything, sailed on her annual trip to the New Hebrides, and we returned with her, praising the Lord and reinvigorated alike in spirit and in body.

CHAPTER LXXVII.
THE GOSPEL IN LIVING CAPITALS.

IN Heathendom every true convert becomes at once a Missionary. The changed life, shining out amid the surrounding darkness, is a Gospel in largest Capitals which all can read. Our Islanders, especially, having little to engage or otherwise distract attention, become intense and devoted workers for the Lord Jesus, if once the Divine Passion for souls stirs within them.

A Heathen has been all his days groping after peace of soul in dark superstition and degrading rites. You pour into his soul the light of Revelation. He learns that God is love, that God sent His Son to die for him, and that he is the heir of Life Eternal in and through Jesus Christ. By the blessed enlightenment of the Spirit of the Lord he believes all this. He passes into a third heaven of joy, and he burns to tell every one of this Glad Tidings. Others see the change in his disposition in his character in his whole life and actions; and amid such surroundings, every Convert is a burning and a shining light. Even whole populations are thus brought into the Outer Court of the Temple; and Islands, still Heathen and Cannibal, are positively eager for the Missionary to live amongst them, and would guard his life and property now in complete security, where a very few years ago everything would have been instantly sacrificed on touching their shores! They are not Christianized, neither are they Civilized, but the light has been kindled all round them, and though still only shining afar, they cannot but rejoice in its beams.But even where the path is not so smooth, nor any welcome awaiting them, Native Converts show amazing zeal. For instance, one of our Chiefs, full of the Christ-kindled desire to seek and to save, sent a message to an inland Chief, that he and four attendants would come on Sabbath and tell them the Gospel of Jehovah God. The reply came back sternly forbidding their Visit, and threatening with death any Christian that approached their village. Our Chief sent in response a loving message, telling them that Jehovah had taught the Christians to return good for evil, and that they would come unarmed to tell them the story of how the Son of God came into the world and died in order to bless and save His enemies. The Heathen Chief sent back a stern and prompt reply once more, "If you come, you will be killed."On Sabbath morning, the Christian Chief and his four companions were met outside the village by the Heathen Chief, who implored and threatened them once more. But the former said, "We come to you without weapons of war! We come only to tell you about Jesus. We believe that He will protect us to-day."

As they steadily pressed forward towards the village, spears began to be thrown at them. Some they evaded, being all except one most dexterous warriors; and others they literally received with their bare hands, striking them and turning them aside in an incredible manner. The Heathen, apparently thunderstruck at these men thus approaching them without weapons of war, and not even flinging back their own spears which they had turned aside, desisted from mere surprise, after having thrown what the old Chief called "a shower of spears." Our Christian Chief called out, as he and his companions drew up in the midst of them on the village Public Ground:

"Jehovah thus protects us. He has given us all your spears! Once we would have thrown them back at you and killed you. But now we come not to fight, but to tell you about Jesus. He has changed our dark hearts. He asks you now to lay down all these your other weapons of war, and to hear what we can tell you about the love of God, our great Father, the only living God."The Heathen were perfectly overawed. They manifestly looked upon these Christians as protected by some Invisible One! They listened for the first time to the story of the Gospel and of the Cross. We lived to see that Chief and all his tribe sitting in the School of Christ. And there is perhaps not an Island in these Southern Seas, amongst all those won for Christ, where similar acts of heroism on the part of Converts cannot be recited by every Missionary to the honor of our poor Natives and to the glory of their Saviour.Larger and harder tests were sometimes laid upon their new faith. Once the war on Tanna drove about one hundred of them to seek refuge on Aniwa. Not so many years before, their lives would never have been thus intrusted to the inhabitants of another Cannibal Island. But the Christ-Spirit was abroad upon Aniwa. The refugees were kindly cared for, and in process of time were restored to their own lands, by our Missionary ship the *Dayspring*. The Chiefs, however, and the Elders of the Church laid the new laws before them very clearly and decidedly. They would be helped and sheltered, but Aniwa was now under law to Christ, and if any of the Tannese broke the public rules as to moral conduct, or in any way disturbed the Worship of Jehovah, they would at once be expelled from the Island and sent back to Tanna. In all this, the Chief of the Tanna party, my old friend Nowar, strongly supported our Christian Chiefs. The Tannese behaved well, and many of them wore clothing and began to attend Church; and the heavy drain upon the poor resources of Aniwa was borne with a noble and Christian spirit, which greatly impressed the Tannese and commended the Gospel of Christ.

CHAPTER LXXVIII.
THE DEATH OF NAMAKEI.

IN claiming Aniwa for Christ, and winning it as a small jewel for His crown, we had the experience which has ever marked God's path through history,—He raised up around us and wonderfully endowed men to carry forward His own blessed work. Among these must be specially commemorated Namakei, the old Chief of Aniwa. Slowly, but very steadily, the light broke in upon his soul, and he was ever very eager to communicate to his people all that he learned. In Heathen days he was a Cannibal and a great warrior; but from the first, as shown in the preceding chapter he took a warm interest in us and our work,—a little selfish, no doubt, at the beginning, but soon becoming purified, as his eyes and heart were opened to the Gospel of Jesus.

On the birth of a son to us on the Island, the old Chief was in ecstasies. He claimed the child as his heir, his own son being dead, and brought nearly the whole inhabitants in relays to see the *white* Chief of Aniwa! He would have him called Namakei the Younger, an honor which I fear we did not too highly appreciate. As the child grew, he took his hand and walked about with him freely amongst the people, learning to speak their language like a Native, and not only greatly interesting them in himself, but even in us and in the work of the Lord. This, too, was one of the bonds, however purely human, that drew them all nearer and nearer to Jesus.

It was this same child, who, in the moment of our greatest peril, when the Mission House was once surrounded by savages who had resolved to murder us, managed in some incredible way to escape, and appeared, to our horror and amazement, dancing with glee amongst the armed warriors. He threw his arms around the neck of one after another, and kissed them, to their great surprise,—at last, he settled down like a bird upon the ringleader's knee, and therefrom prattled to them all, while we from within gazed on in speechless and helpless terror! He roundly scolded them for being "Naughty! Naughty!" The frowning faces began to relax into broad grins, another spirit came over them, and, one after another, they rapidly slipt away. The Council of Death was broken up; and we had a new illustration of the Lord's precious work,—"A little Child shall lead them."

The death of Namakei had in it many streaks of Christian romance. He had heard about the Missionaries annually meeting on one or other of the Islands, and consulting about the work of Jehovah. What ideas he had formed of a Mission Synod one cannot easily imagine; but in his old age, and when very frail, he formed an impassioned desire to attend our next meeting on Aneityum, and see and hear all the Missionaries of Jesus gathered together from the New Hebrides. Terrified that he would die away from home, and that that might bring great reverses to the good work on Aniwa, where he was truly beloved, I opposed his going with all my might. But he and his relations and his people were all set upon it, and I had at length to give way. His few booklets were then gathered together, his meager wardrobe was made up, and a small Native basket carried all his belongings. He assembled his people and took an affectionate farewell, pleading with them to be "strong for Jesus," whether they ever saw him again or not, and to be loyal and kind to Missi. The people wailed aloud, and many wept bitterly. Those on board the *Dayspring* were amazed to see how his people loved him. The old Chief stood the voyage well. He went in and out to our meeting of Synod, and was vastly pleased with the respect paid to him on Aneityum. When he heard of the prosperity of the Lord's work, and how Island after Island was learning to sing the praises of Jesus, his heart glowed, and he said, "Missi, I am lifting up my head like a tree. I am growing tall with joy!"

On the fourth or fifth day, however, he sent for me out of the Synod, and when I came to him, he said, eagerly, "Missi, I am near to die! I have asked you to come and say farewell. Tell my daughter, my brother, and my people to go on pleasing Jesus, and I will meet them again in the fair World."

I tried to encourage him, saying that God might raise him up again and restore him to his people; but he faintly whispered, "O Missi, death is already touching me! I feel my feet going away from under me. Help me to lie down under the shade of that banyan tree."

So saying, he seized my arm, we staggered near to the tree, and he lay down under its cool shade. He whispered again, "I am going! O Missi, let me hear your words raising up in prayer, and then my Soul will be strong to go."

Amidst many choking sobs, I tried to pray. At last he took my hand, pressed it to his heart, and said in a stronger and clearer tone, "O my Missi, my dear Missi, I go before you, but I will meet you again in the Home of Jesus. Farewell!"

That was the last effort of dissolving strength; he immediately became unconscious, and fell asleep. My heart felt like to break over him. He was my first Aniwan Convert—the first who ever on that Island, of love and tears opened his heart to Jesus; and as he lay there on the leaves and grass, my soul soared upward after his, and all the harps of God seemed to thrill with song as Jesus presented to the Father this trophy of redeeming love. He had been our true and devoted friend and fellow-helper in the Gospel; and next morning all the members of our Synod followed his remains to the grave. There we stood, the white Missionaries of the Cross from far distant lands, mingling our tears with Christian Natives of Aneityum, and letting them fall over one who only a few years before was a blood-stained Cannibal, and whom now we mourned as a brother, a saint, an Apostle amongst his people. Ye ask an explanation? The Christ entered into his heart, and Namakei became a new Creature. "Behold, I make all things new."

CHAPTER LXXIX.
CHRISTIANITY AND COCOANUTS.

NASWAI, the friend and companion of Namakei, was an inland Chief. He had, as his followers, by far the largest number of men in any village on Aniwa. He had certainly a dignified bearing, and his wife Katua was quite a lady in look and manner as compared with all around her. She was the first woman on the Island that adopted the clothes of civilization, and she showed considerable instinctive taste in the way she dressed herself in these. Her example was a kind of Gospel in its good influence on all the women; she was a real companion to her husband, and went with him almost everywhere.

Naswai was younger and more intelligent than Namakei, and in everything, except in translating the Scriptures, he was much more of a fellow-helper in the work of the Lord. For many years it was Naswai's special delight to carry my pulpit Bible from the Mission House to the Church every Sabbath morning, and to see that everything was in perfect order before the Service began. He was also the Teacher in his own village School, as well as an Elder in the Church. His addresses were wonderfully happy in graphic illustrations, and his prayers were fervid and uplifting. Yet his people were the worst to manage on all the Island, and the very last to embrace the Gospel.

He died when we were in the Colonies on furlough in 1875; and his wife Katua very shortly pre-deceased him. His last counsels to his people made a great impression on them. They told us how he pleaded with them to love and serve the Lord Jesus, and how he assured them with his dying breath that he had been "a new creature" since he gave his heart to Christ, and that he was perfectly happy in going to be with his Saviour.

I must here recall one memorable example of Naswai's power and skill as a preacher. On one occasion the *Dayspring* brought a large deputation from Fotuna to see for themselves the change which the Gospel had produced on Aniwa. On Sabbath, after the Missionaries had conducted the usual Public Worship, some of the leading Aniwans addressed the Fotunese; and amongst others, Naswai spoke to the following effect: "Men of Fotuna, you come to see what the Gospel has done for Aniwa. It is Jehovah the living God that has made all this change. As Heathens, we quarrelled, killed, and ate each other. We had no peace and no joy in heart or house, in villages or in lands; but we now live as brethren and have happiness in all these things. When you go back to Fotuna, they will ask you, 'What is Christianity?' And you will have to reply, 'It is that which has changed the people of Aniwa.' But they will still say, 'What is it?' And you will answer, 'It is that which has given them clothing and blankets, knives and axes, fish-hooks and many other useful things; it is that which has led them to give up fighting, and to live together as friends.' But they will ask you, 'What is it like?' And you will have to tell them, alas, that you cannot explain it that you have only seen its workings, not itself, and that no one can tell what Christianity is but the man that loves Jesus, the Invisible Master, and walks with Him and tries to please Him. Now, you people of Fotuna, you think that if you don't dance and sing and pray to your gods, you will have no crops. We once did so too, sacrificing and doing much abomination to our gods for weeks before our planting season every year. But we saw our Missi only praying to the Invisible Jehovah, and planting his yams, and they grew fairer than ours. You are weak every year before your hard work begins in the fields, with your wild and bad conduct to please your gods. But we are strong for our work, for we pray to Jehovah, and He gives quiet rest instead of wild dancing, and makes us happy in our toils. Since we followed Missi's example, Jehovah has given us large and beautiful crops, and we now know that He gives us all our blessings."

Turning to me, he exclaimed, "Missi, have you the large yam we presented to you? Would you not think it well to send it back with these men of Fotuna, to let their people see the yams which Jehovah grows for us in answer to prayer? Jehovah is the only God who can grow yams like that!"

Then, after a pause, he proceeded, "When you go back to Fotuna, and they ask you, 'What is Christianity?' you will be like an inland Chief of Erromanga, who once came down and saw a great feast on the shore. When he saw so much food and so many different kinds of it, he asked, 'What is this made of?' and was answered, 'Cocoanuts and yams.' 'And this?' 'Cocoanuts and bananas.' 'And this?' 'Cocoanuts and taro.' 'And this?' 'Cocoanuts and chestnuts,' etc. etc. The Chief was immensely astonished at the host of dishes that could be prepared from the cocoanuts. On returning, he carried home a great load of them to his people, that they might see and taste the excellent food of the shore-people. One day, all being assembled, he told them the wonders of that feast; and, having roasted the cocoanuts, he took out the kernels, all charred and spoiled, and distributed them, amongst his people. They tasted the cocoanut, they began to chew it, and then spat it out, crying, 'Our own food is better than that!' The Chief was confused, and only got laughed at for all his trouble. Was the fault in the cocoanuts? No; but they were spoiled in the cooking! So your attempts to explain Christianity will only spoil it.

Tell them that a man must live as a Christian, before he can show others what Christianity is."

On their return to Fotuna they exhibited Jehovah's yam, given in answer to prayer and labor; they told what Christianity had done for Aniwa; but did not fail to qualify all their accounts with the story of the Erromangan Chief and the cocoanuts.

CHAPTER LXXX.
NERWA'S BEAUTIFUL FAREWELL.

THE Chief of next importance on Aniwa was Nerwa, a keen debater, all whose thoughts ran in the channels of logic. When I could speak a little of their language I visited and preached at his village; but the moment he discovered that the teaching about Jehovah was opposed to their Heathen customs, he sternly forbade us. One day, during my address, he blossomed out into a full-fledged and pronounced Agnostic (with as much reason at his back as the European type!), and angrily interrupted me:

"It's all lies you come here to teach us, and you call it worship! You say your Jehovah God dwells in Heaven. Who ever went up there to hear Him or see Him? You talk of Jehovah as if you had visited His Heaven. Why, you cannot climb even to the top of one of our cocoanut trees, though we can and that with ease! In going up to the roof of your own Mission House you require the help of a ladder to carry you. And even if you could make your ladder higher than our highest cocoanut tree, on what would you lean its top? And when you get to its top, you can only climb down the other side and end where you began! The thing is impossible. You never saw that God; you never heard Him speak; don't come here with any of your white lies, or I'll send my spear through you."

He drove us from his village, and furiously threatened murder, if we ever dared to return. But very shortly thereafter the Lord sent us a little orphan girl from Nerwa's village. She was very clever, and could soon both read and write, and told over all that we taught her. Her visits home, or at least amongst the villagers where her home had been, her changed appearance and her childish talk, produced a very deep interest in us and in our work.

An orphan boy next was sent from that village to be kept and trained at the Mission House, and he too took back his little stories of how kind and good to him were Missi the man and Missi the woman. By this time Chief and people alike were taking a lively interest in all that was transpiring. One day the Chief's wife, a quiet and gentle woman, came to the Worship and said, "Nerwa's opposition dies fast. The story of the Orphans did it! He has allowed me to attend the Church, and to get the Christian's book."

We gave her a book and a bit of clothing. She went home and told everything. Woman after woman followed her from that same village, and some of the men began to accompany them. The only thing in which they showed a real interest was the children singing the little hymns which I had translated into their own Aniwan tongue, and which my wife had taught them to sing very sweetly and joyfully. Nerwa at last got so interested that he came himself, and sat within earshot, and drank in the joyful sound. In a short time he drew so near that he could hear the preaching, and then began openly and regularly to attend the Church. His keen reasoning faculty was constantly at work. He weighed and compared everything he heard, and soon out-distanced nearly all of them in his grasp of the ideas of the Gospel. He put on clothing, joined our School, and professed himself a follower of the Lord Jesus. He eagerly set himself, with all his power, to bring in a neighboring Chief and his people, and constituted himself at once an energetic and very pronounced helper to the Missionary.

On the death of Naswai, Nerwa at once took his place in carrying my Bible to the Church, and seeing that all the people were seated before the stopping of the bell. I have seen him clasping the Bible like a living thing to his breast, as if he would cry, "Oh, to have this treasure in my own words of Aniwa!"

When the Gospels of Matthew and Mark were at last printed in Aniwan, he studied them incessantly, and soon could read them freely. He became the Teacher in his own village School, and delighted in instructing others. He was assisted by Ruwawa, whom he himself had drawn into the circle of Gospel influence; and at our next election these two friends were appointed Elders of the Church, and greatly sustained our hands in every good work on Aniwa.

After years of happy useful service, the time came for Nerwa to die. He was then so greatly beloved that most of the inhabitants visited him during his long illness. He read a bit of the Gospels in his own Aniwan, and prayed with and for every visitor. He sang beautifully, and scarcely allowed any one to leave his bedside without having a verse of one or other of his favorite hymns, "Happy Land," and "Nearer, my God, to Thee."

On my last visit to Nerwa, his strength had gone very low, but he drew me near his face, and whispered, "Missi, my Missi, I am glad to see you. You see that group of young men? They came to sympathize with me; but they have never once spoken the name of Jesus, though they have spoken about everything else! They could not have weakened me so, if they had spoken about Jesus! Read me the story of Jesus; pray for me to Jesus. No! stop, let us call them, and let me speak with them before I go."

I called them all around him, and he strained his dying strength, and said, "After I am gone, let there be no bad talk, no Heathen ways. Sing Jehovah's songs, and pray to Jesus, and bury me as a Christian. Take good care of my Missi, and help him all you can. I am dying happy and going to be with Jesus, and it was Missi that showed me this way. And who among you will take my place in the village School and in the Church? Who amongst you all will stand up for Jesus?"

Many were shedding tears, but there was no reply; after which the dying Chief proceeded, "Now let my last work on Earth be this—We will read a chapter of the Book, verse about, and then I will pray for you all, and the Missi will pray for me, and God will let me go while the song is still sounding in my heart!"

At the close of this most touching exercise, we gathered the Christians who were near by close around, and sang very softly in Aniwan, "There is a Happy Land." As they sang, the old man grasped my hand, and tried hard to speak, but in vain. His head fell to one side, "the silver cord was loosed, and the golden bowl was broken."

CHAPTER LXXXI.
RUWAWA.

His great friend, Ruwawa the Chief, had waited by Nerwa like a brother till within a few days of the latter's death, when he also was smitten down apparently by the same disease. He was thought to be dying, and he resigned himself calmly into the hands of Christ, One Sabbath afternoon, sorely distressed for lack of air, he instructed his people to carry him from the village to a rising ground on one of his plantations. It was fallow; the fresh air would reach him; and all his friends could sit around him. They extemporized a rest—two posts stuck into the ground, slanting, sticks tied across them, then dried banana leaves spread on these and also as a cushion on the ground—and there sat Ruwawa, leaning back and breathing heavily. After the Church Services, I visited him, and found half the people of that side of the Island sitting round him, in silence, in the open air. Ruwawa beckoned me, and I sat down before him. Though suffering sorely, his eye and face had the look of ecstasy.

"Missi," he said, "I could not breathe in my village; so I got them to carry me here, where there is room for all. They are silent and they weep, because they think I am dying. If it were God's will, I would like to live and to help you in His work. I am in the hands of our dear Lord, If he takes me, it is good; if He spares me, it is good! Pray, and tell our Saviour all about it."

I explained to the people that we would tell our Heavenly Father how anxious we all were to see Ruwawa given back to us strong and well to work for Jesus, and then leave all to His wise and holy disposal. I prayed, and the place became a very Bochim. When I left him, Ruwawa exclaimed, "Farewell, Missi; if I go first, I will welcome you to Glory; if I am spared, I will work with you for Jesus; so all is well!"

One of the young Christians followed me and said, "Missi, our hearts are very sore! If Ruwawa dies, we have no Chief to take his place in the Church, and it will be a heavy blow against Jehovah's Worship on Aniwa."

I answered, "Let us each tell our God and Father all that we feel and all that we fear; and leave Ruwawa and our work in His holy hands."

We did so with earnest and unceasing cry. And when all hope had died out of every heart, the Lord began to answer us; the disease began to relax its hold, and the beloved Chief was restored to health. As soon as he was able, though still needing help, he found his way back to the Church, and we all offered special thanksgiving to God. He indicated a desire to say a few words; and although still very weak, spoke with great pathos thus:

"Dear Friends, God has given me back to you all. I rejoice thus to come here and praise the great Father, who made us all, and who knows how to make and keep us well. I want you all to work hard for Jesus, and to lose no opportunity of trying to do good and so to please Him. In my deep journey away near to the grave, it was the memory of what I had done in love to Jesus that made my heart sing. I am not afraid of pain,—my dear Lord Jesus suffered far more for me, and teaches me how to bear it. I am not afraid of war or famine or death, or of the present or of the future; my dear Lord Jesus died for me, and in dying I shall live with him in Glory. I fear and love my dear Lord Jesus, because He loved me and gave Himself for me."

Then he raised his right hand, and cried in a soft, full-hearted voice: "My own, my dear Lord Jesus!" and stood for a moment looking joyfully upward, as if gazing into his Saviour's face. When he sat down, there was a long hush, broken here and there by a smothered sob, and Ruwawa's words produced an impression that is remembered to this day.

In 1888, when I visited the Islands, Ruwawa was still devoting himself heart and soul to the work of the Lord on Aniwa. Assisted by Koris, a Teacher from Aneityum, and visited annually by our ever dear and faithful friends, Mr. and Mrs. Watt, from Tanna, the good Ruwawa carried forward all the work of God on Aniwa, along with others, in our absence as in our presence. The meetings, the Communicants' Class, the Schools, and the Church Services are all regularly conducted and faithfully attended. "Bless the Lord, O my soul!"

CHAPTER LXXXII.
LITSI SORÉ AND MUNGAW.

LITSI, the only daughter of Namakei, had both in her own career and in her connection with poor dear Mungaw, an almost unparalleled experience. She was entrusted to us when very young, and became a bright, clever, and attractive Christian girl. Many sought her hand, but she disdainfully replied, "I am Queen of my own Island, and when I like I will ask a husband in marriage, as your great Queen Victoria did!"

Her first husband, however won, was undoubtedly the tallest and most handsome man on Aniwa; but he was a giddy fool, and, on his early death, she again returned to live with us at the Mission House. Her second marriage had everything to commend it, but it resulted in indescribable disaster. Mungaw, heir to a Chief, had been trained with us, and gave every evidence of decided Christianity. They were married in the Church, and lived in the greatest happiness. He was able and eloquent, and was first chosen as a deacon, then as an Elder of the Church, and finally as High Chief of one half of the Island. He showed the finest Christian spirit under many trying circumstances. Once, when working at the lime for the building of our Church, two bad men, armed with muskets, sought his life for blowing the conch to assemble the workers. Hearing of the quarrel, I rushed to the scene, and heard him saying, "Don't call me coward, or think me afraid to die. If I died now, I would go to be with Jesus. But I am no longer a Heathen; I am a Christian, and wish to treat you as a Christian should."

Two loaded muskets were leveled at him. I seized one in each of my hands, and held their muzzles aloft in air, so that, if discharged, the balls might pass over his head and mine; and thus I stood for some minutes pleading with them.

Others soon coming to the rescue, the men were disarmed; and, after much talk, they professed themselves ashamed, and promised better conduct for the future. Next day they sent a large present as a peace-offering to me, but I refused to receive it till they should first of all make peace with the young Chief. They sent a larger present to him, praying him to receive it, and to forgive them. Mungaw brought a still larger present in exchange, laid it down at their feet in the Public Ground, shook hands with them graciously, and forgave them in presence of all the people. His constant saying was, "I am a Christian, and I must do the conduct of a Christian."

In one of my furloughs to Australia I took the young Chief with me, in the hope of interesting the Sabbath Schools and Congregations by his eloquent addresses and noble personality. The late Dr. Cameron of Melbourne, having heard him, as translated by me, publicly declared that Mungaw's appearance and speech in his Church did more to show him the grand results of the Gospel amongst the Heathen than all the Missionary addresses he ever listened to or read.

Our lodging was in St. Kilda. My dear wife was suddenly seized with a dangerous illness on a visit to Taradale, and I was telegraphed for. Finding that I must remain with her, I got Mungaw booked for Melbourne, on the road for St. Kilda, in charge of a railway guard. Some white wretches, in the guise of gentlemen, offered to see him to the St. Kilda Station, assuring the guard that they were friends of mine, and interested in our Mission. They took him, instead, to some den of infamy in Melbourne. On refusing to drink with them, he said they threw him down on a sofa, and poured drink or drugs into him till he was nearly dead. Having taken all his money (he had only two or three pounds, made up of little presents from various friends), they thrust him out to the street, with only one penny in his pocket.

On becoming conscious, he applied to a policeman, who either did not understand or would not interfere. Hearing an engine whistle, he followed the sound, and found his way to Spencer Street Station, where he proffered his penny for a ticket, all in vain. At last a sailor took pity on him, got him some food, and led him to the St. Kilda Station. There he stood for a whole day, offering his penny for a ticket by every train, only to meet with refusal after refusal, till he broke down, and cried aloud in such English as desperation gave him:

"If me savvy road, me go. Me no savvy road, and stop here me die. My Missi Paton live at Kilda. Me want go Kilda. Me no money. Bad fellow took all! Send me Kilda."

Some gentle Samaritan gave him a ticket, and he reached our house at St. Kilda at last. There for above three weeks the poor creature lay in a sort of stupid doze. Food he could scarcely be induced to taste, and he only rose now and again for a drink of water. When my wife was able to be removed thither also, we found dear Mungaw dreadfully changed in appearance and in conduct. Twice thereafter I took him with me on Mission work; but, on medical advice, preparations were made for his immediate return to the Islands. I intrusted him to the kind care of Captain Logan, who undertook to see him safely on board the *Dayspring*, then lying at Auckland. Mungaw was delighted, and we hoped everything from his return to his own land and people. After some little trouble, he was landed safely home on Aniwa.

But his malady developed dangerous and violent symptoms, characterized by long periods of quiet and sleep, and then sudden paroxysms, in which he destroyed property, burned houses, and was a terror to all.

On our return he was greatly delighted; but he complained bitterly that the white men "had spoiled his head," and that when it "burned hot" he did all these bad things for which he was extremely sorry. He deliberately attempted my life, and most cruelly abused his dear and gentle wife; and then, when the frenzy was over, he wept and lamented over it. Many a time he marched round and round our house with loaded musket and spear and tomahawk, while we had to keep doors and windows locked and barricaded; then the paroxysm passed off, and he slept, long and deep, like a child. When he came to himself, he wept and said, "The white men spoiled my head! I know not what I do. My head burns hot, and I am driven."

One day, in the Church, he leaped up during Worship with a loud yelling war-cry, rushed off through the Imrai to his own house, set fire to it, and danced around till everything he possessed was burned to ashes. Nasi, a bad Tannese Chief living on Aniwa, had a quarrel with Mungaw about a cask found at the shore, and threatened to shoot him. Others encouraged him to do so, as Mungaw was growing every day more and more destructive and violent. When any person became outrageous or insane on Aniwa, as they had neither asylum nor prison, they first of all held him fast and discharged a musket close to his ear; and then, if the shock did not bring him back to his senses, they tied him up for two days or so; and finally, if that did not restore him, they shot him dead. Thus the plan of Nasi was favored by their own customs. One night, after Family Worship—for amidst all his madness, when clear moments came, he poured out his soul in faith and love to the Lord—he said, "Litsi, I am melting! My head burns. Let us go out and get cooled in the open air."

She warned him not to go, as she heard voices whispering under the verandah. He answered a little wildly, "I am not afraid to die. Life is a curse and burden. The white men spoiled my head. If there is a hope of dying, let me go quickly and die!"

As he crossed the door, a ball crashed through him, and he fell dead. We got the mother and her children away to the Mission House; and next morning they buried the remains of poor Mungaw under the floor of his own hut, and enclosed the whole place with a fence. It was a sorrowful close to so noble a career. I shed many a tear that I ever took him to Australia. What will God have to say to those white fiends who poisoned and maddened poor dear Mungaw?

After a while the good Queen Litsi was happily married again. She became possessed with a great desire to go as a Missionary to the people and tribe of Nasi, the very man who had murdered her husband. She used to say, "Is there no Missionary to go and teach Nasi's people? I weep and pray for them, that they too may come to know and love Jesus."

I answered, "Litsi, if I had only wept and prayed for you, but stayed at home in Scotland, would that have brought you to know and love Jesus as you do?"

"Certainly not," she replied.

"Now then," I proceeded, "would it not please Jesus, and be a grand and holy revenge, if you, the Christians of Aniwa, could carry the Gospel to the very people whose Chief murdered Mungaw?"

The idea took possession of her soul. She was never wearied talking and praying over it. When at length a Missionary was got for Nasi's people, Litsi and her new husband offered themselves as the head of a band of six or eight Aniwan Christians and were engaged there to open up the way and assist, as Teachers and Helpers, the Missionary and his wife. There she and they have labored ever since. They are "strong" for the Worship. Her son is being trained up by his cousin, an Elder of the Church, to be "the good Chief of Aniwa"; so she calls him in her prayers, as she cries on God to bless and watch over him, while she is serving the Lord in at once serving the Mission family and ministering to the Natives in that foreign field.

Many years have now passed; and when lately I visited that part of Tanna, Litsi ran to me, clasped my hand, kissed it with many sobs, and cried, "O my father! God has blessed me to see you again. Is my mother, your dear wife, well? And your children, my brothers and sisters? My love to them all! Oh my heart clings to you!"

We had sweet conversation, and then she said more calmly, "My days here are hard. I might be happy and independent as Queen of my own Aniwa. But the Heathen here are beginning to listen. The Missi sees them coming nearer to Jesus. And oh, what a reward when we shall hear them sing and pray to our dear Saviour! The hope of that makes me strong for anything."

CHAPTER LXXXIII.
THE CONVERSION OF NASI.

NASI, the Tanna-man, was a bad and dangerous character, though some readers may condone his putting an end to Mungaw in the terrible circumstances of our case. During a great illness that befell him, I ministered to him regularly, but no kindness seemed to move him. When about to leave Aniwa, I went specially to visit him. On parting I said, "Nasi, are you happy? Have you ever been happy?"

He answered gloomily, "No! Never."

I said, "Would you like this dear little boy of yours to grow up like yourself, and lead the life you have lived?"

"No!" he replied warmly! "I certainly would not."

"Then," I continued, "you must become a Christian, and give up all your Heathen conduct, or he will just grow up to quarrel and fight and murder as you have done; and, O Nasi, he will curse you through all Eternity for leading him to such a life and to such a doom!"

He was very much impressed, but made no response. After we had sailed, a band of our young Native Christians held a consultation over the case of Nasi. They said, "We know the burden and terror that Nasi has been to our dear Missi. We know that he has murdered several persons with his own hands, and has taken part in the murder of others. Let us unite in daily prayer that the Lord would open his heart and change his conduct, and teach him to love and follow what is good, and let us set ourselves to win Nasi for Christ, just as Missi tried to win us."

So they began to show him every possible kindness, and one after another helped him in his daily tasks, embracing every opportunity of pleading with him to yield to Jesus and take the new path of life. At first he repelled them, and sullenly held aloof. But their prayers never ceased, and their patient affection continued to grow. At last, after long waiting, Nasi broke down, and cried to one of the Teachers, "I can oppose your Jesus no longer. If He can make you treat me like that, I yield myself to Him and to you. I want Him to change me too. I want a heart like that of Jesus."

He rubbed off the ugly thick-daubed paint from his face; he cut off his long heathen hair; he went to the sea and bathed, washing himself clean; and then he came to the Christians and dressed himself in a shirt and a kilt. The next step was to get a book,—his was the translation of the Gospel according to St. John. He eagerly listened to every one that would read bits of it aloud to him, and his soul seemed to drink in the new ideas at every pore. He attended the Church and the School most regularly, and could in a very short time read the Gospel for himself. The Elders of the Church took special pains in instructing him, and after due preparation he was admitted to the Lord's Table—my brother Missionary from Tanna baptizing and receiving him. Imagine my joy on learning all this regarding one who had sullenly resisted my appeals for many years, and how my soul praised the Lord who is "Mighty to save!"

During a recent visit to Aniwa, in 1886, God's almighty compassion was further revealed to me, when I found that Nasi the murderer was now a Scripture Reader, and able to comment in a wonderful and interesting manner on what he read to the people! On arriving at the Island, after my tour in Great Britain (1884-85), all the inhabitants of Aniwa seemed to be assembled at the boat-landing to welcome me, except Nasi. He was away fishing at a distance, and had been sent for, but had not yet arrived. On the way to the Mission House, he came rushing to meet me. He grasped my hand, and kissed it, and burst into tears. I said, "Nasi, do I now at last meet you as a Christian?"

He warmly answered, "Yes, Missi; I now worship and serve the only Lord and Saviour Jesus Christ. Bless God, I am a Christian at last!"

My soul went out with a silent cry, "Oh, that the men at home who discuss and doubt about conversion, and the new heart, and the power of Jesus to change and save, could but look on Nasi, and spell out the simple lesson,— He that created us at first by His power can create us anew by His love!"

CHAPTER LXXXIV.
THE APPEAL OF LAMU.

MY first Sabbath on Aniwa, after this tour in Great Britain and the Colonies, gave me a blessed surprise. Before daybreak I lay awake thinking of all my experiences on that Island, and wondering whether the Church had fallen off in my four years' absence, when suddenly the voice of song broke on my ears! It was scarcely full dawn, yet I jumped up and called to a man that was passing, "Have I slept in? Is it already Church-time? Or why are the people met so early?"

He was one of their leaders, and gravely replied, "Missi, since you left, we have found it very hard to live near to God! So the Chief and the Teachers and a few others meet when daylight comes in every Sabbath morning, and spend the first hour of every Lord's Day in prayer and praise. They are met to pray for you now, that God may help you in your preaching, and that all hearts may bear fruit to the glory of Jesus this day."

I returned to my room, and felt wonderfully "prepared" myself. It would be an easy and a blessed thing to lead such a Congregation into the presence of the Lord! They were there already.

On that day every person on Aniwa seemed to be at Church, except the bedridden and the sick. At the close of the Services, the Elders informed me that they had kept up all the Meetings during my absence, and had also conducted the Communicants' Class, and they presented to me a considerable number of Candidates for membership. After careful examination, I set apart nine boys and girls, about twelve or thirteen years of age and advised them to wait for at least another year or so, that their knowledge and habits might be matured. They had answered every question, indeed, and were eager to be baptized and admitted; but I feared for their youth, lest they should fall away and bring disgrace on the Church. One of them with very, earnest eyes, looked at me and said, "We have been taught that whosoever believeth is to be baptized. We do most heartily believe in Jesus, and try to please Jesus."

I answered, "Hold on for another year, and then our way will be clear."

But he persisted, "Some of us may not be living then; and you may not be here. We long to be baptized by you, our own Missi, and to take our place among the servants of Jesus."

After much conversation I agreed to baptize them, and they agreed to refrain from going to the Lord's Table for a year, that all the Church might by that time have knowledge and proof of their consistent Christian life, though so young in years. This discipline, I thought, would be good for them; and the Lord might use it as a precedent for guidance in future days.

Of other ten adults at this time admitted, one was specially noteworthy. She was about twenty-five, and the Elders objected because her marriage had not been according to the Christian usage on Aniwa. She left us weeping deeply. I was writing late at night in the cool evening air, as was my wont in that oppressive tropical clime, and a knock was heard at my door. I called out, "*Akai era?*" (= Who is there?)

A voice softly answered, "Missi, it is Lamu. Oh, do speak with me!"

This was the rejected candidate, and I at once opened the door.

"Oh, Missi," she began, "I cannot sleep, I cannot eat; my soul is in pain. Am I to be shut out from Jesus? Some of those at the Lord's Table committed murder. They repented, and have been saved. My heart is very bad; yet I never did any of those crimes of Heathenism; and I know that it is my joy to try and please my Saviour Jesus. How is it that I only am to be shut out from Jesus?"

I tried all I could to guide and console her, and she listened to all very eagerly. Then she looked up at me and said, "Missi, you and the Elders may think it right to keep me back from showing my love to Jesus at the Lord's Table; but I know here in my heart that Jesus has received me; and if I were dying now, I know that Jesus would take me to Glory and present me to the Father."

Her look and manner thrilled me. I promised to see the Elders and submit her appeal. But Lamu appeared and pled her own cause before them with convincing effect. She was baptized and admitted along with other nine. And that Communion Day will be long remembered by many souls on Aniwa.

It has often struck me, when relating these events, to press this question on the many young people, the highly privileged white brothers and sisters of Lamu, Did you ever lose one hour of sleep or a single meal in thinking of your Soul, your God, the claims of Jesus, and your Eternal Destiny?

And when I saw the diligence and fidelity of these poor Aniwan Elders, teaching and ministering during all those years, my soul has cried aloud to God, Oh, what could not the Church accomplish if the educated and gifted Elders and others in Christian lands would set themselves thus to work for Jesus, to teach the ignorant, to protect the tempted, and to rescue the fallen!

CHAPTER LXXXV.
WANTED! A STEAM AUXILIARY.

IN December 1883 I brought a pressing and vital matter before the General Assembly of the Presbyterian Church of Victoria. It pertained to the New Hebrides Mission, to the vastly increased requirements of the Missionaries and their families there, and to the fact that the *Dayspring* was no longer capable of meeting the necessities of the case,—thereby incurring loss of time, loss of property, and risk and even loss of precious lives. The Missionaries on the spot had long felt this, and had loudly and earnestly pled for a new and larger Vessel, or a Vessel with Steam Auxiliary power, or some arrangement whereby the work of God on these Islands might be overtaken, without unnecessary exposure of life, and without the dreaded perils that accrue to a small sailing Vessel such as the *Dayspring* alike from deadly calms and from treacherous gales.

The Victorian General Assembly, heartily at one with the Missionaries, commissioned me to go home to Britain in 1884, making me at the same time their Missionary delegate to the Pan-Presbyterian Council at Belfast, and also their representative to the General Assemblies of the several Presbyterian Churches in Great Britain and Ireland. And they empowered and authorized me to lay our proposals about a new Steam Auxiliary Mission Ship before all these Churches, and to ask and receive from God's people whatever contributions they felt disposed to give towards the sum of £6000, without which this great undertaking could not be faced.

A few days after my arrival I was called upon to appear before the Supreme Court of the English Presbyterian Church, then assembled at Liverpool. While a hymn was being sung, I took my seat in the pulpit under great depression. But light broke around, when my dear friend and fellow-student, Dr. Oswald Dykes, came up from the body of the Church, shook me warmly by the hand, whispered a few encouraging words in my ear, and, returned to his seat. God helped me to tell my story, and the audience were manifestly interested.

Next, by kind invitation, I visited and addressed the United Presbyterian Synod of Scotland, assembled in Edinburgh. My reception there was not only cordial,—it was enthusiastic. Though as a Church they had no denominational interest in our Mission, the Moderator, amidst the cheers of all the Ministers and Elders, recommended that I should have free access to every Congregation and Sabbath School which I found it possible to visit, and hoped that their generous-hearted people would contribute freely to so needful and noble a cause. My soul rose in praise; and I may here say, in passing, that every Minister of that Church whom I wrote to or visited treated me in the same spirit throughout all my tour.

Having been invited by Mr. Dickson, an Elder of the Free Church, to address a midday meeting of children in the Free Assembly Hall, I was able by all appearances, greatly to interest and impress them. At the close, my dear and noble friend, Principal Cairns, warmly welcomed and cheered me, and that counted for much amid all anxieties; for I had learned that very day, at headquarters, that the Free Church authorities were resolved, in view of a difference of opinion betwixt the *Dayspring* Board at Sydney and the Victorian Assembly as to the new Steam Auxiliary, to hold themselves absolutely neutral.

Having letters from Andrew Scott, Esq., Carrugal, my very dear friend and helper in Australia, to Dr. J. Hood Wilson, Barclay Free Church, Edinburgh, I resolved to deliver them that evening; and I prayed the Lord to open up all my path, as I was thus thrown solely on Him for guidance and bereft of the aid of man. Dr. Wilson and his lady, neither of whom I had ever seen before, received me as kindly as if I had been an old friend. He read my letters of introduction, conversed with me as to plans and wishes (chiefly through Mrs. Wilson, for he was suffering from sore throat) and then he said with great warmth and kindliness:

"God has surely sent you here to-night! I feel myself unable to preach to-morrow. Occupy my pulpit in the forenoon and address my Sabbath School, and you shall have a collection for your Ship."

Thereafter, I was with equal kindness received by Mr. Balfour, having a letter of introduction from his brother, and he offered me his pulpit for the evening of that day. I lay down blessing and praising Him, the Angel of whose Presence was thus going before me and opening up my way. That Lord's Day I had great blessing and joy; there was an extraordinary response financially to my appeals and my proposal was thus fairly launched in the Metropolis of our Scottish Church life. I remembered an old saying, Difficulties are made only to be vanquished. And I thought in my deeper soul,—Thus our God throws us back upon Himself; and if these £6000 ever come to me, to the Lord God alone, and not to man, shall be all the glory!

On the Monday following, after a long conversation and every possible explanation, Colonel Young, of the Free Church Foreign Missions Committee, said, "We must have you to address the Assembly on the evening devoted to Missions." Thus I had the pleasure and honor of addressing that great Assembly; and though no notice was taken of my proposals in any "finding" of the Court, yet many were thereby interested deeply in our work, and requests now poured in upon me from every quarter to occupy pulpits and receive collections for the new Ship.

At the meeting in the Assembly Hall of the Church of Scotland, which along with others, I was cordially invited to address, the good and noble Lord Polwarth occupied the chair. That was the beginning of a friendship in Christ which will last and deepen as long as we live. From that night he took the warmest personal interest, not only by generously contributing to my fund, but by organizing meetings at his own Mansion House, and introducing me to a wide circle of influential friends.

Nor, whilst the pen leads on my mind to recall these Border memories, must I fail to record how John Scott Dudgeon, Esq., Longnewton, a greatly esteemed Elder of the Church went from town to town in all that region, and from Minister to Minister, arranging for me a series of happy meetings. I shared also the hospitality of his beautiful home, and added himself and his much-beloved wife to the precious roll of those who are dear for the Gospel's sake and for their own. Her Majesty's Commissioner to the General Assembly for the year was that distinguished Christian as well as nobleman, the Earl of Aberdeen. He graciously invited me to meet the Countess and himself at ancient Holyrood. After dinner he withdrew himself for a lengthened time from the general company, and entered into a close and interested conversation about our Mission, and especially about the threatened annexation of the New Hebrides by the French.

There also I had the memorable pleasure of meeting, and for a long while conversing with that truly noble and large-hearted lady, his mother, the much-beloved Dowager-Countess well known for her life-long devotion to so many schemes of Christian philanthropy. At her own home, Alva House, she afterwards arranged meetings for me, as well as in Halls and Churches in the immediately surrounding district; and her letters of interest in the work, of sympathy, and of helpfulness, from time to time received, were amongst the sustaining forces of my spiritual life.

When one sees men and women of noble rank thus consecrating themselves in humble and faithful service to Jesus, there dawns upon the mind a glimpse of what the prophet means, and of what the world will be like, when it can be said regarding the Church of God on Earth,—"Kings have become thy nursing fathers, and their Queens thy nursing mothers."

CHAPTER LXXXVI.
MY CAMPAIGN IN IRELAND.

MY steps were next directed towards Ireland, immediately after the Church meetings at Edinburgh; first to 'Derry, where the Presbyterian Assembly was met in annual conclave, and thereafter to Belfast, where the Pan-Presbyterian Council was shortly to sit. The eloquent fervor of the Brethren at 'Derry was like a refreshing breeze to my spirit; I never met Ministers anywhere, in all my travels, who seemed more wholehearted in their devotion to the work which the Lord had given them to do.

I addressed the Assembly at 'Derry and also the Council at Belfast. The memory of seeing all those great and learned and famous men—for many of the leaders were eminently such—so deeply interested in the work of God, and particularly in the Evangelizing of the Heathen World and bringing thereto the knowledge of Jesus, was to me, so long exiled from all such influences, one of the great inspirations of my life. I listened with humble thankfulness, and blessed the Lord who had brought me to sit at their feet.

On the rising of the Council, I entered upon a tour of six weeks among the Presbyterian Congregations and Sabbath Schools of Ireland. It had often been said to me, after my addresses in the Assemblies and elsewhere, "How do you ever expect to raise £6000? It can never be accomplished, unless you call upon the rich individually, and get their larger subscriptions. Our ordinary Church people have more than enough to do with themselves. Trade is dull," etc.

I explained to them, and also announced publicly, that in all similar efforts I had never called on or solicited any one privately, and that I would not do so now. I would make my appeal, but leave everything else to be settled betwixt the individual conscience and the Saviour—I gladly receiving whatsoever was given or sent, acknowledging it by letter, and duly forwarding it to my own Church in Victoria. Again and again did generous souls offer to go with me, introduce me, and give me opportunity of soliciting subscriptions; but I steadily refused—going, indeed, wherever an occasion was afforded me of telling my story and setting forth the claims of the Missions, but asking no one personally for anything, having fixed my soul in the conviction that one part of the work was laid upon me, but that the other lay betwixt the Master and His servants exclusively.

"On what then do you really rely, looking at it from a business point of view?" they would somewhat appealingly ask me.

I answered, "I will tell my story; I will set forth the claims of the Lord Jesus on the people; I will expect the surplus collection, or a retiring collection, on Sabbath; I will ask the whole collection, less expenses, at week-night meetings; I will issue Collecting Cards for Sabbath Scholars; I will make known my Home-Address, to which everything may be forwarded, either from Congregations or from private donors; and I will go on, to my utmost strength, in the faith that the Lord will send me the £6000 required. If He does not so send it, then I shall expect He will send me grace to be reconciled to the disappointment, and I shall go back to my work without the Ship."

This, in substance, I had to repeat hundreds of times; and as often had I to witness the half-pitying or incredulous smile with which it was received, or to hear the blunt and emphatic retort, "You'll never succeed! Money cannot be got in that unbusiness-like way."

I generally added nothing further to such conversation; but a Voice, deep, sweet, and clear, kept sounding through my soul—"The silver and the gold are Mine."

During the year 1884, as is well known, Ireland was the scene of many commotions and of great distress. Yet at the end of my little tour amongst the Presbyterian people of the North principally, though not exclusively, a sum of more than £600 had been contributed to our Mission Fund. And there was not, so far as my knowledge went, one single large subscription; there were, of course, many bits of gold from those well-to-do, but the ordinary collection was made up of the shillings and pence of the masses of the people. Nor had I ever in all my travels a warmer response, nor ever mingled with any Ministers more earnestly devoted to their Congregations or more generally and deservedly beloved.

CHAPTER LXXXVII.
SCOTLAND'S FREE-WILL OFFERINGS.

RETURNING to Scotland, I settled down at my headquarters, the house of my brother James in Glasgow; and thence began to open up the main line of my operations, as the Lord day by day guided me. Having the aid of no Committee, I cast myself on Minister after Minister and Church after Church, calling here, writing there, and arranging for three meetings every Sabbath, and one, if possible, every week-day, and drawing-room meetings, wherever practicable, in the afternoons. My correspondence grew to oppressive proportions, and kept me toiling at it every spare moment from early morn till bedtime. Indeed, I never could have overtaken it, had not my brother devoted many days and hours of precious time, answering letters regarding arrangements issuing the "Share" receipts for all moneys the moment they arrived, managing all my transactions through the bank, and generally tackling and reducing the heap of communications, and preventing me falling into hopeless arrears.

I printed, and circulated by post and otherwise, ten thousand copies of a booklet, "Statement and Appeal,"—containing, besides my Victorian Commission and my Glasgow address, a condensed epitome of the results of the New Hebrides Mission and of the reasons for asking a new Steam Auxiliary Ship. To this chiefly is due the fact, as well as to my refusing to call for subscriptions, that the far greater portion of all the money came to me by letter. On one day, though no doubt a little exceptional, as many as seventy communications reached me by post; and every one of these contained something for our fund-ranging from "a few stamps," and "the widow's mite," through every variety of figure up to the wealthy man's fifty or hundred pounds. I was particularly struck with the number of times that I received £1, with such a note as, "From a servant-girl that loves the Lord Jesus;" or "From a servant-girl that prays for the conversion of the Heathen." Again and again I received sums of five and ten shillings, with notes such as—"From a working-man who loves his Bible;" or "From a working-man who prays for God's blessing on you and work like yours every day in Family Worship." I sometimes regret that the graphic, varied, and intensely interesting notes and letters were not preserved; for by the close of my tour they would have formed a wonderful volume of leaves from the human heart.

I also addressed every Religious Convention to which I was invited, or to which I could secure access. The Perth Conference was made memorable to me by my receiving the first large subscription for our Ship, and by my making the acquaintance of a beautiful type of Christian merchant. At the close of the meeting, at which I had the privilege of speaking, an American gentleman introduced himself to me. We at once entered into each other's confidence, as brothers in the Lord's service. I afterwards learned that he had made a competency for himself and his family, though only in the prime of life; and he still carried on a large and flourishing business—but why? to devote *the whole profits*, year after year, to the direct service of God and His cause among men? He gave me a cheque for the largest single contribution with which the Lord had yet cheered me. God, who knows me, sees that I have never coveted money for myself or my family; but I did envy that Christian merchant the joy that he had in having money, and having the heart to use it as a steward of the Lord Jesus!

Thereafter I was invited to the annual Christian Conference at Dundee. A most peculiar experience befell me there. Being asked to close the forenoon meeting with prayer and the benediction, I offered prayer, and then began, "May the love of God the Father—" but not another word would come in English; everything was blank except the words in Aniwan, for I had long begun to *think* in the Native tongue, and after a dead pause, and a painful silence, I had to wind up with a simple "Amen!" I sat down wet with perspiration. It might have been wiser, as the Chairman afterwards suggested, to have given them the blessing in Aniwan, but I feared to set them alaughing by so strange a manifestation of the "tongues." Worst of all, it had been announced that I was to address them in the afternoon; but who would come to hear a Missionary that stuck in the benediction? The event had its semi-comical aspect, but it sent me to my knees during the interval in a very fever of prayerful anxiety. A vast audience assembled, and if the Lord ever manifestly used me in interesting His people in Missions, it was certainly then and there. As I sat down, a devoted Free Church Elder from Glasgow handed me his card, with "I. O. U. £100." This was my first donation of a hundred pounds, and my heart was greatly cheered. I praised the Lord, and warmly thanked His servant. A Something kept sounding these words in my ears, "My thoughts are not as your thoughts;" and also, "Cast thy burden upon the Lord, and He will sustain thee."

During my address at that meeting three colored girls, not unlike our Island girls, sat near the platform, and eagerly listened to me. At the close, the youngest, apparently about twelve years of age, rose, salaamed to me in Indian fashion, took four silver bangles from her arm, and presented them to me, saying, "Padre, I want to take shares in your Mission Ship by these bangles, for I have no money, and may the Lord ever bless you!"

I replied, "Thank you, my dear child; I will not take your bangles, but Jesus will accept your offering, and bless and reward you all the same."

As she still held them up to me, saying, "Padre, do receive them from me, and may God ever bless you!" a lady, who had been seated beside her, came up to me, and said, "Please, do take them, or the dear girl will break her heart. She has offered them up to Jesus for your Mission Ship."

I afterwards learned that the girls were orphans, whose parents died in the famine; that the lady and her sister, daughters of a Missionary, had adopted them to be trained as Zenana Missionaries, and that they intended to return with them, and live and die to aid them in that blessed work amongst the daughters of India. Oh, what a reward and joy might many a lady who reads this page easily reap for herself in Time and Eternity by a similar simple yet far-reaching service! Take action when and where God points the way; wait for no one's guidance.

The most amazing variety characterize the gifts and the givers. One donor sent me an anonymous note to this effect, "I have been curtailing my expenses. The first £5 saved I enclose that you may invest it for me in the Bank of Jesus. I am sure He gives the best interest, and the most certain returns."

In Glasgow a lady called at my brother's house, saying, "Is the Missionary at home? Can I see him alone? If not, I will call again." Being asked into my room, she declined to be seated, but said, "I heard you tell the story of your Mission in the City Hall, and I have been praying for you ever since. I have called to give you my mite, but not my name. God bless you. We shall meet in Heaven!" She handed me an envelope, and was off almost before I could thank her. It was £49 in bank-notes.

Another dear Christian friend carne to see me, and at the close of a delightful conversation, said: "I have been thinking much about you since I heard you in the Clark Hall, Paisley. I have come to give a little bit of dirty paper for your Ship. God sent it to me, and I return it to God through you with great pleasure." I thanked her warmly, thinking it a pound, or five at the most; on opening it, after she was gone, it turned out to be £100. I felt bowed down in humble thankfulness, and pressed forward in the service of the Lord.

CHAPTER LXXXVIII.
ENGLAND'S OPEN BOOK.

THE time now arrived for my attempting something amongst the Presbyterians of England. But my heart sank within me; I was a stranger to all except Dr. Dykes, and the New Hebrides Mission had no special claims on them. Casting myself upon the Lord, I wrote to all the Presbyterian Ministers in and around London, enclosing my "Statement and Appeal," and asking a Service, with a retiring collection, or the surplus above the usual collection, on behalf of our Mission Ship. All declined, except two. I learned afterwards that the London Presbytery had resolved that no claim beyond their own Church was to be admitted into any of its pulpits for a period of months, under some special financial emergency. My dear friend, Dr. J. Hood Wilson, kindly wrote also to a number of them, on my behalf, but with a similar result; though at last other two Services were arranged for with a collection, and one without. Being required at London, in any case, in connection with the threatened Annexation of the New Hebrides by the French, I resolved to take these five Services by the way, and immediately return to Scotland, where engagements and opportunities were now pressed upon me, far more than I could overtake. But the Lord Himself opened before me a larger door, and more effectual, than any that I had tried in vain to open up for myself.

The Churches to which I had access did nobly indeed, and the Ministers treated me as a very brother. Dr. Dykes most affectionately supported my Appeal, and made himself recipient of donations that might be sent for our Mission Ship. Dr. Donald Fraser, and Messrs. Taylor and Mathieson, with their Congregations, generously contributed to the Fund. And so did the Mission Church in Drury Lane—the excellent and consecrated Rev. W. B. Alexander, the pastor thereof, and his wife, becoming my devoted personal friends and continuing to remember in their work-parties ever since the needs of the Natives on the New Hebrides. Others also, whom I cannot wait to specify, showed a warm interest in us and in our department of the Lord's work. But my heart had been foolishly set upon adding a large sum to the fund for the Mission Ship, and when only about £150 came from all the Churches in London to which I could get access, no doubt I was sensible of cherishing a little guilty disappointment. That was very unworthy in me, considering all my previous experiences; and God deserved to be trusted by me far differently, as the sequel will immediately show.

That widely-known and deeply-beloved servant of God, Mr. J. E. Mathieson, of the Mildmay Conference Hall, had invited me to address one of their annual meetings on behalf of Foreign Missions, and also to be his guest while the Conference lasted. Thereby I met and heard many godly and noble disciples of the Lord, whom I could not otherwise have reached though every Church I had asked in London had been freely opened to me. These devout and faithful and generous people, belonging to every branch of the Church of Christ, and drawn from every rank and class in society, from the humblest to the highest, were certainly amongst the most open-hearted and the most responsive of all whom I ever had the privilege to address. One felt there, in a higher degree than almost anywhere else, that every soul was on fire with love to Jesus and with genuine devotion to His Cause in every corner of the Earth. There it was a privilege and a gladness to speak; and though no collection was asked, or could be expected, my heart was uplifted and strengthened by these happy meetings, and by all that Heavenly intercourse.

But see how the Lord leads us by a way we know not! Next morning after my address, a gentleman who had heard me, the Hon. Ion Keith-Falconer, handed me a cheque from his father-in-law for £300, by far the largest single donation at that time towards our Mission Ship; and immediately thereafter I received from one of the Mildmay lady Missionaries £50, from a venerable friend of the founder £20, from "Friends at Mildmay" £30; and through my dear friend and brother, Mr. Mathieson, many other donations were in due course forwarded to me.

My introduction, however, to the Conference at Mildmay did far more for me than even this; it opened up a series of drawing-room meetings in and around London, where I told the story of our Mission and preached, the Gospel to many in the higher walks of life, and received most liberal support for the Mission Ship. It also brought me invitations from many quarters of England, to Churches, to Halls, and to County Houses and Mansions.

Lord Radstock got up a special meeting, inviting by private card a large number of his most influential friends; and there I met for the first time one whom I have since learned to regard as a very precious personal friend. Rev. Sholto D. C. Douglas, clergyman, of the Church of England, who then, and afterwards at Douglas-Support in Scotland, not only most liberally supported our fund, but took me by the hand as a brother, and promoted my work by every means in his power.

The Earl and Countess of Tankerville also invited me to Chillingham Castle, and gave me an opportunity of addressing a great assembly there, then gathered together from all parts of the County. The British and

Foreign Bible Society received me in a special meeting of the Directors; and I was able to tell them how all we, the Missionaries of these Islands whose language had never before been reduced to writing, looked to them, and leant upon them, and prayed for them and their work—without whom our Native Bibles never could have been published. After the meeting the Chairman gave me £5, and one of the Directors a check for £25 for our Mission Ship.

I was also invited to Leicester, and made the acquaintanceship of a godly and gifted servant of the Lord Jesus, the Rev. F. B. Meyer, B. A. (now of London), whose books and booklets on the higher aspects of the Christian Life are read by tens of thousands, and have been fruitful of blessing. There I addressed great meetings of devoted workers in the Lord's vineyard; and the dear friend who was my host on that occasion, a Christian merchant, has since contributed £10 per annum for the support of a Native Teacher on the New Hebrides.

It was my privilege also to visit and address the Müller Orphanages at Bristol, and to see that saintly man of faith and prayer moving about as a wise and loving father amongst the hundreds, even thousands, that look to him for their daily bread and for the bread of Life Eternal. At the close of my address, the venerable founder thanked me warmly and said, "Here are £50, which God has sent to me for your Mission." I replied saying, "Dear friend, how can I take it? I would rather give you £500 for your Orphans if I could, for I am sure you need it all!"

He replied, with sweetness and great dignity, "God provides for His own Orphans. This money cannot be used for them. I must send it after you by letter. It is the Lord's gift."

Often, as I have looked at the doings of men and Churches, and tried to bring all to the test as if in Christ's very presence, it has appeared to me that such work as Müller's and Barnardo's, and that of my own fellow-countryman, William Quarrier, must be peculiarly dear to the heart of our blessed Lord. And were He to visit this world again, and seek a place where His very Spirit had most fully wrought itself out into deeds, I fear that many of our so-called Churches would deserve to be passed by, and that His holy, tender, helpful, divinely-human love would find its most perfect reflex in these Orphan Homes. Still and forever, amidst all changes of creed and of climate, this, this is "pure and undefiled Religion" before God and the Father!

But in this connection I must not omit to mention that the noble and world-famous servant of God, the Minister of the Tabernacle, invited me to a garden-party at his home, and asked me to address his students and other Christian workers. When I arrived I found a goodly company assembled under the shade of lovely trees, and felt the touch of that genial humor, so mighty a gift when sanctified, which has so often given wings to C. H. Spurgeon's words, when he saluted me as "The King of the Cannibals!" On my leaving, Mrs. Spurgeon presented me with her husband's *Treasury of David*, and also "£5 from the Lord's cows"—which I afterwards learned was part of the profits from certain cows kept by the good lady, and that everything produced thereby was dedicated to the work of the Lord. I praised God that He had privileged me to meet this extraordinarily endowed man, to whom the whole Christian World had been so specially indebted, and who had consecrated all his gifts and opportunities to the proclamation of the pure and precious Gospel.

Of all my London associations, however, the deepest and the most imperishable is that which weaves itself around the Honorable Ion Keith-Falconer, who has already passed to what may truly be called a Martyr's crown. At that time I met him at his father-in-law's house at Trent; and on another occasion spent a whole day with him at the house of his noble mother, the Countess-Dowager of Kintore. His soul was then full of his projected Mission to the Arabs, being himself one of the most distinguished Orientalists of the day; and as we talked together, and exchanged experiences, I felt that never before had I visibly marked the fire of God, the holy passion to seek and to save the lost, burning more steadily or brightly on the altar of any human heart. The heroic founding of the Mission at Aden is already one of the precious annals of the Church of Christ. His young and devoted wife survives, to mourn indeed, but also to cherish his noble memory; and, with the aid of others, and the banner of the Free Church of Scotland, to see the "Keith-Falconer Mission" rising up amidst the darkness of blood-stained Africa, as at once a harbor of refuge for the slave, and a beacon-light to those who are without God and without hope The servant does his day's work, and passes on through the gates of sleep to the Happy Dawn; but the Divine Master lives and works and reigns, and by our death, as surely as by our life, His holy purposes shall be fulfilled.

CHAPTER LXXXIX.
FAREWELL SCENES.

ON returning to Scotland, every day was crowded with engagements for the weeks that remained, and almost every mail brought me contributions from all conceivable corners of the land. My heart was set upon taking out two or three Missionaries with me to claim more and still more of the Islands for Christ; and with that view I had addressed Divinity Students at Edinburgh, Glasgow, and Aberdeen. Again and again, by conversation and correspondence, consecrated young men were just on the point of volunteering; but again and again the larger and better known fields of labor turned the scale, and they finally decided for China or Africa or India. Deeply disappointed at this, and thinking that God directed us to look to our own Australia alone for Missionaries for the New Hebrides, I resolved to return, and took steps towards securing a passage by the Orient Line to Melbourne. But just then two able and devoted students, Messrs. Morton and Leggatt, offered themselves as Missionaries for our Islands; and shortly thereafter a third, Mr. Landells, also an excellent man; and all, being on the eve of their License as preachers, were approved of, accepted, and set to special preparations for the Mission field, particularly in acquiring practical medical knowledge.

On this turn of affairs I managed to have my passage delayed for six weeks, and resolved to cast myself on the Lord that He might enable me in that time to raise at least £500, in order to furnish the necessary outfit and equipment for three new Mission Stations, and to pay the passage money of the Missionaries and their wives, that there might be no difficulty on this score amongst the Foreign Mission Committees on the other side. And then the idea came forcibly, and for a little unmanned me, that it was wrong in me to speak of these limits as to time and money in my prayers to God. But I reflected, again, how it was for the Lord's own glory alone in the salvation of the Heathen, and for no personal aims of mine; and so I fell back on His promise, "Whatsoever ye shall ask in My Name," and believingly asked it in His Name, and for His praise and service alone. I think it due to my Lord, and for the encouragement of all His servants, that I should briefly outline what occurred in answer to these prayers.

Having gone to the center of one of the great shipbuilding districts of Scotland, and held a series of meetings, and raised a sum of about £55 only after nine services and many Sabbath School collecting cards, my heart was beginning to sink, as I did not think my health would stand another six weeks of incessant strain; when, at the close of my last meeting in a Free

Church, an Elder and his wife entered the vestry and said, "We are deeply interested in you and in all your work and plans. You say that you have asked £500 more. We gave you the first £100 at the Dundee Conference; and it is a joy to us to give you this £100 too, towards the making up of your final sum. We pray that you may speedily realize your wish, and that God's richest blessing may ever rest upon your head."

Another week passed by, and at the close of it a lady called upon me, and, after delightful conversation about the Mission, said, "How near are you to the sum required?" I explained to her what is recorded above, and she continued, "I gave you one little piece of paper at the beginning of your efforts. I have prayed for you every day since. God has prospered me, and this is one of the happiest moments of my life, when I am now able to give you another little bit of paper."

So saying, she put into my hand £100. I protested, "You are surely too generous. Can you afford a second £100?"

She replied to this effect, and very joyfully, as one who had genuine gladness in the deed, "My Lord has been very kind to me, in my business. My wants are simple, and are safe in His hands. I wait not till death forces me, but give back whatever I am able to the Lord now, and hope to live to see much blessing thereby through you in the conversion of the Heathen."

My last week had come, and I was in the midst of preparations for departure, when amongst the letters delivered to me was one to this effect:

"Restitution money which never now can be returned to its owner. Since my Conversion I have labored hard to save it. I now make my only possible amends by returning it to God through you. Pray for me and mine, and may God bless you in your work!" I rather startled my brother and his wife at our breakfast table by shouting out in unwontedly excited tones,— "Hallelujah! The Lord has done it! Hallelujah!" But my tones softened down into intense reverence, and my words broke at last into tears, when I found that this, the second largest subscription ever received by me (£1000, by one friend, have since been given to the "John G. Paton Mission Fund"), came from a converted tradesman who had consecrated his all to the Lord Jesus, and whose whole leisure was now centered upon seeking to bless and save those of his own rank and class, amongst whom he had spent his early and unconverted days. Jesus said unto him, "Go home to thy friends, and tell them how great things the Lord hath done for thee, and hath had compassion on thee."

Bidding farewell to dear old Glasgow, so closely intertwined with all my earlier and later experiences, I started for London, accompanied by my brother James. We were sitting at breakfast at Mrs. Mathieson's table,

Mildmay, when a telegram was put into my hands announcing a "thank-offering" from Lord and Lady Polwarth, received since our departure from Glasgow. The Lord had now literally exceeded my prayers. With other gifts, repeated again by friends at Mildmay, the special fund for outfit and traveling expenses for new Missionaries had risen above the £500, and now approached £650.

In a Farewell Meeting at Mildmay the Lord's servants, being assembled in great numbers from all quarters of London, dedicated me and my work very solemnly to God, amid songs of praise and many prayers and touching "last words." And when at length Mr. Mathieson, intimating that I must go, as another company of Christian workers were elsewhere waiting also to say Good-by, suggested that the whole audience should stand up, and, instead of hand-shaking, quietly breathe their benedictory Farewell as I passed from the platform down through their great Hall, a perfect flood of emotion overwhelmed me. I never felt a humbler man, nor more anxious to hide my head in the dust, than when all these noble, gifted, and beloved followers of Jesus Christ, and consecrated workers in His service, stood up and with one heart said, "God speed" and "God bless you," as I passed on through the Hall. To one who had striven and suffered less, or who less appreciated how little we can do for others compared with what Jesus had done for us, this scene might have ministered to spiritual pride; but long ere I reached the door of that Hall, my soul was already prostrated at the feet of my Lord in sorrow and in shame that I had done so little for Him, and I bowed my head and could have gladly bowed my knees to cry, "Not unto us; Lord, not unto us!"

CHAPTER XC.
WELCOME TO VICTORIA AND ANIWA.

ON the 28th October, 1885, I sailed for Melbourne, and in due course safely arrived there by the goodness of God. The Church and people of my own beloved Victoria gave me a right joyful welcome, and in public assembly presented me with a testimonial, which I shrank from receiving, but which all the same was the highly-prized expression of their confidence and esteem.

During my absence at the Islands, to which I immediately proceeded, they unanimously elected me Moderator of their Supreme Court, and called me back to fill that highest Chair of honor in the Presbyterian Church. God is my witness how very little any or all of these things in themselves ever have been coveted by me; but how, when they have come in my way, I have embraced them with a single desire thereby to promote the Church's interest in that Cause to which my whole life and all my opportunities are consecrated—the Conversion of the Heathen World.

My Mission to Britain was to raise £6000, in order to enable the Australian Churches to provide a Steam Auxiliary Mission Ship, for the enlarged and constantly enlarging requirements of the New Hebrides. I spent exactly eighteen months at home; and when I returned, I was enabled to hand over to the Church that had commissioned and authorized me no less a sum than £9000. And all this had been forwarded to me, as the freewill offerings of the Lord's stewards, in the manner illustrated by the preceding pages. "Behold! What God hath wrought!"

Of this sum £6000 are set apart to build or acquire the new Mission Ship. The remainder is added to what we call our Number II. Fund, for the maintenance and equipment of additional Missionaries. It has been the dream of my life to see one Missionary at least, with trained Native Teachers, planted on every Island of the New Hebrides, and then I could lie down and whisper gladly, "Lord, now lettest Thou Thy servant depart in peace!"

As to the new Mission Ship, unexpected delay has arisen. There are differences of opinion about the best way of carrying out the proposal. There must be an understanding betwixt New South Wales and Victoria and the other Colonies, as to the additional annual expenditure. And the perplexity as to the wisest course has deepened, since the Colonial Government began to run Mail Ships regularly from Australia to Fiji, willing on certain terms of subsidy, to call at one or other harbor in the

New Hebrides. Meantime, let all friends who are interested in us and our work understand—that the money so generously intrusted to me has been safely handed over to my own Victorian Church, and is deposited at good interest in the bank, to be spent at their discretion in due time, when all details are settled, and, as nearly as possible in the altered circumstances, exclusively for the purposes for which it was asked and bestowed.

To me personally, this delay is confessedly a keen and deep disappointment. But the special work laid upon me has, however, been accomplished. The Colonial Churches have now all the responsibility of the further steps. In this, as in many a harder trouble of my checkered life, I calmly roll all my burden upon the Lord. I await with quietness and confidence His wise disposal of events. His hand is on the helm; and whither He steers us, all shall be well.

But let me not close this chapter, till I have struck another and a Diviner note. I have been to the Islands again, since my return from Britain. The whole inhabitants of Aniwa were there to welcome me, and my procession to the old Mission House was more like the triumphal march of a Conqueror than that of a humble Missionary. Everything was kept in beautiful and perfect order. Every Service of the Church, as previously described in this book, was fully sustained by the Native Teachers, the Elders, and the occasional visit, once or twice a year, of an ordained Missionary from one of the other Islands. Aniwa, like Aneityum, is a Christian land. Jesus has taken possession, never again to quit those shores. GLORY, GLORY TO HIS BLESSED NAME!

My Home has since been at Melbourne. My life-work now (1892), and probably during the remainder of my active days, will be to visit and address the Congregations and Sabbath Schools of the Presbyterian Churches of Australasia, telling them, as in this book, the story of my experiences, and inspiring the Christian people of these Colonies to support the New Hebrides Mission, and to claim all these Islands for the Lord Jesus Christ.

Reader, in your life, as in mine, one last Chapter still awaits us. By His grace, who has sustained me from childhood till now, I would work out that Chapter, and live through these closing scenes. With this book still open before you, I implore you to go alone before your blessed Saviour, and pledge yourself so to live, and so to die, in the service and fellowship of the Lord Jesus, that you and I, who have companied with each other through these pages, may meet again and renew our happy intercourse in our FATHER'S HOUSE.

CHAPTER XCI.
GOOD NEWS FROM TANNA, 1891.

(By the Editor.)

WHILST this page of manuscript passes through my hands, there is laid before me a brilliant letter from Mrs. Watt of Tanna, which, I am sure, she will pardon me for utilizing thus. It is written from Port Resolution, in the closing days of 1891. Its main theme is the building of the SCOTCH CHURCH, in the very heart of the district where my brother's years of anguish and toil were endured. Friends in Scotland gave Mr. and Mrs. Watt the money wherewith to purchase materials, and St. Paul's Parish Church, Glasgow, provided the Bell. But let us hear how she paints the scene, and unveils to us the Island life,—alike Pagan and Christian.

When they returned from Scotland and found their way to Kwamera, after galling delays among the Islands, one of their first duties was the making of "the annual contribution of arrow-root," the proceeds "to go to line the roof of the Kwamera Church,—the Church itself having been built in the same way," that is, by the sacred arrow-root! Then they went round to Port Resolution for the erection of the SCOTCH CHURCH,—"A Memorial of Workers and Work on Tanna." She tells how they "improvized a derrick by lashing together the masts of the two boats, and, with the aid of these and blocks and tackle, got the principals into their proper position. And though carpenters or builders may laugh at it," she adds, "we heaved a sigh of relief when the last one was secured." Listen to this: "Mr. Gray (neighbor Missionary) and Mr. Watt were the only skilled workmen. The others were all inexperienced, being Natives. We had them all divided into two relays, and they came turn about, each alternate day; and I can assure you there are no Natives in the Group, or indeed in any land, who would have come more faithfully, or worked more heartily, than these much-abused Tannese! The work went on every day, Sabbaths excepted, from 6 A.M. till 6 P.M., for forty days. On ten of these days Mr. Gray gave very valuable assistance; in truth, I do not see how we could have done without him. Day by day the women prepared food; the boys pulled drinking cocoanuts; and every one worked willingly, while crowds came and gazed on in wonder as the edifice arose." And if there be any shallow arm-chair critic of Missions ready to sneer at such toils, let him first digest what this devoted lady Missionary says: "Church Building may not be considered by some as Mission work; yet we believe this Church erection has been the means of much good to this people. We have had better attendances, both on week-days and on Sabbaths, than ever before. And we managed to keep up the daily morning and evening meetings during all the building time,—as, after the devotional part was over, the builders went out, but the rest remained for lessons." What more blessed than thus to work and pray! To teach their hands to work, and their hearts to sing praises to the Lord!

Now let us pass on, and look in upon them at the opening and dedication of this SCOTCH CHURCH ON TANKA to the Lord God. "On a fixed day, Wednesday 28th October, exactly twelvemonths to a day from our leaving Liverpool, Natives from far and near assembled for the occasion. Mr. and Mrs. Gray, with their two children, a Mr. Voullaire, a German who has come to Tanna as a Trader, and our neighbor Mr. Bramwell, joined us. So that, when we all met for the Opening Services, we were a somewhat mixed company, speaking a medley of languages,—English, Scotch, German, Fijian, Aneityumese, Aniwan, and at least two of the Tannese languages! The building was well filled; but the bigger crowd was gathered outside; for our Heathen onlookers were afraid to enter the sacred edifice. The Service was beautiful. All seemed very happy. After it, there was an exchange of gifts, we giving fifty fathoms of prints and calicoes, some handkerchiefs, two pots full of cooked rice, a pile of raw yams and taro, and two pieces of salt beef. Our neighbor gave some print, some tins of luncheon beef, and some uncooked rice. The Natives gave two cooked pigs, and native puddings *ad libitum*. These things being divided to the satisfaction of all, we had speeches, when doubtless some good impressions were made. On the Sabbath following we had a good attendance, Mr. Gray addressing the people. On the Sabbath following that we made our first money collection on Tanna." I again ask to my readers to listen, and to lay to heart what the lady Missionary tells us of these once cruel and cannibal souls. "We asked the people to give it as a thank-offering for the remarkable exemption from accident during the building of the Church though at times the work was rather dangerous. The collection was £3: 5s. We were much pleased with the hearty way the people responded to this, the first call to give a free gift to the Lord. One man, whose whole purse was 17s., gave 1s. himself, and gave 1s. to each of his three sons, so that they too might have something to give. Knowing how meanly the Tannese treated the Spirits whom they worshiped in Heathenism,—giving them the scraggiest fish, the poorest bananas, and the smallest yams,—we rejoiced in this Christian liberality!!"

Referring to exaggerated Newspaper rumors she says: "Tanna bulks largely in some minds, though it is only a small Island, a little larger than Arran! We had noticed that our Civil War was telegraphed not only to the Australian papers, but to San Francisco, and even to the *London Standard.* We have been receiving letters of condolence from friends, who think our lives in danger!" Now, mark what the presence of the Gospel and the

Missionary has brought about, as compared with former days: "Personally, the said Civil War has not affected us in the slightest. The Grays, who were in the center of the scene of action, and who more than once had the bullets whizzing over and around their house, were so assured of their complete safety that Mrs. Gray stayed there bravely alone with their children, while Mr. Gray came up here to assist at our Church building!"

But she does not pretend that all is Christlike: "The list of killed and wounded has been unusually large for Tanna, while the atrocities committed have been worse than we ever heard of before. Indignities were offered to the dead of both sexes. And, in one case at least, a mutilated woman was left unburied to be eaten by dogs,—and would have been completely devoured, had not one of our Teachers come on the scene next day, and, unaided, dug a grave and buried her." And then the writer lets in the lurid light of the Nether Pit in this closing picture: "One instance of the disgusting depravity of the people shocked me much. A man, who even attends Service in the district where the above dreadful affair took place, on seeing the poor mutilated form of the woman, addressed it thus—'If only the Gospel had not reached my Village, how I would have enjoyed a feast off you!' I cannot tell you how much this has preyed upon my mind; or how glad I feel at realizing that Jesus is an Almighty Saviour, and can save to the uttermost, else I would despair of these People!"

This may be commended to the attention of those who still affect to believe that the Cannibalism of my brother's book is overdrawn. That half-civilized Tanna man, smacking his lips at the thought of what might have been his but for the Gospel, outweighs all cavils, and is tenfold stronger than arguments. Also let us ask all readers to ponder the dear lady's parting shot at unsympathetic and disparaging critics: "Some have said that the backwardness of the Gospel on Tanna is due to the want of faith on the part of her Missionaries; but I agree with our fellow-laborer, Mr. Gray, who declares that it is only gigantic Faith that could have toiled so many years amongst such a People!" Dear sister in the Lord, courageous, much-enduring, free of all mock-modesty, conscious of thy Cross, I thank thee for that word—it is the right one—"Gigantic faith!"

Milton Keynes UK
Ingram Content Group UK Ltd.
UKHW031146311024
450535UK00004B/154